A real phenomenon, *QS-9000 Pioneers: Registered Companies Share Their Strategies for Success* is the most highly endorsed book concerning quality management with endorsements from world-renowned quality gurus.

"The important value of *QS-9000 Pioneers* for its readers, together with its presentation of QS-9000 itself, is its well-researched and well-documented case studies of a number of companies that have gone through the full QS-9000 cycle. Every company has its own unique considerations and, while a generalized methodology is useful for guidance, it is this case study information that is especially valuable for all men and women interested in QS-9000 and its implementation under the particular circumstances of their own organization."

Dr. Armand V. Feigenbaum
President and Chief Executive Officer
General Systems Company, Inc., USA

"In the rapidly changing industrial world, QS-9000 is a motivating force to improve the competitive power of companies. Chowdhury and Zimmer fill a great need by providing a book that assists in the implementation of a good quality system; it relates not only to the automotive industry but also to all manufacturing organizations."

Dr. Genichi Taguchi
President
Ohken Associates, Japan

"*QS-9000 Pioneers* is valuable because it details successful techniques in implementing the automotive industry's common quality requirements and helps readers understand what it takes to get things done properly the first time."

Philip B. Crosby
Author
Quality Is Still Free

"American car buyers are happy with the quality improvement they have found in recent-model vehicles, but they are expecting more improvement. QS-9000 is the means by which OEM suppliers will make added contributions to automotive quality. Since most suppliers have yet to embrace the standards, *QS-9000 Pioneers* is the key to informing them about how to get on the automotive quality improvement bandwagon."

J. D. Power III
Founder and President
J. D. Power and Associates, USA

"This excellent new book explains most convincingly that appropriately defined quality management systems do work—and work dramatically well. Viewed from a variety of management perspectives—cost reduction, competitive advantage, customer requirements, and increased operational productivity—QS-9000 creates added value."

Joseph R. Dunbeck
Chief Executive Officer
Registrar Accreditation Board, USA

QS-9000
PIONEERS

REGISTERED COMPANIES SHARE THEIR STRATEGIES FOR SUCCESS

SUBIR CHOWDHURY
KEN ZIMMER

Cases reviewed by
Harvard University's *Roy D. Shapiro*
Massachusetts Institute of Technology's *Janice A. Klein*
University of Chicago's *William A. Golomski*

ASQC
Quality Press
611 East Wisconsin Avenue
Milwaukee, Wisconsin 53202

IRWIN
Professional Publishing®
Chicago • Bogotá • Boston • Buenos Aires
Caracas • London • Madrid • Mexico City
Sydney • Toronto

Cover artwork by Betty Klooster Tyler

This publication is designed to provide accurate and
authoritative information in regard to the subject matter
covered. It is sold with the understanding that neither the
author nor the publisher is engaged in rendering legal, accounting,
or other professional service. If legal advice or other expert
assistance is required, the services of a competent professional
person should be sought.

From a Declaration of Principles jointly adopted by a Committee
of the American Bar Association and a Committee of Publishers.

Times Mirror
Higher Education Group

Library of Congress Cataloging-in-Publication Data

Chowdhury, Subir.
    QS-9000 pioneers : registered companies share their strategies for
success / Subir Chowdhury, Ken Zimmer ; foreword by Armand V. Feigenbaum ;
cases reviewed by Harvard University's Roy D. Shapiro, Massachusetts Institute
of Technology's Janice A. Klein, University of Chicago's William A. Golomski.
        p.   cm.
    Includes bibliographical references and index.
    ISBN 0-7863-0865-6
    1. Automobile industry and trade—United States—Quality control—Quality
management—Standards.   2. Automobiles—Parts—Design and construction—
Quality control—Quality management.   3. ISO 9000 Series Standards.
4. Case studies.   5. QS-9000 Quality System Requirements.   I. Zimmer, Ken.
II. Title.
TL278.C46   1996
629.23'068'5—dc20   96–10433

Printed in the United States of America
1 2 3 4 5 6 7 8 9 0 BS 3 2 1 0 9 8 7 6

To our families
for their continuous support

ACKNOWLEDGMENTS

The authors gratefully acknowledge the efforts of all who assisted in the completion of this book:

To all the contributors and their organizations for sharing their successful implementation strategies.

To Roy D. Shapiro of Harvard University's Graduate School of Business Administration, Janice A. Klein of the Massachusetts Institute of Technology's Sloan School of Management, and William A. Golomski of the University of Chicago's Graduate School of Business for their detailed review and guidance.

To Cynthia Zigmund and Carrie Sestak of Irwin Professional Publishing, and Tripp Martin of Peterson Spring for their continual support.

FOREWORD

For companies in today's automotive industry, quality leadership means managing all parts of the organization in the ways that provide complete satisfaction for the users of the company's products and services. The accelerating quality expectations of today's demanding and well-informed car and truck buyer make this kind of quality-driven strategic and operating emphasis a key to business success in the brutally competitive automotive and truck markets.

The basis for accomplishing this essential business result is clear, well-structured quality systems that put in place throughout the company sound, consistent, visible, and continuously improving quality activities and cross-functionally integrated processes that every man and woman in the organization understands, believes in, and is part of. The basic measure of the success of this *systems discipline*—there is no better term to sum it up—is to provide the foundation for products and services that generate the buyer enthusiasm that is the centerpoint of complete customer satisfaction and of continuing buyer loyalty and buyer retention.

In these times when supplier content is so important in every automotive or truck product, a principal quality systems requirement for accomplishing this kind of customer satisfaction is to fully align the key quality processes of the producer organization with those of the supplier organization. While quality systems applications in the automotive industry have continued to make progress toward this objective, the explosive growth in buyer quality expectations and the duplications and overlaps in some of the earlier producer and supplier quality requirements have made necessary much further improvement in full and effective producer and supplier quality alignment.

The significance of QS-9000 is that it provides this major advance in an integrated automotive and truck quality systems structure to the benefit both of car and truck buyers and of the companies that serve them. It brings together fundamental quality systems areas that are keys to good professional quality practice. It provides the approach for their application. It structures requirements among segments that are ISO 9000 based, sector-specific, and customer-specific. And, importantly, it harmonizes Chrysler's, Ford's, and General Motors' quality systems requirements (together with input from the truck manufacturers) into a cohesive framework.

I can also emphasize, from the experience of the General Systems Company throughout the automotive and truck industry, that it is essential to recognize that while the quality system is the foundation, it is effectiveness in its implementation that makes successful results real and lasting in producer–supplier alignment and in complete customer satisfaction. Leadership, management commitment, recognition of quality (as a business strategic factor), organizationwide involvement, sound procedures, and effective evaluation and auditing are just some of the essential factors in successful implementation throughout an organization.

The important value of *QS-9000 Pioneers* for its readers, together with its presentation of QS-9000 itself, is its well-researched and well-documented case studies of a number of companies that have gone through the full QS-9000 cycle. Every company has its own unique considerations and, while a generalized methodology is useful for guidance, it is this case-study information that is especially valuable for all men and women interested in QS-9000 and its implementation under the particular circumstances of their own organizations.

And the business value of this approach will continue to grow. The reason, as we at General Systems Company know from our projects in the United States and throughout the world, is that the increasing expectations of the automotive and truck buyer will make the quality improvements of the past few years a warm-up practice for what lies ahead. Because continued quality leadership is fundamental to long-term automotive business success, quality systems discipline that is effectively implemented is becoming an increasingly basic, long-term business asset for companies both small and large. Their competitive success in today's rapidly changing automotive markets will depend on it.

Dr. Armand V. Feigenbaum
President and Chief Executive Officer
General Systems Company, Inc.
Pittsfield, Massachusetts

PREFACE

The American auto industry alone employs more than 2 million people directly, and more than 6.7 million people work in related industries. The auto industry accounts for about 3.6 percent of the gross domestic product in the United States. Therefore, the introduction of a major change like *Quality System Requirements QS-9000* has a tremendous impact on the U.S. automotive industry as well as on its global suppliers.

For years the U.S. automakers have been criticized by their supplier base for inconsistent multiple quality requirements. These suppliers have been requesting Chrysler, Ford, and General Motors to unify their quality requirements—the main reason being the cost associated with attempting to comply with three different standards, namely, Chrysler's *Supplier Quality Assurance Manual,* Ford's *Q-101 Quality System Standard,* and General Motors–North American Operations' *Targets for Excellence.* For the first time ever the original equipment manufacturers (OEMs) have jointly provided unified quality system requirements, known as QS-9000.

QS-9000 was developed by the Chrysler, Ford, and General Motors Supplier Quality Requirements Task Force. In developing QS-9000, the task force intended that it would be implemented in the spirit of continuous improvement, which will enrich quality systems overall. QS-9000 applies to all suppliers of manufacturing, service parts, and related materials including suppliers who have design responsibilities. Appropriately enough, this includes Chrysler's, Ford's, and General Motors' internal suppliers.

PURPOSE OF THE BOOK

In the 1995 Automotive Industry Action Group (AIAG) quality survey, a majority of respondents stated that actual case studies would help their companies to achieve QS-9000 registration. The purposes of this book are to assist the reader in understanding the new quality system requirements and to provide guidelines for effective implementation of QS-9000 by organizations of any size. The implementation techniques are described via successful case studies from the QS-9000 registered pioneering companies.

IMPORTANCE OF ACTUAL CASES

This book tells the true stories behind the companies, teams, and individuals who rose to the challenge of these demanding quality requirements. Through a series of case studies profiling suppliers to the world's leading automakers, this is the first book to reveal the best practices of the registered companies who continue to lead the way. Successful cases showing the requirements, milestones, pitfalls, and expected returns are shared. This book will be a formula for "instant knowledge" on subject areas that apply to the reader's organization.

ABOUT THE BOOK

As of this writing, only 40 companies are QS-9000 registered. Approximately 40,000 automotive suppliers worldwide will attempt to achieve QS-9000 registration within the next two years. An excellent way to learn about the implementation of QS-9000 is to study what real organizations have done to achieve registration. This book provides actual achievement stories of QS-9000 registered companies. After analyzing the experiences of these successful companies, readers will gain knowledge that will be useful in deriving their own approach to QS-9000. Readers will also be acquainted with various methods for translating techniques into action for implementation purposes.

The first three chapters of the book provide readers with the history, a basic explanation, and an implementation methodology of QS-9000. The remaining chapters are case studies from registered companies; these studies were provided directly by members of the contributing organizations. Each case is unique in its style and content. Contributing organizations vary from small companies to large corporations with respect to number of employees and sales. Therefore, the philosophy and methodology of implementation vary in each organization; the reader may choose from a variety of techniques to best fit his or her own organization. Throughout the book, all place names are in the United States unless otherwise noted, and all monetary figures are in current U.S. dollars.

INTENDED AUDIENCE

This book is for anyone interested in QS-9000 registration: quality professionals, consultants, registrars, manufacturing professionals, managers, engineers, and educators. Its unique blend of case studies and review of best practices makes it ideal for training and education purposes. This book will serve academia as well.

CONTENTS

CHAPTER 5

STEERING QS-9000 ON THE ROAD TO SUCCESS: DELPHI SAGINAW STEERING SYSTEMS, GENERAL MOTORS CORPORATION 67

CHAPTER 6

10 COMMANDMENTS FOR ACHIEVING QS-9000: DRAKE PRODUCTS CORPORATION 93

CHAPTER 7

JOURNEY TO MANUFACTURING EXCELLENCE: J. B. TOOL & MACHINE, INC. 107

CHAPTER 14

FAST TRACK TO QS-9000: SATURN ELECTRONICS & ENGINEERING, INC.   217

CHAPTER 15

TEAM APPROACH TO QS-9000: STEMCO INC.   235

CHAPTER 16

JOURNEY TO REGISTRATION: ZENER ELECTRONICS   245

APPENDIX A

CASE CONTRIBUTORS

APPENDIX B

QS-9000 REGISTRARS

APPENDIX C

QS-9000 ACCREDITATION BODIES

APPENDIX D

RESOURCES

APPENDIX E

ACRONYMS

APPENDIX F

GLOSSARY

APPENDIX G

BIBLIOGRAPHY

CHAPTER 1

Background

The intent of this chapter is to provide a brief history behind the QS-9000 quality system requirements. For the purpose of adopting and implementing QS-9000, an in-depth understanding of its history is not absolutely necessary; however, a brief background will be helpful to the reader in fully appreciating the intention of the quality system requirements. Because QS-9000 is based on the ISO 9000 International Standard, it is important to provide an overview of the ISO 9000 series international standards.

INTRODUCTION TO ISO 9000

The ISO 9000 series standards were developed by a European-based organization, international in scope, to promote the development of international standards. This organization, known as the International Organization for Standardization, is composed of over 200 technical committees with active members from 92 countries. The United States is represented by the American National Standards Institute (ANSI).

Founded in 1946, the organization utilizes *ISO* as the prefix for its numerical standards and (although not an acronym for the International Organization for Standardization) uses *ISO* as an easily remembered version of its name. The significance in the name *ISO* is that it is from the Greek word *isos*, meaning "equal."

The standards in the ISO 9000 series are not product standards and do not include technical requirements. They do represent elements of a generic quality management system that are essential

1

in achieving quality assurance. The standards are basic and uncomplicated, presenting a universally applicable systems approach to fundamental business practices.

The ISO 9000 standards are based on British BS 5750 quality system standards, which were approved in 1987 by ISO Technical Committee 176. The basic ISO 9000 series consists of three conformance standards and two guidance standards.

Conformance standards are used for external quality assurance, which develops a customer's confidence in its supplier's products and services. Conformance standards differ in comprehensiveness and can be easily adapted to various types of organizations. Three conformance standards are ISO 9001, ISO 9002, and ISO 9003. These are described below:

• *ISO 9001, Quality Systems: Model for Quality Assurance in Design, Development, Production, Installation, and Servicing,* includes all elements in ISO 9002 and ISO 9003. ISO 9001 deals with design and development inputs, outputs, and changes, but does not prescribe specific design and development methodology. ISO 9001 applies to organizations responsible for the entire product life cycle.

• *ISO 9002, Quality Systems: Model for Quality Assurance in Production, Installation, and Servicing,* focuses on production and installation. ISO 9002 covers most elements of ISO 9001, except that in ISO 9002 design function is excluded. ISO 9002 is applicable to those industries in which customers provide designs and specifications of the product.

• *ISO 9003, Quality Systems: Model for Quality Assurance in Final Inspection and Test,* focuses only on detection and control of problems during testing and final inspection. ISO 9003 normally applies to those organizations whose products or services are relatively less complicated and are required to be assessed by inspection and testing.

Guidance standards are used for internal quality assurance, which develops management's confidence in the organization's overall quality achievement. These standards provide guidance to the organization for the purpose of quality management. Two guidance standards are ISO 9000-1 and ISO 9004-1.

• *ISO 9000-1, Quality Management and Quality Assurance Standards: Guidelines for Selection and Use,* explains fundamentally accepted quality concepts. ISO 9000-1 also provides guidance on the selection and use of conformance standards, and directs the use of ISO 9004-1.

• *ISO 9004-1, Quality Management and Quality System Elements: Guidelines*, applies to the internal quality management of organizations disregarding external requirements. ISO 9004-1 elaborates most of the conformance standards elements.

Other standards in the ISO 9000 series include the following:

- *ISO 9000-2, Quality Management and Quality Assurance Standards, Part 2: Generic Guidelines for the Application of ISO 9001, ISO 9002, and ISO 9003.*

- *ISO 9000-3, Quality Management and Quality Assurance Standards, Part 3: Guidelines for the Application of ISO 9001 to the Development, Supply, and Maintenance of Software.*

- *ISO 9004-2, Quality Management and Quality System Elements, Part 2: Guidelines for Services.*

- *ISO 10011-1, Guidelines for Auditing Quality Systems, Part 1: Auditing.*

- *ISO 10011-2, Guidelines for Auditing Quality Systems, Part 2: Qualification Criteria for Quality Systems Auditors.*

- *ISO 10011-3, Guidelines for Auditing Quality Systems, Part 3: Management of Audit Programs.*

- *ISO 10012-1, Quality Assurance Requirements for Measuring Equipment, Part 1: Metrological Confirmation System for Measuring Equipment.*

- *ISO/DIS 10013, Guidelines for Developing Quality Manuals.*

- *ISO 8402, Quality Management and Quality Assurance: Vocabulary.*

In general, people associate the certifiable standards (i.e., ISO 9001, ISO 9002, and ISO 9003) with the topic of ISO 9000 because most of the other standards are considered as quality system guidelines.

INTRODUCTION TO QS-9000

As the result of a June 1988 American Society for Quality Control (ASQC) Automotive Division workshop on concerns of suppliers and original equipment manufacturers (OEMs), workshop participants from Chrysler, Ford, and General Motors approached the Automotive Division about providing a neutral forum where the automotive suppliers' concerns over duplication of effort and documentation required to satisfy OEM requirements could be addressed. The Chrysler, Ford, and General Motors Supplier Quality Requirements Task Force was established.

The task force was given the mandate to harmonize all existing supplier documents and procedures. It was understood that each company would handle individually the company-specific, division-specific, and commodity-specific requirements. Five major documents were produced between 1990 and 1994. In December 1992, the task force was given the challenge to produce a single document that would govern supplier evaluation and approval.

Quality System Requirements QS-9000 was introduced by Chrysler, Ford, and General Motors to their North American supply base in August 1994. The Supplier Quality Requirements Task Force also introduced *Quality System Assessment (QSA)* at the same time. QSA is used to determine conformance to the quality system requirements via a list of questions directly related to Sections I and II of QS-9000. Chrysler's *Supplier Quality Assurance Manual,* Ford's *Q-101 Quality System Standard,* and General Motors–North American Operations' *Targets for Excellence,* with input from the truck manufacturers, were harmonized to form QS-9000. The foundation for *Quality System Requirements QS-9000* is ISO 9001:1994, Section 4. Because the types of applications required by the customer needed to be made more specific, over 100 additional auditable requirements were added to ISO 9001.

The Automotive Industry Action Group (AIAG) Truck Advisory Quality Committee was drafting an Industry Sector Quality System Standard prior to the development of QS-9000. Also based on ISO 9001, it was expanded with additional requirements specific to the heavy truck industry. Member companies of the Truck Advisory Group agreed to adopt QS-9000 in mid-1994.

> **Quality System Requirements QS-9000** *is in the process of being translated into French, German, Chinese, Mexican Spanish, and Castilian Spanish.*

Even though QS-9000 was introduced in North America during August 1994, the European and Australian rollouts of QS-9000 took place in June 1995. Ford's Australian Operations' supplier quality improvement manager, Mr. Frank Scarano, stated, "Australia is the only country in the world where the whole auto industry has adopted QS-9000." Two Japanese automakers, Toyota and Mitsubishi, have adopted QS-9000 in their operations in Australia. As of this writing *Quality System Requirements QS-9000* is in the process of being translated into French, German, Chinese, Mexican Spanish, and Castilian Spanish.

Understanding QS-9000

This chapter provides the reader with a detailed overview of the *Quality System Requirements QS-9000*. This overview is not intended to serve as a replacement of the actual *QS-9000* document, but to guide the reader in cross-referencing the QS-9000 sections with key points described in Chapters 4 through 16. A quick review of the QS-9000 sections provided in Chapter 2 will also enhance the reader's understanding of the situations described in the case studies that follow.

QS-9000 OVERVIEW

"Quality System Requirements QS-9000 is the development of fundamental quality systems that provide for continuous improvement, emphasizing defect prevention and the reduction of variation and waste in the supply chain." This is the goal of QS-9000 as stated in the second edition of *Quality System Requirements QS-9000*. It defines the fundamental quality system expectations Chrysler, Ford, General Motors, truck manufacturers, and other subscribing companies have of their internal and external suppliers. QS-9000 applies to all suppliers of production materials, production or service parts, or heat treating, painting, plating or other finishing services directly to Chrysler, Ford, General Motors or other OEM customers subscribing to the Quality System Requirements.

Harmonization of standards, processes, and quality-related procedures—including *Advanced Product Quality Planning and*

Control Plan: Reference Manual (Chrysler, Ford, General Motors 1995), *Fundamental Statistical Process Control: Reference Manual* (Chrysler, Ford, General Motors 1995), *Measurement Systems Analysis: Reference Manual* (Chrysler, Ford, General Motors 1995), *Potential Failure Mode and Effects Analysis: Reference Manual* (Chrysler, Ford, General Motors 1995), and *Production Part Approval Process* (Chrysler, Ford, General Motors 1995)—has assisted the U.S. automotive supplier base in meeting the QS-9000 requirements. The latest versions of these manuals are available through the Automotive Industry Action Group (AIAG).

The QS-9000 structure is based on three sections (Figure 2–1):

- *Section I: ISO 9000 Based Requirements* includes all 20 elements of ISO 9001.
- *Section II: Sector-Specific Requirements* contains three basic parts, namely, Production Part Approval Process, Continuous Improvement, and Manufacturing Capabilities.
- *Section III: Customer-Specific Requirements* consists of specific requirements of Chrysler, Ford, General Motors, and truck manufacturers.

F I G U R E 2–1

QS-9000 Structure

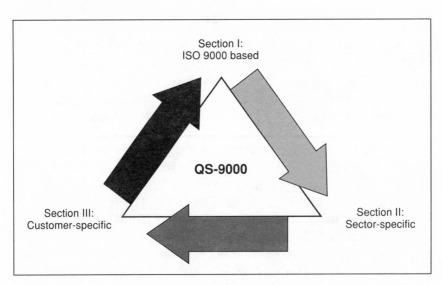

SECTION I: ISO 9000 BASED REQUIREMENTS

Section I of QS-9000 is based on 20 elements of ISO 9001. It also has some additional requirements for the automotive industry as mentioned in the *Quality System Requirements QS-9000*. In this section each element will be discussed.

Element 4.1: Management Responsibility

It is the responsibility of management to develop an effective quality system. The focus is on the senior management to organize and plan for quality. The quality responsibility should not be deputed to the lower levels of management. Senior management must be dedicated to quality. Just being passively involved in quality-related activities is not enough; upper management's commitment to quality must be an active function. The major responsibilities include the establishment of a quality policy, quality verification, and quality system review. There are six subclauses (three of which are QS-9000 specific) under element 4.1.

4.1.1: Quality Policy
Executive management must define the quality policy for the organization and document it. The policy must include objectives for quality and the organization's commitment to quality. The executive management must assure that the policy is relevant to organizational goals and customer needs. Executive management must implement, communicate, and maintain the quality policy at all levels of the organization.

4.1.2: Organization

4.1.2.1: Responsibility and Authority The organization must define the responsibility, authority, and interrelation of all personnel who manage, perform, and verify work affecting the quality of product and service to customers. This refers to personnel who must initiate action to prevent the occurrence of any product nonconformity; identify and record any problems related to product, process, and quality system; initiate and recommend solutions through designated channels; verify their implementation; and control further processing, delivery, or installation of nonconforming product until the condition has been corrected.

4.1.2.2: Resources The executive management must identify resource requirements and make sure the organization has adequate resources and trained personnel to execute any verification activities, which include inspection, testing, monitoring, design reviews, and internal quality system audits.

4.1.2.3: Management Representative Executive management must appoint a member of management who, irrespective of other responsibilities, must have defined authority to establish, implement, and maintain the quality system in accordance with the international standard. The management representative reports on the performance of the quality system to the executive management for review and as a basis for improvement of the quality system. The management representative's responsibility may also include liaison with external bodies on matters relating to the quality system.

Organizational Interfaces (QS-9000 specific) During concept development, prototype, and production, the supplier must have systems in place to ensure management of appropriate activities with reference to the *Advanced Product Quality Planning and Control Plan* reference manual. A multidisciplinary approach for decision making must be used.

4.1.3: Management Review
Executive management must regularly review all elements of the entire quality system to maintain its effectiveness and suitability. Records of quality system reviews must be maintained.

4.1.4: Business Plan (QS-9000 specific)
The supplier must utilize a formal, documented, comprehensive business plan, which typically includes the following: cost objectives, customer satisfaction plans, financial planning, growth projections, health and safety issues, human resource development, internal quality objectives, market-related issues, and research and development plans. The short-term and long-term goals and plans should be based on analysis of competitive products. Goals and plans should also be based on benchmarking activities within the automotive industry. This requirement is intended to encourage strategic business planning. Contents of the business plan are not subject to third-party assessment.

4.1.5: Analysis and Use of Company-Level Data (QS-9000 specific)

Trends in quality, operational performance, and current quality levels for key product and service features must be documented by the supplier. Operational performance is defined as productivity, efficiency, and effectiveness. Company-level data should undergo analysis and competitive comparisons to benchmarks. Data in trend format should be compared with progress toward business objectives. This is to develop priorities for problem solving and to support review status, decision making, and long-term planning.

4.1.6: Customer Satisfaction (QS-9000 specific)

The supplier must have documented processes to determine customer satisfaction; these processes must include frequency of determination and assurance of objectivity and validity. Customer satisfaction and dissatisfaction trends must be documented and supported by objective information. Upper management should review these trends and compare them with competitors' trends.

Element 4.2: Quality System

The supplier must establish and maintain a documented quality system that ensures product conformity to requirements. There are three subclauses under element 4.2.

4.2.1: General

A quality manual must be prepared consistent with the international standard requirements. The quality manual must include or make reference to the quality system procedures. It must outline the documentation structure used in the quality system.

4.2.2: Quality System Procedures

The supplier must prepare quality system procedures covering the requirements of the international standard and stated quality policy. The supplier must implement the quality system and its documented procedures effectively. The degree of documentation required for procedures depends on the methods used, the skills required, and the training obtained by personnel responsible for carrying out the related activities.

4.2.3: Quality Planning

The supplier must define and document how the requirements for quality will be met. Quality planning must be documented in a format that is suitable to the supplier's method of operation, and it must be consistent with all other requirements of the supplier's quality system. The supplier must consider activities that are appropriate in meeting the specified requirements for products or projects. Such activities include the following:

- Clarifying standards of acceptability for all requirements.
- Ensuring the compatibility of design, the production process, servicing, installation, inspection, and test procedures.
- Identifying and preparing quality records.
- Identifying any controls, processes, equipment, fixtures, skills, and resources necessary for the required quality achievement.
- Identifying extraordinary measurement requirements.
- Identifying suitable verification at appropriate stages in the realization of product.
- Preparing a quality plan (control plan in QS-9000).
- Updating quality control, inspection, and testing techniques.

QS-9000 specific   The *Advanced Product Quality Planning (APQP) and Control Plan* reference manual must be utilized. The following are also QS-9000 specific requirements:

   • *Use of cross-functional teams.* Cross-functional teams must be established and the supplier must implement an advanced product quality planning process. Teams should be utilized to prepare for production of new or changed products. Appropriate techniques as identified in the *Advanced Product Quality Planning (APQP) and Control Plan* reference manual should be used by the cross-functional teams. Teams should typically include areas of responsibility such as quality, engineering, production, manufacturing, design, and all other appropriate personnel.

   • *Feasibility reviews.* Suppliers are required to investigate and verify the manufacturing feasibility of proposed products in the early stages of the planning process, prior to contracting and production. Portions of the feasibility review are used to identify the specific design suitability. Areas of consideration for feasibility review are engineering performance specifications, manufacturing tolerances, adequate capacity, material handling, cost, and statistical process control.

• *Process Failure Mode and Effects Analysis (Process FMEAs)*. The objective of the *Process FMEA* is defect prevention rather than defect detection. The *Process FMEA* is a living document and should be considered in all manufacturing operations. It assumes that the product as designed will meet the design intent.

• *The Control Plan*. Suppliers must prepare control plans, which are to be utilized as living documents throughout the product life cycle. The control plan is an integral part of an overall quality process. A control plan is a written description of the system for controlling parts and processes. As defined in the *APQP and Control Plan* reference manual, the control plan must cover three distinct phases as appropriate:

1. *Prototype*—a description of the dimensional measurements, material, and performances tests occurring during prototype build.
2. *Prelaunch*—a description of the dimensional measurements, material, and performance tests that will occur after prototype and before normal production.
3. *Production*—a comprehensive documentation of product/ process characteristics, process controls, tests, and measurement systems occurring during normal production.

Control plans must be reviewed and updated as appropriate when the product is changed, the processes are changed, or the processes become unstable and/or noncapable.

Element 4.3: Contract Review

To meet customer requirements, the supplier must first understand what the requirements are. There are four subclauses under element 4.3.

4.3.1: General
The supplier must establish and maintain procedures for contract review. These procedures must be documented and cover the co-ordination of such activities.

4.3.2: Review

Before the submission of a tender (an offer made by a supplier in response to an invitation to satisfy a contract award to supply product) or the acceptance of a contract or order (agreed requirements between supplier and customer transmitted by any means), the supplier must review the tender, contract, or order. The basic review process requirements are as follows: the supplier is capable of meeting the contract or order requirements; the contract does not differ from the original inquiry or tender; and the contract requirements are well defined and well documented. The supplier must ensure that all customer requirements, including QS-9000 Section III requirements, are met.

4.3.3: Amendment to a Contract

The supplier must identify how any amendments to a contract are made and properly transferred to the appropriate functions within the organization.

4.3.4: Records

The supplier must maintain records of contract reviews. The contract review procedure should include all interested parties, a method to obtain understanding of the contract requirements, provisions for modifying the contract, a draft quality plan, and a verification checklist.

Element 4.4: Design Control

Inadequate design is often the root cause of many problems associated with quality. Basic quality aspects of any product (performance, safety, durability, dependability, etc.) are determined during the design and development stage. There are nine subclauses under element 4.4.

4.4.1: General

The supplier must have a documented procedure to control the product design and must verify that the design meets customer-specific and/or regulation-specific requirements.

4.4.2: Design and Development Planning

For each design activity, the supplier must develop design plans that define it. All design and development activities must be assigned to qualified personnel who have appropriate resources. As the design evolves, the plans must be updated.

QS-9000 specific Suggested qualified skills for the supplier's design activity are computer-aided design (CAD), computer-aided engineering (CAE), design for assembly (DFA), design for manufacturing (DFM), design of experiments (Taguchi and classical), failure mode and effects analysis (FMEAs), finite element analysis, geometric dimensioning and tolerancing (GD&T), quality function deployment (QFD), reliability engineering plans, simulation techniques, and value engineering (VE).

4.4.3: Organizational and Technical Interfaces
A variety of cross-functional organizational sources typically contribute to design. The organizational and technical interfaces must be defined, and the necessary information must be documented, transmitted, and reviewed regularly.

4.4.4: Design Input
Design input may be in the form of product descriptions or product performance, with specifications. All design input requirements applicable to the product must be identified and documented. The selection for design input adequacy must be reviewed. Any inadequate, vague, or contradictory design input requirements must be resolved. Design input must be factored into the result of any contract review activities.

Design Input—Supplemental (QS-9000 specific) Suppliers must have adequate resources and facilities to utilize computer-aided product design, engineering, and analysis. Suppliers must also provide technical guidance to subcontractors if such functions are subcontracted. The computer-aided design and computer-aided engineering systems must be capable of two-way interface with customer systems. The customer may waive the requirement for computer-aided systems.

4.4.5: Design Output
Design output may be in the form of technical documents such as drawings, specifications, analyses, and software. Design output must be documented and must meet the requirements of design input. Design output must recognize all design characteristics that are

crucial to safety and to the product's appropriate functions. Design output documents must be reviewed before the release date.

Design Output—Supplemental (QS-9000 specific)   To optimize the design, the supplier's design output must be documented with specific design tools, which include design FMEA, quality function deployment (QFD), design of experiments (DOE), value engineering (VE), and geometric dimensioning and tolerancing (GD&T).

4.4.6: Design Review
Documented design reviews must be planned and conducted at the appropriate stages of design. Design review representatives must be from all functional areas related to design. The supplier must maintain records of the design review.

4.4.7: Design Verification
To best ensure that the design output requirements meet the design input requirements, a design verification plan should be established. Design verification must be performed and recorded. Design verification may include such activities as utilizing existing proven designs and comparing them with new designs; performing tests, demonstrations, and alternative calculations; and reviewing design stage documents prior to release.

Design Verification—Supplemental (QS-9000 specific)   The supplier must have an extensive prototype program and must use the same tooling, processes, and subcontractors as used in production whenever possible (the customer may waive this requirement). Performance testing activities must include (as appropriate) product life, reliability, and durability; and all performance testing activities must be tracked to monitor conformance and timely completion. The supplier must also supply technical leadership in the development of the product if these services are contracted.

4.4.8: Design Validation
Because design validation ensures that the product conforms to defined user needs, it must be performed. Design validation follows successful design verification and is usually completed under defined operating conditions. Validation not only may be appropriate on the final product but also may be necessary at earlier stages. If there are different intended uses of the product, multiple validations may be required.

4.4.9: Design Changes
Although it is not uncommon for designs to be modified or changed, all such modifications or changes must be properly identified, documented, reviewed, and approved prior to their implementation.

Design Changes—Supplemental (QS-9000 specific)   All design changes must have written customer approval or waiver of approval prior to production implementation. For proprietary designs, studies considering fit, function, performance, durability, and impact on form must be conducted with the customer so that all effects of the change can be properly evaluated.

Element 4.5: Document and Data Control

Element 4.5, Document and Data Control, can be one of the most challenging elements. For many organizations, hundreds of documents are used in daily operational activities. Element 4.5 deals with such documents as well as with data control. There are three subclauses under element 4.5.

4.5.1: General
Procedures must be established and maintained by the supplier to control all documents and data. These may include external documents, such as customer drawings and standards. Document and data control may apply to both paper and electronic methods of documentation.

Reference Documents (QS-9000 specific)   The supplier must have currently released documents (engineering standards and drawings, inspection instructions, operations sheets, quality assurance procedures, quality manual, work instructions, etc.) available at all appropriate manufacturing locations if customer drawings or specifications reference such documents.

Document Identification for Special Characteristics (QS-9000 specific)   The customer's special characteristic symbol or the supplier's equivalent notation must be used to mark the supplier's process control guidelines and similar documents, indicating process steps that affect special characteristics. Appendix C of QS-9000 provides a list of common recommended symbols and identifications.

4.5.2: Document and Data Approval and Issue

The proper control of documents in any organization can be difficult. Before documents and data are issued, they must be reviewed and approved for adequacy by authorized personnel. To avoid invalid and/or obsolete documents, the supplier must establish a master list or similar procedure and make it available. The list or procedure must identify the current revision status of the documents. The main focuses of document control are to ensure that appropriate documents are available to users functioning within the quality system and to ensure that invalid and/or obsolete documents are removed or otherwise assured against unintended use. Obsolete documents that are required to be retained must be properly identified.

Engineering Specifications (QS-9000 specific)   A procedure must be established to ensure the timely review, distribution, and implementation of all customer standards, specifications, and changes. Maintenance of changes must be kept in all of the supplier's documentation. Implementation of changes must include updates to all appropriate documents.

4.5.3: Document and Data Changes

The supplier must identify changes in documents and data. The changes must be reviewed and approved by the supplier. The functions/organizations that performed the original review (unless specifically designated) must have access to pertinent background information upon which to base the review and approval. The nature of the change must be identified in the document where practicable.

Element 4.6: Purchasing

The supplier must have a system that ensures the conformance of the product or service purchased based on contractual requirements. There are four subclauses under element 4.6.

4.6.1: General

Documented procedures must be established and maintained to ensure purchased product conforms to specified requirements.

Approved Materials for Ongoing Production (QS-9000 specific)   Suppliers must purchase materials from an approved subcontractor list.

Materials used to manufacture parts must satisfy governmental and safety regulations.

4.6.2: Evaluation of Subcontractors
The requirements for the evaluation of subcontractors are to establish and maintain quality records of acceptable subcontractors, to evaluate and select subcontractors on the basis of ability to meet requirements inclusive of the quality system, and to describe the type and extent of control over subcontractors.

Subcontractor Development (QS-9000 specific)   Suppliers must perform subcontractor quality system development using QS-9000 as the basic quality system requirement. Assessment can be accomplished by the customer, an original equipment manufacturer (OEM) second party, or an accredited third-party registrar.

Scheduling Subcontractors (QS-9000 specific)   The supplier must require 100 percent on-time delivery, provide appropriate planning information to enable subcontractors to meet delivery schedules, and monitor the delivery performance including tracking of premium excessive freight.

4.6.3: Purchasing Data
Purchasing documents containing data must clearly define the product ordered. Requirements for purchasing data include the type, class, grade, or other precise identification; the title, number, and issue of the quality system standard to be used; the title or other positive identification; and applicable issues of specifications, process requirements, inspection instructions, drawings, and other relevant data (including requirements for approval or qualification of product, procedures, process equipment, and personnel). Prior to release, the supplier must review and approve the purchasing documents for adequacy.

Restricted Substances (QS-9000 specific)   Suppliers must have a process to satisfy governmental and safety regulations concerning purchased products and manufacturing processes.

4.6.4: Verification of Purchased Product
This requirement considers two situations to verify subcontracted product. In the first situation, the supplier must specify verification arrangements and the method of product release in the purchasing

documents. In the second situation, the supplier's customer must be afforded the right to verify that the subcontracted product conforms to specified requirements; this verification is completed at the subcontractor's location.

Element 4.7: Control of Customer-Supplied Product

Customer-supplied product is any product that is owned by the customer and furnished to the supplier (who accepts full responsibility for the product while in possession of it) for the purpose of meeting contract requirements. The supplier must establish and maintain documented procedures for the control of verification, storage, and maintenance of customer-supplied product. This element includes customer-owned tooling and returnable packaging.

Element 4.8: Product Identification and Traceability

Where appropriate (where product identity is not inherently obvious), the supplier must establish and maintain documented procedures for identifying the product by suitable means from receipt, production, delivery, and installation. In the event that traceability is a specified requirement, the supplier must establish and maintain documented procedures for unique identification of individual product or batches.

Element 4.9: Process Control

The supplier must identify, plan, and control the production, installation, and servicing processes that directly affect quality. Controlled situations must include the following: the use of proper production, installation, and servicing equipment; an appropriate working environment; compliance with quality plans, reference standards, and documented procedures; control of process parameters and product characteristics; documented procedures defining the manner of production, installation, and servicing for work that affect quality; appropriate maintenance of equipment; processes and equipment approval; and criteria for workmanship. To ensure that the specified requirements are met where the results of processes cannot be fully verified by subsequent inspection and testing, the processes must be carried out by qualified operators and/or must require continuous monitoring. Records for qualified people, equipment, or processes must be kept.

Government Safety and Environmental Regulations (QS-9000 specific)
Compliance with all applicable government, safety, and environmental regulations must be ensured by the supplier and be evidenced by appropriate documentation.

Designation of Special Characteristics (QS-9000 specific)   The supplier must provide documentation showing compliance with all customer requirements for designation and control of special characteristics.

Preventive Maintenance (QS-9000 specific)   The supplier must identify key processes requiring preventive maintenance, and must document and plan the activities based on process/equipment performance.

There are seven subclauses under element 4.9 that are *QS-9000 specific.*

4.9.1: Process Monitoring and Operator Instructions

For all operational employees the supplier must prepare documented process monitoring and operator instructions that are accessible at the work station. Process monitoring and operator instructions must include 13 individual requirements, as appropriate, which are as follows: corrective action instructions, current engineering level/date, customer and supplier special characteristics, inspection and test instructions, material identification, operation name and number keyed to a process flow chart, part name and number, relevant engineering and manufacturing standards, required tools and gauges, revision dates and approvals, statistical process control (SPC), tool change intervals and setup instructions, and visual aids.

4.9.2: Preliminary Process Capability Requirements

Preliminary process capability studies are required for special characteristics of new processes that must meet customer requirements.

4.9.3: Ongoing Process Performance Requirements

Ongoing process performance requires the application of statistical process control for performance evaluation. This requirement is defined by the customer. Continuous improvement is required regardless of demonstrated process capability, with the highest priority on special characteristics.

4.9.4: Modified Preliminary or Ongoing Capability Requirements

Modified preliminary or ongoing capability requirements may be required by the customer; in such cases, the control plan must be annotated.

4.9.5: Verification of Job Setups

The supplier must verify job setups as producing parts that meet all customer requirements. For setup personnel, documentation must be available, and, where applicable, statistical verification is required.

4.9.6: Process Changes

When change occurs in the part number, engineering change level, manufacturing location, material/component subcontractor, or production process environment, the process changes by definition. The supplier must maintain a record of process change effective dates.

4.9.7: Appearance Items

Appearance items must be manufactured with proper controls. When the customer designates manufacturing parts as "Appearance Items," the supplier must provide appropriate lighting for evaluation; masters for color, grain, and texture; maintenance of appearance masters; and verification that personnel making appearance evaluations are qualified.

Element 4.10: Inspection and Testing

This element reviews three areas of inspection and testings: receiving, in-process, and final inspection. There are five subclauses under element 4.10.

4.10.1: General

In order to ensure that the specified requirements for the product are met, the supplier must establish and maintain documented procedures for inspection and testing. These procedures must be detailed in the quality plan.

Acceptance Criteria (QS-9000 specific) "Zero defects" must be the acceptance criteria for attribute data sampling plans.

Accreditation Laboratories (QS-9000 specific)   Accredited laboratories must be used by the supplier when required.

4.10.2: Receiving Inspection and Testing
The importance of receiving inspection is that it allows suppliers to verify that subcontractors are fulfilling their contractual obligations.

4.10.2.1 Suppliers must ensure that incoming products are not used or processed until they are verified as conforming to the requirements. Verifications of conformance must be in accordance with the quality plan.

4.10.2.2 Consideration must be given to the amount of control exercised at the subcontractor's premises in determining the amount and nature of receiving inspection.

4.10.2.3 To permit recall and replacement of nonconforming product, incoming product must be identified and recorded by the supplier when incoming product is released for urgent production prior to verification.

Incoming Product Quality (QS-9000 specific)   The supplier must monitor incoming product quality utilizing one or more of the following: receipt of statistical data, receiving inspection and/or testing, second- or third-party assessments, part evaluation by accredited contractors or test laboratory. Subcontractor warrants or certifications must include test results and must be used in combination with one or more of the other methods.

4.10.3: In-Process Inspection and Testing
The supplier must inspect and test products as required by the quality plan, and must hold product until the required inspection and test have been completed. All process activities should be directed toward defect prevention methods.

4.10.4: Final Inspection and Testing
The supplier must complete all final inspection and testing in accordance with the quality plan. The quality plan and/or documented procedures involving final inspection and testing must require that all specified inspections and tests have been completed.

Until all activities specified in the quality plan have been satisfactorily completed, product must not be dispatched.

Layout Inspection and Functional Testing (QS-9000 specific) The results of layout inspection and functional verification required for all products must be available for customer review.

4.10.5: Final Inspection and Testing
The supplier must establish and maintain records that provide evidence of whether the product has passed or failed inspections per the acceptance criteria. Procedures for the control of nonconforming product must be applied when the product fails to pass inspection. Records must identify the inspection authority who releases the product.

Element 4.11: Control of Inspection, Measuring, and Test Equipment

There are four subclauses (two of which are *QS-9000 specific*) under element 4.11.

4.11.1: General
The supplier must establish and maintain documented procedures to control, calibrate, and maintain its inspection, measuring, and test equipment to demonstrate the conformance of product to specified requirements. The supplier must use equipment in a manner that assures that the measurement uncertainty is known and consistent with required measurement capability. Test software and hardware must be checked to prove they are capable of verifying the product's acceptability. Technical measurement data must be available when required by the customer.

4.11.2: Control Procedure
Supplier requirements for calibration of equipment, testing accuracy, handling of equipment, checking procedures documentation, and equipment identification are specified in this element. The supplier must:

- Identify the appropriate measurements, required accuracy, and appropriate instruments.
- Calibrate to recognized standards at prescribed intervals.

- Define calibration process and control of calibration service providers.
- Ensure that the equipment is capable of required accuracy and precision.
- Identify instruments with a suitable indicator or approved identification record.
- Maintain calibration records for instruments.
- Assess and document the validity of previous inspection and test results when instruments are found to be out of calibration.
- Ensure that the environmental conditions are suitable.
- Ensure the handling is such that fitness for use is maintained.
- Safeguard inspection, measuring, and test facilities from adjustments that would invalidate calibration.

4.11.3: Inspection, Measuring, and Test Equipment Records (QS-9000 specific)

Records of calibration on all inspection, measuring, and test equipment must include customer notification if suspect material has been shipped; revisions following engineering changes; gauge conditions and actual readings as received for calibration or verification.

4.11.4: Measurement System Analysis (QS-9000 specific)

Appropriate evidence is required indicating that statistical studies have been conducted to analyze the variation present in the results of each type of measuring and test equipment system.

Element 4.12: Inspection and Test Status

The status of product must be identified as conforming or nonconforming. The supplier must establish a quality system for identifying the inspection status of product during all manufacturing stages. The supplier must identify the inspection authority responsible for the product's release.

Product Location (QS-9000 specific)   The product's location in the manufacturing process does not establish appropriate indication of inspection and test status unless inherently obvious.

Supplemental Verification (QS-9000 specific) Supplemental verification requirements must be met, when required by the customer.

Element 4.13: Control of Nonconforming Product

A nonconforming product is a product or service that fails to meet customer specifications or requirements. There are four subclauses (two of which are *QS-9000 specific*) under element 4.13.

4.13.1: General
The supplier must establish and maintain a procedure to prevent the unintentional use or installation of a nonconforming product. Control of nonconforming product must provide for identification, segregation, evaluation, documentation, disposition, and notification to concerned functions.

Suspect Product (QS-9000 specific) Suspect product will be treated the same as nonconforming product under this element.

4.13.2: Review and Disposition of Nonconforming Product
The supplier must define responsibility for review and authority for the disposition of nonconforming product. Nonconforming product must be reviewed according to documented procedures. Nonconforming product may be reworked, accepted with or without repair by concession, rejected or scrapped, or regraded for alternative application. The supplier may need to notify customers and obtain approval before dispositioning nonconforming material. Reinspection of repaired and/or reworked product must be in accordance with the quality plan.

4.13.3: Control of Reworked Product (QS-9000 specific)
The supplier must provide instructions for reworked product. Reduction programs must be implemented by the supplier. There can be no visible rework on the exterior of products for service applications without the customer's prior approval.

4.13.4: Engineering Approved Product Authorization (QS-9000 specific)
The supplier must obtain written customer approval whenever the product or process is different from that currently approved. This requirement is applicable to subcontractors' products and services.

Element 4.14: Corrective and Preventive Action

Corrective action focuses on eliminating actual causes of nonconformities, whereas preventive action focuses on eliminating causes of potential nonconformities of the product. There are three subclauses under element 4.14.

4.14.1: General

The supplier must establish, document, and maintain procedures for implementing corrective and preventive actions. Actions taken to eliminate the causes of actual or potential nonconformities must be appropriate to the size of the problem.

Problem Solving Methods (QS-9000 specific) Disciplined problem solving methods must be used when an internal or external nonconformance occurs. The supplier must respond in a fashion prescribed by the customer when external nonconformances occur.

4.14.2: Corrective Action

The supplier's procedures for corrective action must include the following: handle customer complaints and nonconformity reports effectively; investigate and analyze the problem and record results; decide the effective corrective action; and ensure that effective corrective actions are implemented.

Returned Product Test/Analysis (QS-9000 specific) Parts returned from the customer must be analyzed by the supplier, and records of the analysis must be made available upon request.

4.14.3: Preventive Action

The supplier's procedures for preventive action must include the following: use available information such as work operations, quality records, service reports, and customer complaints to detect, analyze, and eliminate potential causes of nonconformities; decide the effective preventive action; ensure that effective preventive actions are implemented; and ensure that management reviews the relevant information on actions taken.

Element 4.15: Handling, Storage, Packaging, Preservation, and Delivery

There are six subclauses under element 4.15.

4.15.1: General

The supplier must establish, document, and maintain procedures for handling, packaging, storage, preservation, and delivery of product.

4.15.2: Handling

Methods of handling product that prevent damage or deterioration are required by the supplier.

4.15.3: Storage

To prevent damage or deterioration of the product, the supplier must use designated storage areas and appropriate methods for authorizing receipt to and dispatch from these areas. The condition of product in stock must be assessed appropriately for the detection of deterioration.

Inventory (QS-9000 specific)   To continuously optimize inventory turns, ensure stock rotation, and minimize inventory levels, an inventory management system must be established and documented.

4.15.4: Packaging

The supplier must control packing, packaging, and marking processes according to customer specifications.

Customer Packaging Standards (QS-9000 specific)   Customer packaging standards apply to unique customer packaging, including service part packaging standards.

Labeling (QS-9000 specific)   To ensure that all materials are shipped and labeled according to customer requirements, an effective system must be developed by the supplier.

4.15.5: Preservation

When the product is under the supplier's control, the supplier must apply appropriate methods for preservation and segregation of the product.

4.15.6: Delivery

After final inspection and test, the supplier must arrange for the protection of the product's quality. Where contractually specified, this protection must be extended to include delivery to destination.

Supplier Delivery Performance Monitoring (QS-9000 specific)   The supplier must establish systems to support 100 percent on-time delivery to the customer. The supplier must implement corrective actions to improve delivery performance if the 100 percent on-time shipment requirement is not maintained. The supplier must adhere to established lead-time requirements, track performance to customer delivery, and ship all materials in conformance with customer requirements.

Production Scheduling (QS-9000 specific)   The supplier's production scheduling activity must be order driven; an ultimate goal of one-piece flow in a synchronous manner is highly encouraged.

Shipment Notification System (QS-9000 specific)   To track shipment of products, an advanced shipment notification system must be in place. The supplier must have full software capacity in using this system and must have a backup method in the event of the computerized system's failure.

Element 4.16: Control of Quality Records

Quality records must provide evidence of product quality and effectiveness of the quality system. The supplier must establish and maintain documented procedures for handling, maintaining, and disposing of quality records. Quality records must be legible, readily retrievable, and stored in a suitable environment to prevent loss and damage. Retention times of quality records must be established and recorded; where contractually agreed, these records must be available for evaluation by the customer. Records may be electronic, hard copy, or both.

Record Retention (QS-9000 specific)   Unless otherwise specified, records of tooling, purchase orders, and production part approvals must be maintained during active production and service life, plus one year. Quality performance records must be maintained for one year after the year of creation and records of internal audits and management reviews for three years.

Superseded Parts (QS-9000 specific)   Copies of pertinent documents from superseded parts must be kept in a new-part file.

Element 4.17: Internal Quality Audits

Internal quality audits assess the effectiveness of the quality system. Quality audits must be scheduled according to the status and importance of the activity to be audited. Audits must be carried out by personnel independent of the activity being audited. Documented procedures for internal quality audits of the quality system must be established and maintained. Audit results must be recorded and communicated to the appropriate personnel. Corrective action must be performed in a timely manner. Follow-up audits must verify and record the effectiveness of corrective action.

Inclusion of Working Environment (QS-9000 specific)   Suitability of the working environment must be considered as part of the overall internal audit process.

Element 4.18: Training

Effective training is necessary to achieve quality. Documented procedures for identifying training needs of all personnel performing activities affecting quality must be established and maintained. Records of training must be maintained by the supplier.

Training as a Strategic Issue (QS-9000 specific)   Training effectiveness must be periodically evaluated and the supplier should view training as a strategic issue affecting all personnel.

Element 4.19: Servicing

Documented procedures must be established and maintained to perform and verify that servicing meets specified requirements.

Feedback of Information from Service (QS-9000 specific)   Communication of information on service concerning manufacturing, engineering, and design activities must be in place and properly maintained.

Element 4.20: Statistical Techniques

There are two subclauses under element 4.20.

4.20.1: Identification of Need

The need for statistical techniques must be identified by the supplier as required for establishing, controlling, and verifying process capability and product characteristics.

4.20.2: Procedures

The supplier must identify the adequate statistical methods and must provide documented procedures to implement and control statistical techniques.

Selection of Statistical Tools (QS-9000 specific)   The supplier must include in the control plan appropriate statistical tools used for each process as determined during the advanced quality planning.

Knowledge of Basic Statistical Concepts (QS-9000 specific)   Basic statistical concepts (variation, capability, stability) should be understood as appropriate throughout the supplier's organization.

SECTION II: SECTOR-SPECIFIC REQUIREMENTS

Section II is organized into three parts to cover additional QS-9000 specific requirements:

- Production Part Approval Process.
- Continuous Improvement.
- Manufacturing Capabilities.

In this section each topic is discussed.

Production Part Approval Process

Two areas are covered under Production Part Approval Process:

- 1.1: General.
- 1.2: Engineering Change Validation.

1.1: General

Suppliers must be in full compliance with all requirements described in the *Production Part Approval Process* manual. Production parts are approved by part number, engineering change level, manufacturing location including material subcontractors, and production process environment. Subcontracted material and services are the supplier's responsibility. Any questions regarding the production part approval process are to be referred to the customer's approving authority.

1.2: Engineering Change Validation
The supplier is responsible for engineering change validation.

Continuous Improvement

Three areas are covered under Continuous Improvement:

- 2.1: General.
- 2.2: Quality and Productivity Improvements.
- 2.3: Techniques for Continuous Improvement.

2.1: General
A comprehensive philosophy of continuous improvement must be deployed throughout the supplier's organization. Suppliers must continuously improve in key areas such as quality, service, delivery, and price. Specific action plans for continuous improvement in processes identified as most important to the customer must be developed by suppliers, once the processes are stable and capable.

2.2: Quality and Productivity Improvements
Opportunities for quality and productivity improvements—such as scrap, rework, and repair; excessive variation; wasted labor and materials; and unscheduled machine downtime—must be identified by the supplier.

2.3: Techniques for Continuous Improvement
For continuous improvement efforts, the supplier must use, as appropriate, the following techniques: analysis of motion/ergonomics, benchmarking, capability indices, control charts, cost of quality, cumulative sum charting, design of experiments, evolutionary operation of processes, mistake proofing, overall equipment effectiveness, parts per million analysis, problem solving, theory of constraints, and value analysis.

Manufacturing Capabilities

Four areas are covered under Manufacturing Capabilities:

- 3.1: Facilities, Equipment, and Process Planning and Effectiveness.
- 3.2: Mistake Proofing.
- 3.3: Tool Design and Fabrication.
- 3.4: Tooling Management.

3.1: Facilities, Equipment, and Process Planning and Effectiveness

Suppliers must utilize cross-functional teams while developing facilities, processes, and equipment plans in conjunction with advanced quality planning. Methods must be developed for the purpose of evaluating the effectiveness of current operations and processes.

3.2: Mistake Proofing

Mistake proofing is to be used to assist in preventing the manufacture of nonconforming product. Mistake proofing must be utilized in the planning process.

3.3: Tool Design and Fabrication

Appropriate technical resources must be used in the design and fabrication of tooling. Tools and equipment owned by the customer must be permanently marked so as to identify ownership.

3.4: Tooling Management

The supplier must establish and implement an effective system for tooling management including maintenance and repair, setup, storage, and tool change system for perishable tools.

SECTION III: CUSTOMER-SPECIFIC REQUIREMENTS

While Sections I and II represent a comprehensive harmonization of the Chrysler, Ford, and General Motors quality system requirements, Section III addresses specific requirements of each customer where individual requirements were not harmonized. Section III identifies reference manuals that are company- or customer-specific and that suppliers are expected to utilize as part of their quality system.

As mentioned in Chapter 1, Japanese automakers Toyota and Mitsubishi have recently adopted QS-9000 in their Australian operations. Also, as of this writing, several other international automakers are considering the adoption of QS-9000. Because of the rapidly changing acceptance of QS-9000 throughout the world, the intent here is to give an itemized account of each current customer requirement as mentioned in the second edition of *QS-9000,* and not to detail each issue.

Chrysler–Specific Requirements

- Parts Identified with Symbols:
  — The Shield (S)
  — The Diamond (D)
  — The Pentagon (P)
- Significant Characteristics
- Annual Layout
- Internal Quality Audits
- Design Validation/Production Verification
- Corrective Action Plan
- Packaging, Shipping, and Labeling
- Process Sign-Off
- Chrysler Bibliography:
  — Design Review Guidelines
  — Design Verification Plan and Report
  — Reliability Functions
  — Reliability Testing
  — Test Sample Planning
  — Priority Parts Quality Review
  — Product Assurance Planning Manual

Ford–Specific Requirements

- Control Item Parts
  — Control Plans and FMEAs

- — Shipping Container Label
- — Equipment Standard Parts
- Critical Characteristics
- Setup Verification
- Control Item Fasteners
  - — Material Analysis, Heat-Treated Parts
  - — Material Analysis, Non–Heat-Treated Parts
  - — Lot Traceability
- Heat Treating
- Process Changes and Design Changes for Supplier-Responsible Designs
- Supplier Modification of Control Item Requirements
- Engineering Specification Test Performance Requirements
- System Design Specification
- Ongoing Process Monitoring
- Prototype Part Quality Initiatives
- Quality Operating System (QOS)
- Qualification and Acceptance Criteria for Materials
- Table A: Qualification of All Product Characteristics
- Table B: Ongoing Process and Product Monitoring
- Ford Bibliography
  - — A Quality, Reliability Primer
  - — Heat-Treat System Survey Guidelines
  - — Manufacturing Standards for Heat Treating
  - — Packaging Guidelines for Production Parts
  - — Potential Failure Mode and Effects Analysis Handbook
  - — QOS Assessment and Rating Procedure
  - — Team-Oriented Problem Solving

General Motors–Specific Requirements

- General Procedures and Other Requirements (*Documents*)
  - — C4 Technology Program, GM: Supplier C4 Information
  - — Key Characteristics Designation System
  - — Supplier Submission of Material for Process Approval
  - — Problem Reporting and Resolution Procedure

- Supplier Submission of Match Check Material
- Component Verification and Traceability Procedure
- Continuous Improvement Procedure
- Run at Rate
- Evaluation and Accreditation of Supplier Test Facilities
- Early Production Containment Procedure
- Traceability Identifier Requirements
- Specifications for Part and Component Bar Codes
- Procedure for Suppliers of Material for Prototype
- Packaging and Identification Requirements for Production Parts
- Shipping/Parts Identification Label Standard
- Shipping and Delivery Performance Requirements

- Customer Approval of Control Plans
- UPC Labeling for Commercial Service Applications
- Layout Inspection and Functional Test

Truck Manufacturers–Specific Requirements

Truck manufacturers' additional requirements are available in their respective publications.

APPENDIXES

QS-9000 has eight appendixes in its second edition: (A) The Quality System Assessment Process, (B) Code of Practice for Quality System Registrars, (C) Special Characteristics and Symbols, (D) Local Equivalents for ISO 9001 and 9002 Specifications, (E) Acronyms and Their Meanings, (F) Change Summary, (G) QS-9000 Accreditation Body Implementation Requirements, and (H) Survey Audit Days Table. Because these appendixes are self-explanatory in the *QS-9000* second edition, they are not described in this chapter. Appendixes are very useful to organizations seeking registration as well as registrars. There is also a glossary in *QS-9000*.

THIRD-PARTY REGISTRATION
REQUIREMENTS

As of this writing, the third-party registration requirements are as follows:

- Chrysler: July 31, 1997
- Ford
  - North America: Not required at this time (compliance expected June 1995)
  - Australia: December 1997
- General Motors
  - North America: January 1, 1996 (new suppliers)
  - Worldwide: December 31, 1997 (all suppliers)
- Toyota
  - Australia: June 1998
- Mitsubishi
  - Australia: December 1997

CHAPTER 3

Implementing QS-9000

The benefits of QS-9000 are directly dependent on how effectively the quality system is implemented. Every member of the organization must take active responsibility in the process. The major objective in implementing QS-9000 should not be the achievement of registration only. The primary purpose of QS-9000 implementation should be to improve an organization's quality system. Such a purpose directly impacts product quality, reliability, on-time delivery, costs, and so on. If an organization's quality system is truly effective, internal as well as external customers will notice the positive effects.

An extremely focused effort to examine current business strategies in relation to their impact on the quality system may be necessary. Utilizing the quality system requirements to strengthen the business strategy may require revisions to the quality-related procedures that impact such strategies. As procedures are followed and continuous improvement activities implemented, the organization will experience positive change. The use of teams in a cross-functional environment will assist in the implementation process.

This chapter addresses how to prepare the organization for QS-9000 implementation by describing the basic steps in the process. These steps have common conditions that lead to successful QS-9000 registration, as mentioned in the following chapters via case studies. This chapter also introduces the concepts and methodologies of implementing a quality management system and provides a description of the activities that an organization may use during the implementation process.

A 10-STEP METHODOLOGY FOR QS-9000 IMPLEMENTATION

The 10-step methodology for QS-9000 implementation presented here is based on (1) the authors' extensive research in the subject matter, (2) practical experience in application, and (3) valuable input from QS-9000 registered companies. The authors found several slightly different methodologies concerning QS-9000 implementation either in research or in practical applications. In either case, the steps may be named or arranged differently, or the process expanded or condensed by adding or deleting steps. The steps may vary in sequence depending on the organization's size, philosophy, culture, and so on. In this methodology one should focus on each step and its contents; the focal point is that the steps listed below are the major components of the QS-9000 implementation process. The 10 steps are as follows:

1. Leadership commitment.
2. QS-9000 implementation team.
3. Management representative.
4. Education and training.
5. Organizational awareness.
6. Documentation structure.
7. System evaluation.
8. Internal quality audits.
9. Registrar selection.
10. Third-party assessments.

Leadership Commitment

Understanding the increasing significance of quality, members of top management are taking active roles and responsibilities in such efforts as QS-9000. Because, traditionally, management's focus is on bottom-line results, true commitment will not be realized until QS-9000 is viewed as a tactical advantage. As Dr. W. Edwards Deming stated, 85 percent of quality-related problems are due to management, so successful registration to the quality system requirements would be near impossible without the support of top management.

After the quality system has been successfully implemented, management must demonstrate commitment to its maintenance. Top management's involvement must be apparent in the beginning and should increase over time. To show support, top management should participate directly in the training process. Top management's willingness to be involved in day-to-day activities will assist in addressing employee concerns early and will diminish employees' inclination to test management's commitment. Employees must be able to witness their leadership's commitment. This commitment must gain momentum as it flows through the organization vertically as well as horizontally until everyone is included, familiarized, and committed.

> *The attitude adopted by top management concerning QS-9000 will permeate every level of the organization.*

The attitude adopted by top management concerning QS-9000 will permeate every level of the organization in a very short period of time. Top management must provide support and resources for proper implementation.

QS-9000 Implementation Team

The most significant contributing factor to successful QS-9000 implementation is an empowered, multidisciplined, cross-functional team. It pays to involve as many staff members as possible in the team activities because implementation should be considered as a corporate project. It is important to note that cultural and organizational barriers are detrimental to sharing responsibilities on cross-functional teams. As the team begins to function comfortably and starts to take on complex projects, it should take caution to manage these projects properly. If the organization uses the team approach for implementation, a "champion" should be developed. To develop, the champion must maintain active involvement in the strategic implementation process.

It is important to understand that although the quality system belongs to the entire organization, it is management's responsibility to provide it, manage it, and maintain it. The implementation process will be made easier if management divides the tasks into easily manageable components so that they don't seem impossible. With this in mind, it would be considered wise if the implementation strategy is structured to include discipline, control, and a form of milestone measurement. The same discipline and control should be used to maintain and improve the certifiable system once it is in place and approved.

An effective implementation program requires determination and consistent encouragement. Managing change is key to effective implementation; employees' natural resistance to change will deteriorate as employees begin to feel a sense of ownership in their quality system. The management system is expected to get results, but it is important to remember that there are

> *Employees' natural resistance to change will deteriorate as employees begin to feel a sense of ownership.*

no perfect systems—mistakes and failures should be considered part of the learning process. Proper project management enhances the success of implementation.

Management Representative

After its implementation, the maintenance of the quality system must be properly managed. An important requirement of QS-9000 is that a member of management is charged with ensuring that the quality system is effectively maintained. This representative is required to report on the performance of the quality system to management for review. The selection of the management representative is critical and should be thoroughly thought out. In the best interests of the organization, the management representative should be well respected, be knowledgeable about the organization and the quality system requirements, possess authority, and have strong leadership and project management skills.

The management representative should draw from all levels of management and all functional areas of the organization to form guided, cross-functional teams. The management representative must assist the organization in defining requirements and projects, identifying team member responsibilities, planning projects, implementing projects, reporting completions, and evaluating results.

Education and Training

The importance of education and training cannot be overemphasized in an effective quality system. Training is essential to the achievement of quality. Organizations that do not properly train their personnel at all levels are not taking advantage of employees' full potential. It is recommended that all employees of the organization have at least a basic understanding of QS-9000; this knowledge will add strength toward successful implementation.

There is no universal formula for proper education and training. The organization must determine for itself the appropriate education and training needs of its personnel. The organization should evaluate these needs based on such factors as organizational goals, needs analysis, employee functions, and position. During the implementation phase, all activities should be focused so as not to cause delays in the process.

Organizational Awareness

The organization should approach its personnel through structured, well-organized information channels. During implementation, grapevine communication, which often passes along incorrect or misunderstood information, can hinder proper organizational awareness. Correct, clear, and timely information is crucial to a healthy quality system. Once the flow of information is turned on, it should be maintained with information that provides knowledge and answers questions relating to the organization and to QS-9000.

Every member should be informed of, at minimum, what the quality system requirements are, why the organization is adopting them, how they affect each employee, and what the benefits will be. Sharing accurate information assists in reducing anxiety and increases receptiveness and cooperation. Employees will be able to make better decisions and greater contributions if everyone is working within an accurate and timely communication system.

Because QS-9000 is relatively new to most companies, lack of knowledge and misconceptions may be understandable. Some organizations, even those that possess a great deal of knowledge about QS-9000, continue to seek answers to important questions dealing with interpretations. For this reason, interpretations were created by the International Automotive Sector Group (IASG), which is made up of accreditation bodies recognized by Chrysler, Ford, and General Motors; representatives of the Independent Association of Accredited Registrars (IAAR) and the Independent International Organization for Certification (IIOC); Tier I automotive suppliers; and representatives of the Chrysler/Ford/General Motors Supplier Requirements Task Force. Questions can be submitted to the IASG for interpretation, and copies of the latest IASG-sanctioned interpretations can be obtained from the American Society for Quality Control.

Documentation Structure

The usual structure for documentation in a QS-9000 quality system is a four-level hierarchy. The organization's operations and methods are detailed in these layers at steadily increasing levels. The four levels in hierarchical order are as follows: the quality manual, procedures, job instructions, and other forms of organizational operational documentation (records).

The quality manual describes the organization's quality system and defines its approach and responsibilities. The quality manual should state the organization's commitment to quality through its quality policy.

Procedures describe what is to be done, when, where, why, and by whom. They describe how the organization's quality system functions. Procedures should reflect the principles and practices as defined in the quality manual.

Job instructions describe how individuals do the work. They must be in line with the requirements set forth in the procedures. Job instructions describe the details of any specific task and help ensure consistent working methods.

Records indicate that the quality system is operating. They may include specifications, drawings, files, standards, and charts. All forms of documentation should be kept current, accurate, and accessible. The adequacy and effectiveness of documentation should be monitored throughout the implementation process.

System Evaluation

Although a system evaluation can be accomplished at any stage in the implementation process, an organization typically completes a system evaluation once the organization's leadership is committed, the implementation team formed, the management representative selected, education and training in process, organizational awareness implemented, and the documentation structure in place. An evaluation logically occurs at this point because the organization has a new awareness of what the requirements are but is not sure of where it stands in meeting them.

An effective way to evaluate a system, in order to determine what is missing from the systemwide structure of the organization, is to establish a gap analysis. This analysis assists in directing the organization as it indicates its strengths and weaknesses in comparison to QS-9000. Resources can be shifted to areas where the largest gap exists to close the gap in concert with the organizational time line. A complete system audit against the quality system requirements and the organization's existing documentation may be necessary to generate the information for establishing the gap analysis. Many organizations utilize an independent consultant to perform this initial audit because it provides an objective assessment of the system.

Internal Quality Audits

Many organizations mistakenly underestimate the advantages that a sound internal quality audit program contributes to the quality system. Internal quality audits provide important feedback to the organization when they are utilized to determine the quality system's effectiveness. A structured audit program encompasses all documented elements of the quality system. The information generated from the audits provides management with opportunities to improve the quality system by exposing deficiencies. Follow-up audits verify the effectiveness of the corrective actions taken on the deficiencies. This activity provides management with a cycle of information that should be used to strengthen the entire system.

As described above in system evaluations, gap analysis provides the organization's management with an effective tool to track progress of closing the gaps between current situations and desired situations. Internal audits provide a good source of information to keep the gap analysis current and accurate. The information generated from these audits should also be used to track the effects of actions taken for continuous improvement projects.

Registrar Selection

Third-party registration/certification programs for quality systems have experienced tremendous growth worldwide. The need for quality system registration bodies (i.e., registrars) has obviously increased with the demand. As a consequence, there are significantly more registrars from which to choose. As described in *QS-9000*, "a registrar is a company that conducts quality system assessments to the quality system requirements." Chrysler, Ford, and General Motors recognize only those registrars that have been certified by an appropriate accreditation body.

Seeking a registrar means seeking a long-term partner of the organization. Before a registrar is chosen, organizations should properly gather enough information about the registrar to make the best selection. Organizations should consider cost, industry knowledge, location, and "chemistry" during the selection process. Many organizations have indicated that the chemistry between them and the registrar is very important, especially during the implementation phase. Other suggestions to consider in choosing a registrar are (1) develop a list of questions for interviewing the registrar that focus on specific areas important to the organization, (2) ask the registrar to provide the experiences and backgrounds of the auditors, and (3) make sure the registrar understands and complies with the QS-9000 Code of Practice for Quality System Registrars.

Third-Party Assessments

Third-party assessments are administered by independent certified bodies for the purpose of evaluating an organization with regard to an applicable standard or set of requirements. The results of this evaluation are used to determine the status of the organization's quality system. There are three major types of assessments that deal with QS-9000: preassessment, assessment, and surveillance.

• *Preassessment* is generally used as a broad overview evaluation of an organization's quality system. Although a preassessment is not compulsory for QS-9000, it assists in determining the organization's preparedness for a full assessment, and the information gained can be used to verify or update the organization's gap analysis. An aggressive response to nonconformances uncovered in the preassessment will have a positive impact on preparation for the full assessment.

• *Assessment* is an evaluation of the quality system that includes a document review, an on-site audit, an analysis, and a report. The duration of assessment depends on the size and complexity of the organization to be registered. Appendix H of *QS-9000* as modified in the sanctioned interpretations provides the survey audit days table, which shows the minimum number of man-days spent by the registrar on initial QS-9000 quality system audits and ongoing six-month surveillance audits. During the assessment, any level of personnel may be interviewed by the third-party auditors to determine the effectiveness of the quality system.

• *Surveillance* is a less-intensive audit that registrars conduct at six-month intervals. Its purpose is to confirm that the organization's quality system is effective and has not deteriorated. If the organization's internal audit system is effective, there should not be any indications of major discrepancies in the organization's quality system as the result of a surveillance audit.

IMPLEMENTATION VIA SUCCESSFUL CASE STUDIES

Chapters 4 through 16 describe QS-9000 registered organizations' successful case studies. Each chapter provides valuable information that will assist any organization in its strategic efforts from planning through registration. Although the same topic (e.g., document and data control) is mentioned in several different chapters, in each case the company's approach to the topic is unique, which provides the reader with somewhat different successful techniques on the same subject matter. A general company profile is given at the beginning of each chapter to help the reader preview the company and its products, customers, annual sales, location, and so on.

CHAPTER 4

Motivation for Registration

Aetna Industries, Inc.

GENERAL

- *Headquarters*   : **Center Line, Michigan, U.S.A.**
- *Year Founded*   : **1933**
- *Number of Employees*   : **1,500**

QS-9000 SPECIFIC

- *Registered Location(s)*   : **Center Line, Warren, Sterling Heights (All 9 locations are in these 3 cities of Michigan, U.S.A.)**
- *Number of Employees*   : **1,500**
- *Registration Date*   : **February 6, 1995**
- *Product(s)*   : **Stampings, Roll Forms, Welded Assemblies**
- *Tier I, II, III Supplier* : **Tier I and II**
- *Major Customer(s)*   : **Chrysler, General Motors**
- *Annual Sales*   : **U.S. $200 Million**

INTRODUCTION

This case study is presented to share some of Aetna Industries' perceptions of, and experience with, the third-party registration process, both to ISO and QS-9000. Emphasis is placed on the value and benefits derived from the process, as well as potential pitfalls and obstacles. The focus of this case study is on the experience and insight gained by Aetna that others seeking registration may find of use.

It has been the experience of Aetna Industries that QS-9000 can provide a significant positive contribution to an organization's business management system. This has been validated through ongoing monitoring of key performance measures. These measures include external, internal, and supplier quality performance—which, in turn, have been reflected in the organization's profit performance. It has also been seen, however, that failure to clearly understand the intent behind QS-9000 can quickly lead to the establishment of wasteful activities, such as unnecessary documentation and duplication of effort. These can ultimately undermine the validity and intent of the entire document.

Aetna Industries' early preparation for ISO registration was not prompted by a customer mandate, business dealings in Europe, or the perception that attaining registration would lead to new market opportunities. Initially, registration itself was not even a goal. A review of the ISO 9000 series standard had led to the conclusion that its content simply made good business sense. It was seen as a framework that could be used for the continuing development of the existing quality management system. Alignment of the existing quality management system to ISO 9002 was initiated for this reason. Ultimately, registration was seen to be the only effective way of ascertaining if true alignment had been accomplished.

The real need of the customer is, and always has been, consistent shipment of parts meeting all requirements, delivered on time according to schedule and at a competitive price. Today, price is dictated by the marketplace and is constantly being driven down. The dynamic nature of our business therefore makes continuous improvement vital to survival, both technologically and economically. Aetna Industries has determined it must learn to do more with less. Through long-range planning sessions, a strategy was developed that evolved into what is now termed the Aetna Production System. A key to developing this strategy was that it be a "winning" strategy, not a composite of quality, marketing, or other functional strategies.

There were two main components to this winning strategy. The first was the recognition that all work must be planned and that success results from the effective execution of planned work. The second was a total focus on the elimination of all forms of waste.

The organization did not seek to reinvent the wheel. On the contrary, the study of other companies' successful production systems, together with benchmarking activities, resulted in the adoption of Dr. Shigeo Shingo's principles as the basis of the Aetna Production System.

At Aetna Industries, QS-9000 is now a key component of the Aetna Production System. The Aetna Production System has one goal: the elimination of all forms of waste. It is generally known that poor quality results in many forms of waste, some of the more obvious being rework, scrap, sorting, process downtime, and extra handling/material movement. A structured, properly implemented quality management system must therefore be an essential part of any successful strategy to eliminate waste.

BACKGROUND

Founded in 1933 as Aetna Metal Products, Aetna Industries, Inc., is a privately held producer of stampings, roll-formed products, and welded assemblies for the automotive industry. Based in Center Line, just north of Detroit, Michigan, its annual sales exceed $200 million. Aetna Industries has several manufacturing facilities, all of which are located in Detroit's northern suburbs. It is a Tier I supplier with approximately 1,500 employees. Major customers include Chrysler, General Motors, and CAMI. Aetna Industries is also a supplier to a number of other major Tier I automotive suppliers. The workforce is affiliated with the United Auto Workers (UAW). In addition to being shipped to many major U.S. vehicle assembly plants, product is also shipped to Canada, Mexico, Europe, South America, and Asia.

Aetna attained its initial third-party registration to ISO 9000 in November 1993. This was achieved by two plants, one of which was primarily representative of the organization's stamping operations, the other of its automated weld assembly and roll-forming processes. This followed a decision to go through the registration process with two plants that represented the organization's overall manufacturing processes rather than to attempt to attain registration for the entire organization at one time. It proved to be a good decision in that it both provided a valuable learning experience and enabled the remaining plants to achieve registration more expediently. Registration of the entire organization was accomplished five months later.

The issue of *QS-9000* in August 1994 prompted Aetna to begin upgrading the registration status. A certification assessment was conducted in November 1994, and QS-9000 registration was announced in February 1995. A number of surveillance audits have been conducted since initial registration. Scheduled every six months, each has been instrumental in both reinforcing the value of the registration process and identifying further opportunities for improvement.

MANAGEMENT RESPONSIBILITIES

A structured approach is needed to assess, prepare for, and implement each element of QS-9000. Aetna Industries' approach was based on several guiding principles. The first was a clear definition. A useful definition of the intent of the ISO 9000 series standard is that it is the consistent application of common sense. This definition helped the organization maintain focus and question the value-added impact of each element of the quality management system as it was developed. As implementation progressed, continually questioning the commonsense attributes of each planned implementation element was found to be of vital importance. It was discovered that not doing so could quickly lead to the establishment of wasteful activities and unnecessary documentation.

The additional prescriptive requirements contained in QS-9000 render the above definition somewhat less accurate. Things that are done simply because they are mandated may not be done with a clear understanding of their intent or potential value. Furthermore, the culture, or point of evolution, of an organization may not effectively support the prescribed activity. However, the activity can still be used effectively if determined effort is made to understand the intent of the added requirements and compliance is continuously achieved in a form that adds value to the organization itself.

The essence of the entire implementation of the QS-9000 process can be captured in the following three phrases:

Say what you do, effectively.

Do what you say, effectively.

Demonstrate that you do it, effectively.

At Aetna Industries, these phrases continue to provide guidance throughout the process. The process is as follows: First, clearly identify, in a format that is authorized and controlled, the who, when, where, and how for all activities that impact the quality management system. Second, verify that what actually takes place is as documented. If it is not, determine the preferable practice and either change the procedure or reinstruct the personnel performing the task. In actuality, a modification to both was often the outcome. Third, maintain adequate records or data to substantiate that the prescribed activities are being performed on an ongoing basis.

Who should coordinate the registration initiative? Typically the quality manager, director, vice president, or whoever else is responsible for the management of the quality department might be appointed as management representative. While this may be the appropriate individual in many organizations, it is wrong to assume it is the case for all organizations. Aetna discovered ISO 9000 defined a *business* management system, not just a *quality* management system. Depending on the structure, position, and authority of the quality function, it is possible that effective implementation may be better directed by a member of some other functional area. Equally wrong is the assignment of this responsibility to an individual at a level where he or she cannot be effective, even if he or she reports directly to the president or chief executive officer. The management representative is responsible for assuring that a quality system is established, implemented, and maintained. This responsibility cannot be met by someone (regardless of his or her personal skills and abilities) who is not recognized within the organization to be at a level to command the necessary authority.

LEADERSHIP COMMITMENT

Before embarking on implementation activities, the organization must question why QS-9000 registration is being sought. An obvious reason is that the customer mandates it. This reason alone, however, will not lead to full realization of the potential effective implementation of QS-9000 can bring. On the contrary, if the implementation of QS-9000 is viewed as a necessary course of action for purely external reasons, it will likely inhibit the development of effective procedures and result in the duplication of at least some activities. Senior management commitment is the key. Real commitment to QS-9000 registration will likely not be assured unless it is viewed as a strategic opportunity with the potential to positively impact the bottom line. It is therefore vital to define a reason other than "The customer says so." Before proceeding with the question of implementation, the question "How does QS-9000 registration relate to our business strategy?" should be asked, and answered.

Leadership commitment must then be visible to all employees if implementation efforts are to be effective. Employees test management commitment on a daily basis. The attitude of the workforce is a reflection of management commitment. If management is serious, then the workforce is serious. Alternatively, if the workforce is not serious, it is because it does not believe that management is serious.

> *Real commitment to QS-9000 registration will likely not be assured unless it is viewed as a strategic opportunity with the potential to positively impact the bottom line.*

Commitment can be demonstrated in simple ways. For example, the president of Aetna Industries made a point of informally asking several employees, in various departments, what controlled documents they used on a daily basis. This followed the distribution of an ISO 9000 question-and-answer booklet to all employees. Several senior staff members had a misunderstanding of what document control meant. The telephone switchboard operator, a purchasing buyer, and a sales assistant were among those asked. Their initial response was that they did not know and had not read the booklet. The president told them he would ask them the same question the next day. Within an hour the entire organization was buzzing. All of the employees were asking themselves the same question about controlled documents. By the next day the employees fell into one of two categories: those who knew what controlled documents they used on a daily basis, and those who were still working to find out. One thing everyone knew was that document control was important to the president and was consequently something they should hold important. It was a tremendous learning experience for everyone.

Another key benefit of this simply posed question was that it underscored the importance of ISO 9000 within the organization. The same approach was effectively used to help address perceived gaps throughout the organization as system development continued.

IMPLEMENTATION

After identifying clear business reasons for pursuing registration, it is necessary to determine where an organization is with respect to compliance with QS-9000. An approved lead assessor training course provided knowledge and understanding that better enabled Aetna Industries to do this effectively.

Since QS-9000 requires the quality management system to be documented in the form of a quality manual, it is first necessary to compare any existing manuals with all of the requirements contained in QS-9000. What Aetna Industries discovered in going through this review was that its quality manual already contained most of what was required. However, it also contained a lot of good procedural information, some of which was not effectively implemented. Many of the quality manuals that had been issued sat on the recipients' bookshelves gathering dust. The large size of the manual itself did little to promote interest in it.

One result of Aetna's review was the separation of policy and principles from procedural information. Today, the policy and principles remain as a much-streamlined quality manual. Procedural information was developed and compiled into a separate manual on standard operating procedures. These procedures evolved to become valuable documents for use in (a) effectively implementing the system, (b) providing the framework for recording improvements, (c) identifying training needs, and (d) auditing.

Once the comparison of actual practices with requirements had been completed, it made good sense for Aetna to formulate an implementation plan to address each issue. This structured plan identified the individual responsible for each element of the plan and set realistic timing. It was found that a formal implementation plan served several important purposes. These included the following:

- The development of a realistic implementation timetable.

- The assignment of ownership for each element of the plan.

- A basis for comparison of actual achievements throughout the timetable.

- The potential for faster identification of elements or activities that may have been omitted from the original plan.

The appointed management representative had overall responsibility for this implementation plan and provided a weekly status report to the management team.

DOCUMENT AND DATA CONTROL

The reported number one reason for ISO 9000 and QS-9000 registration failure is lack of adequate document and data control. Just who is responsible for documentation and data? What form should documentation and data take? How far do you go in documenting activities and procedures? Aetna found the answers to these questions by considering the commonsense aspect of each situation. The answer to each question was not always the same when asked in different areas. Furthermore, the right answer two years ago would not necessarily be the right answer today. Such is the nature of continuous improvement.

There are several software packages available that claim to provide a solution to the issue of documentation and data control. This may be true if the software is properly applied, supported, and administered as an integral part of an organization's business activities. However, it may be easier, and more effective, to implement a manual system first and then advance to a computer-based system when the fundamentals are in place and understood. Consider the huge hardware and software industry that grew up after statistical process control (SPC) was mandated in the early 1980s. Most of it facilitated faster, easier data collection and charting. Unfortunately, many users gained little in real process improvements. This was because data collection was looked at as if it were the process, and charts and indices the output. QS-9000 should be viewed as a means to improve performance, just as SPC should be used as a tool to aid in improving the process being monitored.

The use of "master lists" was the subject of some confusion within Aetna Industries as documentation and data control requirements were determined. A major cause of resistance was the general idea that compliance with ISO 9000 and QS-9000 meant there would be a significant increase in the amount of paperwork required. Furthermore, accountability for that paperwork was seen by some as a threat. In reality, the number of forms and documents was actually decreased, even though accountability for the remaining forms and documents did increase. When each department set about identifying the forms, record sheets, and written instructions in use, or supposedly in use, significant duplication, obsolescence, and redundancy were found. In some cases, the document in actual use was an employee-modified version of the issued document. Each department created a master list of those documents over which it had direct control. These lists simply identify each document's name and revision status. Obsolete documents were eliminated. Some documents were combined into one, and still others were updated to reflect the actual needs of those using them. The net result was clear identification and purpose for all documents needed and used. Issue and revision controls were created for each document, and, most important, ownership was established. This involvement of the personnel who use the forms and documents rendered the fear of accountability void. When purpose, use, and application were clearly established, ownership was readily accepted.

Consequently, something that was initially viewed by many to be an unnecessary administrative burden proved to be an opportunity to improve efficiency and eliminate waste. Further evidence of this was seen in the subsequent application, throughout the organization, of document and data control principles that were beyond the original scope of quality system documents. Managing the paperwork challenge became significantly easier when a defined, structured system was developed to handle it effectively over time. The same system proved equally effective for the control of electronic data.

EDUCATION AND TRAINING

An element of QS-9000 itself, the identification of training needs is as important to effective QS-9000 implementation as it is to the entire quality management system. Those coordinating the implementation activities must have a sound knowledge of the QS-9000 requirements. At Aetna, group meeting sessions, booklets, and the company newsletter were all used to inform and educate employees regarding ISO 9000 and QS-9000. Meetings, presented by the president and vice presidents of manufacturing, finance, and quality, were held with all employees from all shifts. A videotape was subsequently produced to satisfy the ongoing need to convey a basic explanation of QS-9000 and how Aetna's quality management system is based on it. This videotape is now used as part of the training curriculum for all employees.

Education and training have emerged as the most important issues regarding the implementation, maintenance, and continuing development of an effective business management system. The fundamental element that distinguishes one organization from another is its people. There are many organizations that manufacture similar products and use the same basic equipment, materials, and technology as Aetna Industries. The same can be said of the vast majority of manufactured product and service providers. What distinguishes one from another starts with those in leadership positions and continues with every individual member of the organization. Without effective ongoing education and training, it is difficult to convey leadership direction consistently. The multitude of specific requirements related to the procedures and work practices that make up any business management system dictate effective ongoing education and training if the status quo alone is to be maintained. Identifying and maintaining improvements, vital to business survival, mandate continuous human resource development.

This realization led Aetna to establish an education and training function within the human resource department. The identification of training needs, and training provision, was previously handled by each individual department. This was done without real consideration for training effectiveness and often led to duplication of effort in determining training providers. There was often inconsistency in the training received from two providers of the same subject matter. This sometimes resulted in confrontation and debate regarding correct application.

The internal education and training function now determines training needs and providers based on input from all departments collectively. It serves as an internal consultant and administers training activities. This has resulted in the development of several essential training and education courses that were previously unavailable. Training investment is continuously monitored and reported as a key performance measure. A direct positive correlation has been shown between training hours, sales per employee, and sales per unit area of manufacturing facilities. These key performance measures are monitored, reported graphically, and reviewed regularly by senior management. Developing an organizationwide training curriculum and providing consistent ongoing training that supports the curriculum are paramount to maintaining and developing an effective business management system.

It is a common misconception that only know-how is required to implement a new system. Success, however, also requires know-*why*. Continuous improvement requires continuous effective change. Human nature is to resist change. Know-why helps people to understand what is being done and therefore enables them to better cope with changing situations. Continued investment in education and training is therefore essential.

INTERNAL AUDITING

A key purpose of auditing is to identify opportunities for positive change and improvement. Sadly, however, auditing has been one of the most poorly utilized tools available to the quality management profession. Unfortunately, the purpose of auditing has often been construed to be to find fault and assign blame. This negative impression of auditing has not been helped by the absence of defined training and qualification criteria for personnel who conducted second-party assessments on behalf of the Chrysler, Ford, General Motors, and major Tier I suppliers. This is indeed unfortunate because, at Aetna Industries, scheduled internal audits, performed by competent personnel, have proved key to problem-solving initiatives, the identification of training needs, and overall continuing development and improvement of the quality management system.

It was not always this way, however. QS-9000 did not make internal auditing a new requirement for automotive suppliers. The way in which Aetna Industries had satisfied customer requirements for internal audits, prior to ISO 9000, was by making auditing a part-time activity for each department manager. A matrix identified what was subject to audit and when audits were to be conducted. There were a number of fundamental problems with this approach. At first, performing internal audits was not exactly high on any manager's priority list. Consequently, most were not performed according to schedule, and many were performed only after repeated reminders. Second, the majority of those performing audits had not been trained in auditing skills and methods, which generally resulted in inaccurate audit results and frustrated audit participants. Third, identified noncompliances, although answered by the function audited, were not generally closed through any form of follow-up or validation.

The internal quality audits element of QS-9000 clearly specifies ongoing auditing of the entire system. However, to derive the most from auditing, as well as to comply fully with QS-9000, it is essential that auditing be recognized, positioned, and staffed appropriately. The solution to this problem was the establishment of an independent internal auditing function staffed with qualified personnel. At Aetna Industries, approved internal auditor training courses and professional certification of auditors through the American Society for Quality Control (ASQC) add credibility both to the individuals performing the audit and to the audit function.

SUBCONTRACTOR DEVELOPMENT

The question of how to address the subcontractor development requirement contained in QS-9000 was the subject of much deliberation at Aetna. A proposed easy answer was to mandate subcontractor registration to QS-9000 in a defined time limit, just as Chrysler and General Motors did for their suppliers. It was quickly concluded that this was not an appropriate course of action and did not fit the established purchasing policy of working with subcontractors in the spirit of a cooperative partnership. Nonetheless, QS-9000 defines quality management system elements that are potentially valuable for all organizations. Furthermore, QS-9000 does mandate subcontractor development, with its Sections I and II as the fundamental basis for that development.

The approach Aetna Industries took was to inform all subcontractors of its intent to perform supplier development activities based on the content of QS-9000. A letter was sent asking each subcontractor to identify its present status in regard to QS-9000 compliance. The letter asked each subcontractor to confirm whether it had developed its quality management system to comply with QS-9000 and, if not already in compliance, when it estimated it would be. The responses to this letter provided an effective database for identifying those subcontractors most in need of assistance. The other major indicators used were quality and delivery performance.

Most, if not all, subcontractors do not want to be developed. What they do want is to develop themselves and be given assistance and support when they feel they need it. Customers are often a contributing cause of poor supplier performance, failing to provide clear requirements, to maintain schedule commitments, and to report performance results consistently. Subcontractor development is a misnomer that would be better called partnership development. As much, or more, emphasis should be placed on developing the customer's part of the relationship as on the subcontractor's.

STATISTICAL TECHNIQUES

The term *statistical techniques* to most automotive suppliers means average and range charts, capability studies, and capability indices. Some may then go on to identify design of experiments and other statistical tools. While all are potentially valuable, if properly used and applied, limiting and judging compliance on these alone is too restrictive. *Statistics* can be defined as the collection, organization, and interpretation of numerical data. Another way of interpreting the definition of statistical techniques is *management by fact, based on data*. Management itself is therefore a process that can and should be controlled.

This viewpoint is expressed out of concern for all the time and resources wasted by many organizations over the past decade in efforts to comply with perceived customer requirements regarding statistical process control. There are probably many organizations that can derive more benefit from acting on data collected from a simple tally sheet than from all their control charts collectively. The point is to do what makes sense, understand what is done, and act accordingly.

REGISTRAR SELECTION

Back in 1993 there were many horror stories about registrars from Europe and their exorbitant cost. First-class airfare and premium hotel accommodation were cited as the norm. Today, based on data collected by the Automotive Industry Action Group, the extremes are significantly more rare, but the registrar selection decision is no less important. Cost is obviously still a major consideration. However, it is important to recognize that the objective when selecting a registrar is to enter into a long-term continuous relationship. A healthy relationship is both constructive and productive. Factors to consider are cost, industry and product knowledge, location, and chemistry. Chemistry is the least tangible but probably the most significant for the long-term relationship.

One very positive experience of the registration process may be the optional preassessment. Aetna Industries elected to take this option and found that it served several key functions. The organization gained an understanding of the third-party audit process without being under the duress of an actual assessment. Areas of noncompliance were identified that internal assessments had overlooked. The knowledge, ability, and professionalism of the registrar were evaluated before time or money had been invested that would have made changing the registrar more difficult. Most important, the company and the registrar got to know each other. In hindsight, a preassessment would today be considered essential.

It is perhaps the registrars themselves that will ultimately determine the future of QS-9000. Their continued professional conduct, objectivity, and ability to interpret and perform assessments will ultimately determine whether suppliers view QS-9000 as an aid to improving business performance or just another obstacle to overcome. The informed supplier will demand that its registrar provide the service for which it is being paid.

THE SURVEILLANCE AUDIT

Following successful registration comes the surveillance audit, which is repeated every six months for a three-year period, after which a complete reassessment is required. In the past, following a customer audit, the normal reaction, on the part of most, was to breathe a sigh of relief because it was over. QS-9000 registration is a process, not an event. It is never over. The surveillance audit helps to assure that the organization remains active in this process. This is perhaps one of its greatest merits. The frequency of surveillance audits is such that a constant focus must be kept on the system and its effectiveness.

> *QS-9000 registration is a process, not an event. It is never over. The surveillance audit ... is perhaps one of its greatest merits.*

In November 1989, Aetna Industries was one of the first organizations to be presented with General Motors' Mark of Excellence award. Pursuit of this award was based solely on the perception that it would identify Aetna Industries as a preferred supplier and lead to increased business opportunities with General Motors. In actuality, neither resulted. Following the presentation of a plaque, a flag was hoisted in front of Aetna's administrative offices for all to see. A year later, at the suggestion of an hourly employee, the flag was voluntarily taken down. The reason for this was that many of those in management and supervisory positions had become complacent. The flag symbolized the attainment of an event, the end of a journey. In reality, ongoing performance had failed to maintain the level of performance on which the award had been based. Removing the flag made it clear to all employees that business survival is contingent on looking to the future, not reflecting on the past. An organization that does not continuously improve is doomed to fail.

The surveillance audit provides continuity to the process. It also maintains the organization's relationship with the registrar. Most important, it serves to confirm continuing compliance with QS-9000 and identifies improvement opportunities.

One of the ways Aetna Industries has sought to further embed the process of maintaining registration is to directly involve those employees closest to it. During the initial assessments and follow-up visits, senior management representatives were directly involved in escorting auditors and answering questions. Other staff members were on hand for support as needed. The most recent surveillance audit was conducted entirely by plant representatives. Senior management was involved only where needed to answer those questions specifically related to management responsibility and review. This promotes further understanding of the auditing process, and QS-9000 requirements, for those involved.

SUMMARY

For any organization, achieving or maintaining a competitive business advantage dictates constantly looking to the future and continuously improving. Learning from past mistakes, and identifying and benchmarking best practices, all while keeping a constant eye on the competition, are essential. Critics of ISO 9000 and QS-9000 have argued that they contain nothing new or revolutionary. One real benefit, of course, is the harmonization of many supplier quality system manuals and assessment tools, resulting in a reduction in the number of audits and assessments a supplier may be subject to. However, when compared to other quality management criteria, the Malcolm Baldrige National Quality Award, for example, QS-9000 does not address many elements considered by some to be essential to total quality management. This is actually where QS-9000 offers the greatest potential advantage. ISO 9000 and QS-9000 define *fundamental* quality system requirements.

Typically, the root cause of product nonconformance, identified both internally at Aetna Industries and at Aetna's subcontractors, is not having followed basic system requirements. Properly implemented, ISO 9000 and QS-9000 provide a sound foundation on which a total quality management (TQM) system can be built. It is the solidarity of the foundation that ensures consistent quality performance. That foundation, however, must be constantly checked and reinforced to ensure its soundness. This should be the prime purpose of both internal and external audits. The media have reported that TQM has failed to deliver over the long term. Perhaps the cause of the reported failure, which apparently followed significant initial improvement, can be found in shortcomings related to the basic fundamental system.

The return on investment for QS-9000 registration costs was not measured directly because improvements have been the result of combined activities. Tangible benefits have been seen in many ways. External quality performance has improved significantly since the registration initiative began. Aetna Industries' target reduction in customer-reported nonconforming product is 50 percent per year. This has been realized for the past three years. Less tangible, but important, benefits have been seen in employee involvement, teamwork, and morale. The only costs considered relevant to attaining and maintaining QS-9000 registration are those paid directly to the registrar. Any other costs are, and have been, justified on the basis of the issue for which they are expended.

The attainment of ISO 9000 registration prior to the issue of QS-9000 made QS-9000 registration somewhat easier. The reason is that ISO 9000 is a descriptive standard. It identifies quality system elements that must be in place. The manner in which those elements are satisfied is left up to each individual organization. QS-9000 adds prescriptive requirements. These impose methods and activities that may require significant changes to an organization's operations. Since these are, reportedly, not new requirements, an existing Tier I automotive supplier should, at least in theory, already be in compliance. In reality, the effective implementation of these prescriptive requirements must be carefully assessed. This is where common sense must prevail in order to avoid doing things just because the customer says so. There is significant potential value in all of the tools and techniques prescribed by QS-9000. However, that value can be realized only if a clear understanding of their use and purpose precedes implementation. What was done to satisfy customer requirements in the past may not fit the business reason(s) identified for pursuing QS-9000 registration today.

Developing Aetna Industries' business management system around ISO 9000 and QS-9000 proved to be an extremely gratifying experience. The process caused every individual to identify his or her contribution to the quality management system. It allowed people to take ownership of their respective jobs and provide direct input into how those jobs could best be done. When such an environment is created, it seems there is no limit to the collective talent and initiative that follow. This leads to the identification and implementation of improvement opportunities and is itself a self-perpetuating process. After all, one of the biggest potential forms of waste in any organization is not using the collective talent of its people. At Aetna Industries, ISO 9000 and QS-9000 continue to help change that for the better.

This case study is contributed by Edward Lawson, Vice President of Quality Assurance, Aetna Industries, Inc., Center Line, Michigan.

CHAPTER 5

Steering QS-9000 on the Road to Success

Delphi Saginaw Steering Systems, General Motors Corporation

GENERAL

- *Headquarters*   : **Saginaw, Michigan, U.S.A.**
- *Year Founded*   : **1906**
- *Number of Employees*   : **14,000**

QS-9000 SPECIFIC

- *Registered Location(s)* : **World Headquarters, 2 Plants at Saginaw, Michigan, and 2 Plants at Athens, Alabama, U.S.A.**
- *Number of Employees*   : **6,725**
- *Registration Date*   : **December 21, 1995**
- *Product(s)*   : **Steering Columns, Pumps Halfshafts, Rack & Pinion Gears**
- *Tier I, II, III Supplier* : **Tier I**
- *Major Customer(s)*   : **General Motors, Chrysler, Toyota, Volkswagen, Daewoo Motors, NUMMI, Renault, Volvo, Peugeot**
- *Annual Sales*   : **U.S. $3 Billion**

INTRODUCTION

Delphi Saginaw Steering Systems is proud to be considered a QS-9000 pioneer—as well as being the first operating division within General Motors, Ford, and Chrysler to achieve QS-9000 registration.

We want to emphasize that we looked upon the implementation of a QS-9000 based quality system first as an *opportunity* and, second, as a customer mandate. When we talked about the process as an opportunity, we recognized at the very beginning that this was a universal quality system requirement that we could employ across Delphi Steering's worldwide operations.

The QS-9000 registration efforts are only partially complete for this division. At this time, we have registration of our world headquarters, which includes engineering and other functional staffs, and registration of two manufacturing plants in Saginaw, Michigan, and two manufacturing plants in Athens, Alabama.

BACKGROUND

Years of Innovation

Delphi Steering can trace its commitment to quality to 1906, when it was founded in Saginaw, Michigan, to produce a revolutionary steering mechanism. Saginaw Steering Gear (SSG) became the first parts manufacturing division of General Motors (GM). By 1934, gear production at SSG was spectacular, with over 1 million units per year. In 1937, the United Auto Workers (UAW) became part of SSG. By 1950, SSG had successfully developed the first power steering systems. In 1995, the company became a division of Delphi Automotive Systems and changed its name to Delphi Saginaw Steering Systems. With GM as its parent company, Delphi Automotive Systems has over 170,000 employees at technical centers, sales offices, and manufacturing locations in over 30 countries. Delphi Automotive Systems has six different product divisions, one of which is Delphi Steering.

Today at Delphi Steering

Today, Delphi Steering is acknowledged as the global leader in the design and manufacture of quality-built steering columns, intermediate shafts, halfshafts, and steering systems. Delphi Steering offers the widest possible range of steering components and systems with full-line capabilities, making us the world's most comprehensive steering supplier.

Our global customers form such a complete list that virtually all automotive manufacturers use Delphi Steering products in their production. Our customers include Austin, BMW, Chrysler, Daewoo Motors, Fiat, Ford, General Motors, Isuzu Motors, Jaguar, Lamborghini, Maserati, Mercedes, Nissan, New United Motor Manufacturing, Inc. (NUMMI), Peugeot, Renault, Rolls-Royce, Saab, Toyota, Volkswagen, and Volvo.

We have been successful in our quality initiatives and have been recognized by several customers, for example, via the Pinnacle Award from Toyota, the Pentastar Award from Chrysler, and Q1 from Ford. Delphi Steering has advanced manufacturing facilities, technology centers, and joint ventures in Europe, Asia, and North and South America, with plants covering more than 700,000 square meters. Over 14,000 employees generate $3 billion in annual sales.

BEFORE QS-9000: THE STATE OF THE QUALITY SYSTEM

Prior to Delphi Steering's quest for QS-9000 registration, our quality system would have been considered a traditional detection-based system. The division had implemented concepts of prevention, statistical analysis, and problem-solving with moderate success.

The theme for quality, which had existed for a number of years, was GM's Targets for Excellence (written for and applied to GM manufacturing divisions and their outside suppliers). Some people in our organization understood that the Quality Network (QN) process, which has existed within GM for a number of years, was our quality system. In reality, Quality Network is our total quality management process, developed jointly by GM and its employees, to achieve customer enthusiasm through people, teamwork, and continuous improvement. Typically, we operated under the philosophy that the responsibility for quality belonged to the quality assurance organization.

STRATEGIC RATIONALE

Delphi Steering's decision to aggressively pursue QS-9000 was a strategic decision. When we made the decision to pursue QS-9000 registration in December 1994, some customers had voiced their expectation that suppliers needed QS-9000 or ISO 9000 registration.

While not all original equipment manufacturers (OEMs) mandated ISO or QS registration, it was quite clear that a world-class quality system was required to meet the customers' quality expectations. As a supplier to virtually every major OEM in the world, we recognized the many benefits that would result from an effort to improve our quality system. The executive staff, composed of the general manager and the directors of each functional staff, viewed QS-9000 as an opportunity aimed at improving our quality system and achieving customer enthusiasm. It was also a way to gain recognition in the marketplace as an organization that strongly supports quality and continuous improvement. We felt that an early success in QS-9000 registration would serve to set us apart and help us take a giant step in the area of quality system improvements.

The executive staff also recognized that this was an enormous challenge—one that would impact the culture and future of the organization. As a result, they invited the UAW to participate as a full partner in the QS-9000 process. Delphi Steering realized that the full cooperation of all employees was required in order to achieve QS-9000 registration. We recognized that our UAW partners needed to be involved at the beginning of the process. Again, this decision was made to help us achieve more than one objective. Certainly joint union and management participation would help us with the specific goal of achieving QS-9000, but it was also an opportunity to enhance our overall union and management relations throughout our domestic facilities.

IMPLEMENTATION PROCESS

The actual implementation process used by Delphi Steering is shown in Figure 5–1. The events are numbered in the order in which they occurred during our actual implementation. They were not all necessarily identified at the start of the process, as the whole process was pioneered while we moved ahead. We need to call attention to the note on Figure 5–1: "Training ongoing throughout process" (e.g., training in the QS requirement, procedure training, training the entire workforce in the quality policy, auditor training, problem-solving training, and escort training). To further underscore the need for training, early in the process we visited two GM facilities that had recently completed ISO 9000 registration. We learned from them firsthand that the training associated with QS-9000 was significant, but we never anticipated that the commitment and required resources would be of the magnitude that resulted throughout the entire implementation process.

QS-9000 Implementation Process

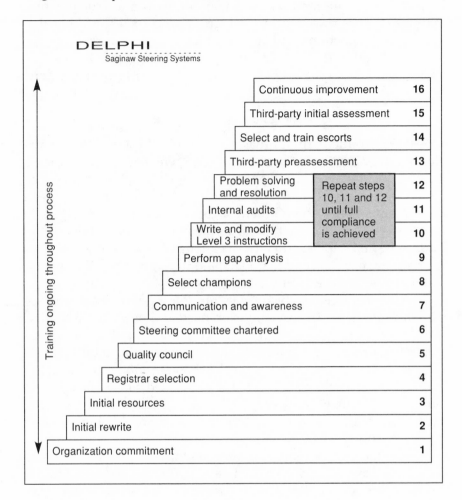

Step 1: Organization Commitment

As mentioned, many of our old quality system procedures did not reflect current operating practices and, more important, did not reflect the requirements necessary to achieve QS-9000 registration. In past years, a project of this magnitude—to rewrite a significant number of quality procedures—would, without question, have been undertaken by one or two people in the quality assurance and engineering groups.

We knew that the new QS-9000 requirement would impact our entire organization and that to successfully meet the challenge we needed to get full organizational commitment to rewrite our procedures. We also wanted to use a cross-functional team that represented all functions and manufacturing sites. We received the necessary commitment, and our team came together as the first major event in the new QS-9000 quality system implementation.

Step 2: Initial Rewrite

QS-9000 introduces an approach to "Quality System Documentation Progression," which spells out requirements for generating a Level 1 document (e.g., a quality manual); Level 2 documents (e.g., procedures); and Level 3 documents (e.g., job instructions). With the organizational commitment achieved, the process began in earnest as we pulled together an 18-member cross-functional team and, as the first step, scheduled a week-long QS-9000 training session. Our rewrite team needed to understand the entire QS-9000 requirement before there was any attempt to rewrite procedures.

While completing this QS-9000 training phase, it became apparent to the team that our division needed a new quality policy. Our first reaction was to draft a divisional quality policy within our quality assurance staff, but after a more careful look at the QS-9000 requirements, we decided to place the challenge of writing a quality policy with our executive staff. They accepted the challenge, and our quality policy was born: "We are committed to achieving customer enthusiasm. Our first priority is to provide high-quality products and services."

The quality assurance staff decided to begin generating a new Delphi Steering quality manual that, when completed, would fully describe our new quality system. This new manual soon became an identifiable symbol and rallying point of the implementation process that was beginning to take shape across the division.

Step 3: Initial Resources

The decision to strongly recommend to our executive staff that we begin our actual implementation process jointly with our UAW labor union as full partners was paramount to our success. A proposed implementation organization chart was put together by our top Quality Network joint representatives working in conjunction with our quality assurance leadership. The proposal taken to our executive staff showed co-champions from union and management leading the charge. Figure 5–2 shows the implementation structure. This chart was shown to the executive staff and the divisional quality council to achieve their buy-in and full support. With its nine members from top union and management, the divisional quality council is our Quality Network governing body.

The executive staff understood that dedicated resources would be required to accomplish such a major undertaking. Shortly after leadership's decision to go forward with the proposed implementation team and to provide the necessary resources, they asked the newly formed implementation team to determine what resources—personnel, equipment, facilities, and training—would be required to accomplish registration. Thus, our first attempt to draft an implementation budget began.

F I G U R E 5–2

QS-9000 Joint Process

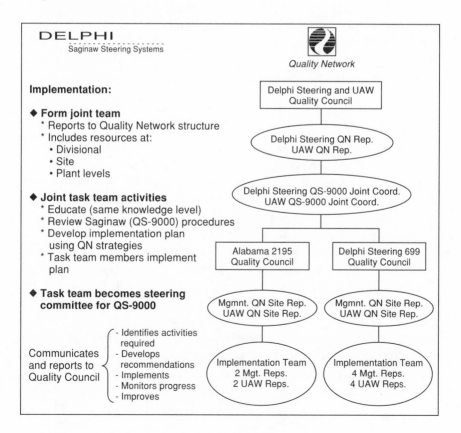

The implementation co-champions, along with members of the divisional quality assurance staff, drafted a proposed budget consisting of resources for people, computers, training, registration, and outside quality consultant costs. The total resources required were communicated to the appropriate staffs with a request for their approval, which was granted after several revisions.

Step 4: Registrar Selection

Our parent organization, Delphi Automotive Systems, provided our division with the opportunity to select from five prescreened registrars. These registrars had earlier met specific quoting criteria generated by a group of quality and purchasing professionals from various divisions of Delphi Automotive Systems.

Our implementation team, along with members of the divisional quality assurance staff, invited three of the registrars to come to Delphi Steering's world headquarters, where each independently presented his company for interview and selection consideration. Out of this process, the implementation team members and participants from quality assurance unanimously selected one registrar who had the highest experience level and displayed the most professional presentation. This registrar has served us for preassessments and initial assessments.

Step 5: Quality Council

The next step in the effort to obtain QS-9000 registration was to get the total commitment of the plant or staff leadership to ensure that a complete understanding of the task at hand was communicated. The plant quality council consists of top UAW and Delphi Steering leaders for that particular facility. The leadership commitment was a critical aspect due to the significant cost, resource, communication, and training efforts that each plant had to budget.

Meetings with each plant's quality council were conducted by the divisional joint QS-9000 coordinators, who had the overall responsibility for communicating the QS-9000 plan. A one-hour overview covering the specific details of how the process worked and the guidelines that would be followed was given to each council.

Realizing the depth of understanding these stakeholders needed, further training was provided to expand the QS-9000 knowledge base of the councils. Each quality council had the responsibility to approve the communication rollout step by step, removing any and all roadblocks and also monitoring the process for improvements. The leadership commitment had to be the driving force in order to get the involvement of the workforce and maintain it.

Step 6: Steering Committee Chartered

Steering committees were recognized as a formal part of the process and took on various responsibilities depending on the plant or function they represented. In most cases, the plant quality council did not officially appoint a steering committee. The committees developed out of need.

In one of the manufacturing facilities, the quality assurance task team became the steering committee. In another plant, the superintendents of the facility became this committee. A formal steering committee was developed at world headquarters. This group was composed of representatives from the various functional staffs within the organization. Certain staffs (such as engineering) found it necessary to have a steering committee within their own group to ensure the various steps in the process were met. Engineering, due to its organizational size, the diversity of products, and the specific documentation requirements it is responsible for, had an enormous challenge and therefore utilized the steering committee concept to help drive the process.

The various steering committees normally met weekly to resolve new issues and assure that the time lines were being met. As with other groups involved in the process of QS-9000 implementation, training needed to be provided to these committees also.

Step 7: Communication and Awareness

Realizing that communication is critical to any effort, we focused our attention on making sure that each employee had the level of understanding necessary to be successful in this endeavor. QS-9000 requirements meant that the employees' knowledge of our quality system had to be increased. The communication started from the top down, with information first given to the quality council then rolled out to all salary and hourly employees.

Training was conducted based on the level of knowledge needed for the task at hand. Training was developed to address different expertise and was normally delivered in two-, four-, and eight-hour blocks depending on each employee's position and knowledge. The communication process utilized different media such as banners, pocket cards, newsletters, check stubs, monthly meetings, and in-plant TV monitors to deliver the message concerning QS-9000. The details of QS-9000, along with its importance to retaining existing business and obtaining new business, had to be conveyed. Our leaders were featured in a series of videos that delivered the QS-9000 message. The implementation teams held the meetings, handed out pocket cards, and conveyed the message of QS-9000. All employees were involved in more than one communication. At subsequent meetings, each employee received a pen with the quality policy printed on it. Employees were asked to sign a large quality policy banner to indicate their support of the policy.

Step 8: Select Champions

Selecting champions is a vital step. The champion should be a dedicated person who will ensure that the process is moving effectively in the right direction. Ideally, the champion should have an in-depth understanding of the current quality system and a basic knowledge of QS-9000. At divisional headquarters, champions were selected for each functional staff group or steering committee. At the plant site, champions were selected for every department. Some plants also appointed a plantwide champion. These were manufacturing superintendents who were relieved of their normal job responsibilities to assist the QS-9000 implementation process.

When there was a significant increase in implementation activity, the executive staff appointed an executive-level manager to champion the QS-9000 process. This sent a very clear message that the division was committed to achieving the goal of QS-9000 registration for world headquarters (including divisional functional staffs and engineering) and four domestic facilities by the end of 1995.

Champions had to monitor the implementation steps and report major obstacles to the quality council or other appropriate leadership team for their respective area. In some cases, the champion selected had the required skills to drive the process but did not have the QS-9000 knowledge base. The implementation team provided the knowledge based on QS-9000 and assisted in driving the process forward.

Step 9: Perform Gap Analysis

Gap analysis examines the current state versus the required or desired state. To measure the gap between the current state of the quality system and the QS-9000 requirements, the implementation team developed a common format. The format included the *Quality System Assessment (QSA)* as a baseline (Figure 5–3).

The results of the gap analysis became the road map and the rationale for allocating resources. Although management initially appeared shocked at the results, in reality they should not have been surprised. The internal audit process had been reporting the same discrepancies, but the appropriate corrective action had yet to be implemented.

F I G U R E 5-3

ISO/QS-9000 Gap Analysis

DELPHI Saginaw Steering Systems										Quality Network
Delphi ISO / QS-9000 Gap Analysis Worksheet Procedure 731 - Management Responsibility for the Quality System									QS-9000 Requirements	
Area Affected:_____ Area Contact Person:_____ Area Superintendent:_____ Date:_____ Page:____										
Action Element	Div.	Plt.	Dept.	Current Situation	Need to Do	Owner	Proj. Comp. Date	Open/ Compelete	Comments	
1. Is the quality policy communicated, understood and maintained throughout the organization? (I.4.1.1)	X	X	X							
2. Are there clearly defined and documented responsibilities and authorities for all personnel affecting quality? (I.4.1.2)	X	X	X							
3. Is authority delegated to personnel to: • Prevent non-conformity reoccurrence? • Identify & record quality problems? • Initiate & verify corrective action? • Control further processing (I.4.1.2)		X X X X	X X X X							
4. Is a multi-disciplinary approach used in the design process with direct input in decision making? (4.1.2)	X	X								
5. Is there a periodic top management review of quality system effectiveness supported by appropriate records? (I.4.1.3)	X	X								

We hired an outside consultant to assist with our gap analysis. The consultant worked with our implementation team members and provided an objective evaluation of our system and a clear interpretation of the requirements. The gap analysis also identified the areas where our workforce required training, and it served as a learning tool for the organization. Taking time to evaluate and communicate the current state of the quality system was a major event.

Step 10: Write and Modify Level 3 Instructions

Step 10 became the natural outcome of the gap analysis. Our Level 3 documents (work and operating instructions) needed our immediate attention. It became obvious that our current Level 3 documents were not in compliance with QS-9000 requirements. Unfortunately, at first we attempted to rewrite our documents without observing our current practices. We quickly learned to update instructions to reflect current practices. We also had to *change* some practices to meet QS-9000 requirements.

Step 11: Internal Audits

Our most important tool to drive continuous improvement, the internal audit, was being underutilized. Our up-front QS-9000 training helped the organization understand the significance of internal auditing. An audit schedule was developed for each plant site and for the divisional functional staffs. The audit checklist was modified to reflect the new QS-9000 requirement. We also strengthened our audit documentation requirement. For each question, objective evidence needed to be gathered to verify compliance or noncompliance.

Our corrective action process included a five-step approach: (1) *identify* the problem, (2) *analyze* the situation, (3) develop the *plan* to resolve the problem, (4) *implement* the corrective action, and (5) *evaluate* the results to make certain the corrective action worked. Nonconformities were reviewed with the leadership team, ensuring that resources would be allocated to correct the problem. To complete the audit cycle, additional auditors were added, which required more training. We chose to hire external accredited professionals to train our auditors.

Step 12: Problem-Solving and Resolution

The corrective action process was painful and expensive; however, the root cause of each problem was identified and corrected. Corrective action *verification* was key to ensuring that the problem was solved. Collecting objective evidence to demonstrate conformance was new to our process and proved to be highly effective. We had to repeat process steps 10, 11, and 12 until we were convinced that full compliance was achieved.

Step 13: Third-Party Preassessment

The original plan was to have one preassessment at one of our manufacturing facilities and then share the experience throughout the division. We realized there were many benefits to scheduling preassessments at each site, so we modified our plan to include preassessments at each facility. This included a preassessment at our divisional headquarters. We went so far as to have our executive staff audited on Element 4.1: Management Responsibility. The third-party preassessment helped us create a greater sense of urgency, provided our leadership team with a clear picture of the actual level of implementation, and allowed the workforce to become familiar with the assessment process. After generating nonconformance reports based on the auditors' findings, we repeated steps 10, 11, and 12 until full compliance was achieved. The results of the gap analysis and preassessments were used to develop a checklist of the requirements that plant and engineering staff champions had to complete (See Figure 5–4 for plant example).

Step 14: Select and Train Escorts

An escort is someone who acts as a guide for the third-party auditor. The escort's responsibilities are to facilitate and keep the audit on schedule. In almost all cases, the QS-9000 champion was the escort. We prepared training modules on how to be an escort and how to respond during an audit. These training modules helped build confidence for a successful initial assessment.

Providing encouragement and preparing for the initial assessment were added steps to boost our confidence level and to allow us to declare, "We are ready." This phrase quickly became optimistically infectious. We created WE ARE READY banners for the plants and functional staffs and used them to proclaim readiness just prior to the facility's actual initial assessment.

Plant 7 Champion Checklist

DELPHI
Saginaw Steering Systems

PLANT 7

Department		Champion #1					Champion #2			
#1	Is the Quality Policy known?									
#2	JIG's / PFP's correct?									
#3	SUS's up-to-date?									
#4	Employee Instruction Manual									
#5	Organizational charts									
#6	Training matrix									
#7	"Call It Right Manual"									
#8	Repair manuals									
#9	Proper charting									
#10	Procedure location									
#11	Customer contact reports									
#12	Review the 5S's									
#13	Information board									
#14	Answer the 5 phases									
#15	Safety / Ergonomics									
#16	Written training plan									
#17	Non-conforming quality issues									
#18	Proper revision levels									
#19	Log books up-to-date									
#20	Team meetings documented									
#21	"Top Ten Issues"									
#22	Preventive maintenance schedule									
#23	Packing instructions									
#24	Gages ID'ed and calibrated									
#25	Are KPC and KCC gauges ID'ed									
#26	Engineering permits									

Step 15: Third-Party Initial Assessment

The day of reckoning finally arrived. It wasn't brutal, but we were still very anxious. Prior to the auditor's arrival, we reviewed their audit schedule and provided feedback. Changes were permitted based on logistics or obvious errors. We did not have the liberty to delete any department from the audit schedule but could add departments if time permitted. The third-party auditors developed the schedule based on floor-plan layouts and products produced. Top leaders from union and management attended the opening meeting to show their support of the effort.

As we visited each area, we took careful notes of the auditors' comments. If nonconformities were discovered, we took immediate action when appropriate. The scheduled daily reviews with the auditors and the people who had been audited that day ensured an understanding of all the findings. The auditors need to experience that the workforce is involved and committed to correcting the problems identified and driving continuous improvement. Top leaders also attended the closing meeting, again demonstrating their support. After the closing meeting, steps 10, 11, and 12 were performed once again to resolve minor nonconformities, and the formal correction report was submitted to the third-party auditors. Delphi Steering was recommended for registration at each plant or site assessed.

Step 16: Continuous Improvement

Our quality system philosophy is based on achieving customer enthusiasm through feedback and continuous improvement. QS-9000 registration requires surveillance audits every four to six months. These third-party audits will support our quality philosophy, reinforce our need for the internal audit process, and maintain our registration. Our workforce is depending on the leadership team to continue to provide vision, direction, and commitment to being a world-class organization.

PROBLEMS ENCOUNTERED

Obviously, with an undertaking of this magnitude, numerous problems were encountered. This section highlights the problems that were the largest for us and may be common to other companies attempting to obtain QS-9000 registration.

Cost of QS-9000 Implementation

One of our earliest problems was that of the insufficient budgeting of financial and human resources. Given the limited information available on the cost of QS-9000 implementation when we established our resource requirements, we could only calculate our best guess. Unfortunately, as the process progressed, we realized that the funds we had budgeted were far short of the amount necessary to make the improvements in our current quality system that would bring us into QS-9000 compliance.

We did not allow this to stop the process. Instead, we recognized that we needed to be more aggressive in reducing costs in other areas and keeping our implementation costs to the minimum level. This forced us to look at the best manual, or "lean," methods of implementing many of the required changes. For example, we didn't procure an expensive on-line document hierarchy system; instead we improved upon our current system and put the discipline and training in place to make a manual method work. As time progresses we will look at upgrading our manual system based on cost savings or valid business case analysis. There also came a point at which each manager realized that the organization would benefit from improving the quality system and being disciplined to live the system.

Program of the Month

Another problem we encountered dealt with our history of too many short-term programs. Our workforce, in many cases, had developed a wait-and-see attitude. They weren't confident that QS-9000 and the push to improve the quality system had long-term management commitment. Our UAW leaders and implementation team members played a very pivotal role by convincing the workforce that QS-9000 *was* a long-term quality initiative and *was* indeed linked to job security.

The UAW chairmen of our local unions sent a letter to all members of their locals indicating that QS-9000 was important to the future of all employees because it was a customer expectation and it was a joint process strongly supported by the UAW. This single event created a new level of desire within the workforce, and the hourly employees started to pull the required information from the implementation teams and other knowledgeable resources within the plant.

Plant managers and the directors of the various functional staffs (such as engineering or purchasing) took a very active, visible role in QS-9000 implementation. "Quality walks," a tool used by management to visit various manufacturing departments to review quality efforts and problem-resolution activities, were increased in frequency and in scope of information reviewed. A quality walk now usually includes the plant manager and several members of the plant staff, as well as UAW representatives. To create a greater sense of urgency for QS-9000, one plant manager held several quality walks each day, covering all shifts.

A site plant manager instituted a process whereby his organizations visibly tracked their progress using large charts brightly coded with red, yellow, and green indicators. He held a meeting every Friday morning where employees reported on the progress made within each department on problem areas or gaps that required correction in their respective areas. It was clear that every department was expected to move from red (a gap to the requirement), to yellow (a corrective process has been started), to green (corrective action is implemented and the area is fully in compliance with QS-9000).

The Priority and Understanding of QS-9000

We initially had a slow start in understanding how QS-9000 fit within the organization. Employees with a good understanding of the quality requirements quickly recognized that QS-9000 was really not a different system, but rather an organized compilation of all the actions needed to have a good quality system and achieve customer enthusiasm.

Many employees, however, viewed QS-9000 as an independent process and, accordingly, resisted it because they didn't understand how it fit the big picture of our normal business practices. Through many hours of training, employees understood that QS-9000 wasn't a redundant process; we were improving our quality system to meet customer requirements, and it was part of our everyday process. As we worked at the process of training and improving our quality system, we believe we saw the

We saw the organization shift from one that felt quality was owned by quality assurance to one where the quality system was owned by everyone.

organization shift from one that felt quality was owned by quality assurance to one where the quality system was owned by everyone.

Training

Training ended up being a massive undertaking. Not only did we need to train our employees in the QS-9000 requirements, but we found we needed to train many of our employees in the *current* procedures. In most cases, the training we were looking for was not available to us in the marketplace. We spent a significant amount of time in the development of training materials.

We found ourselves in a training loop. The more we trained employees, the more questions they asked, causing us to change and improve our procedures. More training had to be given to ensure employees understood the new changes. We believe it is safe to say that all employees in those registered plants have received training that improved their business knowledge and upgraded their skill level as a result of QS-9000.

We used a variety of methods to accomplish the required training. The implementation team members in the plants were key players in training the workforce on QS-9000 and procedures. Certain facilities performed the majority of their training during regularly held departmental meetings. Functional staffs held special training classes for their employees.

Document and Data Control

Document and data control was perhaps the single biggest problem we had and was perhaps the area where the most positive improvements were made in our day-to-day business management. Some of our problem was self-created in that we truly didn't understand the requirement of document and data control. We were making it a much tougher and bigger issue than we needed to. As we continued to struggle with identifying which documents needed to be controlled and how to control them, we learned more about the *real* requirement.

Our system of document control at the onset was not adequate to meet the QS-9000 requirements. Our solution to the problem came in the form of document control centers and document control zones. A document control center is a physical location, such as a cabinet, where all documents that need to be controlled under the requirements of QS-9000 Element 4.5 are maintained. Examples for our organization are Level 1, 2, and 3 documents. Other documents include organization charts, engineering specifications, process flow-charts, and setup sheets. Each document center contains the controlled documents needed by the user group in that area. Manufacturing facilities and functional staffs decided how many document centers they needed within their respective areas, but the requirement to have a document center was universal.

Each document center must also have a "master list" that identifies the documents stored there and the revision date and "owner" of each document. All employees have been trained to go to the document center to see that they have the most recent version of any document that will impact the quality of our products. In many cases, it's as simple as comparing the revision date of the document in hand to the revision date on the master list.

Procedure Rewrites

We found ourselves in a constant state of change with our procedures for a variety of reasons. The primary reason for the numerous changes was that our procedures were out of date and no longer reflected current practice. One major problem we caused for ourselves was to aggressively write or modify procedures to achieve the ultimate state of the quality system.

We soon settled down to a process of making sure we understood the requirements, matching what we were currently doing to the requirements, changing the process or practice as required to close any gaps to the requirements, and then documenting the process in a procedure or operating instruction. We also added one last check, "Does it make business sense?" If the answer was yes, we were satisfied. If not, we kept exploring until we improved our understanding of the requirement or saw the error of our ways.

Understanding the Role of the Implementation Teams

The plan for the implementation teams was for them to become the resident experts on QS-9000 within the confines of the plant. They were there to train all employees and to answer questions. If they didn't have the answer, they were charged with finding one. They were responsible for assisting and monitoring the implementation of the process. These teams physically resided in the plant or area they were serving. It was our expectation that these teams would not own the implementation process. The process needed to be owned by the plant employees and plant leadership, the plant quality councils in our case.

Each facility went through a period when the workforce felt that the implementation team members would actually do the implementing to achieve registration. Obviously, this was prior to the plant personnel truly understanding what registration of our quality system was all about. In our experience, once the group understood that the requirements were in fact the basic quality system we should have conformed with all along, they understood that every employee was an implementor and that someone else could not come in and make it happen. The implementation teams were then allowed to function as the training, counseling, and monitoring experts. These teams met weekly to share lessons and discuss the next steps. In this way we were able to keep the process common within our facilities and rapidly transfer best practices between our plants and staff.

Role and Training of Auditors and Internal Audit Process

Our audit process did not meet QS-9000 requirements. It became painfully evident during the preparation for our assessment that our process was ineffective. We had cut back on resources dedicated to the audit function, provided little training for the auditors we did have, and were not disciplined to respond to the audit discrepancies with a sense of urgency. As a result, we struggled with much of our initial gap analysis.

As a solution to our problem, we held several audit training classes. These were taught by an outside consulting house and included sessions of actual hands-on auditing. We then had the in-plant auditors and divisional functional staff auditors work closely with the implementation teams. This strengthened the audit skills of all employees and also transferred knowledge about the QS-9000 process to the auditors.

AFTER QS-9000 REGISTRATION: STATE OF THE QUALITY SYSTEM

We now believe that we have successfully shifted our quality focus from one of detection to one of prevention, quality planning, and continuous improvement. Our QS-9000 quality system is now recognized as a divisionwide quality system that involves all employees. We believe that we have a good, solid beginning to a quality system that is everyone's responsibility.

A number of other realized benefits to our registration effort show our new, higher-level state of quality:

- We have a quotable, understandable divisionwide quality policy.
- We have a workforce trained in our quality system requirements.
- We have all of our Level 2 QS-9000 related procedures up-to-date.
- We have a new QS-9000 based quality manual.
- All employees have access to current procedures and instructions via our document centers.
- We have the responsibility and authority for our quality system fully defined and fully implemented.
- We have increased the dialogue and ownership of the quality system between the UAW and management.
- Our new, enhanced approach toward quality system audits includes a formalized process to drive continuous improvement of our quality system and of our operations across the division.
- We have used the QS-9000 implementation process as a rallying point around quality.
- The entire organization has risen to a much higher level of discipline regarding the understanding and following of procedures.

LESSONS LEARNED

As we completed our first wave of QS-9000 assessments we stopped to reflect on the lessons learned. We did this several times during the process, which allowed us to change course and improve the process as we moved into a different facility or a different stage in the process. Keep in mind that our plants and functional staffs were following the same generic process but were doing so at different points in time. Consequently, lessons learned in one plant could be quickly transferred to another plant or staff, and modifications in the implementation process could be made as required.

Joint Union and Management Process

We strongly believe the single most important decision was making our implementation process a joint union and management process. This joint process provided the checks and balances to make sure adequate resources were obtained and corrective action was implemented. Quality councils, the mechanism used to monitor the process, were an integral part of General Motors' Quality Network process and existed at the divisional level, at each plant and staff group. These various councils operated with different levels of effectiveness. Regardless of the current state at any council, we were consistent in using that forum as the basis for the implementation in each plant.

The diversity of union and management worked well for us. For example, the union had its implementation team members appointed in advance of management. They kept the organization focused on getting the rest of the employees assigned to the team and getting the process started. Union leadership helped implement some of the corrective actions required to close gaps to the QS-9000 requirement. In some cases gap closure required different work practices on the part of union hourly employees. In a few instances, our employees resisted the changes. Our union leadership helped those employees understand that this was not management just trying to make the job tougher but a quality system requirement and therefore it was necessary for the workforce to comply. The change in our quality system, and corresponding change in our culture, was so massive it could not have been accomplished without the full cooperation of both union and management.

> *Union leadership helped implement some of the corrective actions required to close gaps to the QS-9000 requirement.*

Departmental Champions

We learned quickly that we needed to empower the "correct" level of the organization to implement the required changes. The employees performing the work needed full ownership. Through the use of departmental champions, in both plant departments and staff work groups, we unleashed the real power of the organization. The use of champions necessitated extensive training, but the benefits to the organization were evident in the success of our process. We are confident we will continue to achieve benefits from the quality system training we gave our employees.

Cross-Functional Teams

Our quality system touches all employees. This is good news and bad news. It is great to get everyone involved, but very difficult to make a change because each change impacts so many people or areas. We used cross-functional teams extensively throughout our implementation. The concept of cross-functional teams is not new to our organization; it is the way we run the business. However, companies pursuing registration need to understand that the process should not be done in a vacuum, including only those employees or departments that most impact quality.

Integration of QS-9000 into Our Normal Business Practices

QS-9000 is not a stand-alone process. We have improved our quality system to meet, at a minimum, the QS-9000 requirements. Our goal of being QS-9000 registered by the end of 1995 was considered a major initiative by Delphi Steering. It received the same level of exposure to the executive staff as did other initiatives within the division. Many other processes, such as our product development process, were improved as a result of our QS-9000 initiative. We now recognize our quality system as being compliant with QS-9000 and one of the major business initiatives for continuous improvement within the organization.

Benefits of Document Control

The use of document control centers has been a major success. We believe there is a significant benefit from QS-9000 Element 4.5. All employees now have ready access to all the information they need to perform their jobs. All instructions, whether they are specific employee job instructions, machine setup instructions, or gauge calibrations, are at the latest revision and up-to-date. Most questions that impact the quality of a product can be answered by walking to the document center and looking for the information. We also have a process in place to keep the procedures and instructions current. Our procedure requires us to not only make the change in the required documents but also to communicate that revision to the affected people. The magnitude of any given change may indicate the need for training versus mere communication of a change.

Training

A significant proportion of the training we found necessary was due to neglect. We had always done a fair amount of training; however, it was obvious that we had not done enough. We recognize that training must be continuous. We have improved upon several of our practices to ensure that training continues to receive the priority it deserves. We will look to our joint process to help keep the balance between the cost of training and the need to train our employees appropriately.

Internal Audit Process

The internal audit process is key to assessing compliance to the QS-9000 requirement and to maintaining the system once it is implemented. Our lesson: We needed to increase the resources devoted to that process, provide additional training for those resources, modify our audit checklists, and completely redo the way we schedule and control audits and audit results. We learned that our audit process will be the means to understand the opportunities of our current quality system and to drive improvement. The audit process will be the basis of improving our quality system. We now have a process where results of all audits are reviewed by the appropriate owners for corrective action. The plant quality councils and executive staff review audit results with the intent of improving our current system. Any significant change to our quality system will be part of our routine business planning annual goals and initiatives process, allowing the quality system to receive the attention necessary within the organization to achieve customer enthusiasm.

Leadership Commitment

As with any major change initiative undertaken, leadership commitment is key. Our effort was no exception. We cannot stress enough the importance of having the entire organization perceive that leadership is committed and involved. If the leaders feel committed but the organization perceives otherwise, nothing has been gained. Both the visibility of plant managers during quality walks and the union and management participation in quality councils were critical to motivating the organization.

As the activity increased in the implementation process, an executive-level manager was appointed as overall champion of the QS-9000 effort. This executive champion kept the organization focused, motivated, and on schedule throughout the implementation process.

Use of Registrar and Consultants

Over the course of the registrar selection and the preassessments, we learned to use the registrar to our advantage. We considered the registrar to be our partner and attempted to work proactively with our assessors. Although registrars selected to perform the actual audits cannot consult, we did use our registrar to provide a clear interpretation of the requirements. This was often done by showing them a solution to a problem during a preassessment to make sure it met the requirement. We decided to expose our problems to the registrar during preassessment rather than try to hide them. In this way, we were able to get a better understanding of what the expectation was and to address the requirement in an efficient manner.

SUMMARY

We recognize that we have only just started our journey to full QS-9000 registration for all entities within Delphi Steering. We are currently pursuing QS-9000 registration in our four remaining domestic plants, as well as all global facilities. The majority of our global facilities have already achieved ISO 9000 registration levels and are now beginning their journey to QS-9000.

As with any major change effort, old habits need to be removed, new habits or practices need to be installed, and then the new culture or practices need to be institutionalized. We believe we have modified the old practices, but we have not yet refrozen, or institutionalized, this new quality system. Our current plan is to use our internal audit process to solidify the new practices and the current high level of discipline to the quality system.

We recommend that any company pursuing QS-9000 registration view it as an opportunity to drive major improvements within an organization—as opposed to merely a customer requirement. QS-9000 registration can have a great, far-reaching impact on an organization. We believe our company is better situated to meet the competitive demands of the future as a result of our QS-9000 compliant quality system.

This case study is contributed jointly by Diane M. Fries, Quality Assurance Manager; David M. Carter, Quality Assurance Senior Administrator; Richard H. Hamood, QS-9000 Coordinator and Quality Assurance General Supervisor; and James F. Jackson, UAW QS-9000 Coordinator with Delphi Saginaw Steering Systems, General Motors Corporation, Saginaw, Michigan.

CHAPTER 6

10 Commandments for Achieving QS-9000

Drake Products Corporation

GENERAL

- *Headquarters* : **Grand Rapids, Michigan, U.S.A.**
- *Year Founded* : **1970**
- *Number of Employees* : **300**

QS-9000 SPECIFIC

- *Registered Location(s)* : **Greenville, Michigan, U.S.A.**
  Anderson, South Carolina, U.S.A.
- *Number of Employees* : **300**
- *Registration Date* : **April 27, 1995**
- *Product(s)* : **Custom Injection Moldings**
- *Tier I, II, III Supplier* : **Tier I**
- *Major Customer(s)* : **General Motors, Ford, BMW, Frigidaire**
- *Annual Sales* : **U.S. $50 Million**

INTRODUCTION: IN THE BEGINNING . . .

In the beginning, several years ago at Drake Products Corporation, there was much chaos, especially in the Quality Assurance Department. As in so many corporations, the Quality Assurance Department was separated from the rest of the corporation and left to handle "quality problems" as they became known. Our internal reject levels were well above 10 percent on a daily basis, and customer complaints were received every day. The ISO 9000 series of standards was just becoming known within the United States because of the formation of the European Common Market. These standards, especially ISO 9001, became the backbone for QS-9000.

Drake Products Corporation made the decision to pursue ISO 9001 registration in the last quarter of 1993. It was granted in early 1994. QS-9000 registration followed in 1995. In the same time period, the corporation was in a period of rapid growth. Our corporation grew from a single plant with $8 million in sales to a three-plant operation with sales approaching $50 million. In addition, a separate corporate office was opened in a nearby metropolitan area, Grand Rapids, Michigan. The Service Division was started, and a previous plant site was repurchased. The equipment to start the Service Division was remanufactured equipment from the main plant where new equipment was leased. Also, a State of Michigan Educational Grant for $183,888 was received.

This case study will be the technical director's summary of the experience gained at Drake. Hopefully, readers of this account may learn to avoid many pitfalls in their quest to comply with QS-9000. The most difficult part of any new venture is usually the beginning. Fear of the unknown is present, and the wisdom of pioneers is grossly lacking or, worse, often contradictory. Since the journey to QS-9000 is a new adventure for many, the term *pioneer* is very appropriate.

As a pioneer, Drake has found that simple advice has helped the entire corporation. This simple advice, which will be discussed shortly in the sections below, is given as the "10 commandments" for achieving QS-9000 registration. These 10 commandments are basically self-evident, though putting them into practice is difficult. Nonetheless, they are necessary to consider before any outlay of expenditures is committed.

Registration to QS-9000 has opened many new markets to the Drake Products Corporation and has made the external customer audits a less troublesome chore.

CORPORATE PROFILE:
THE PROMISED LAND ...

Before elaborating on the 10 commandments for achieving QS-9000, it would be wise to give a brief corporate profile. Drake Products Corporation began in 1946 with two injection molding machines. The first order was for little plastic buttons to be used in Gibson refrigerators to hold the shelves to the metal sides. The second order was for plastic glides to keep the metal legs of Samsonite folding chairs from marring floors.

Drake Products Corporation has averaged 25 percent growth over the last 10 years. Today, the corporation is a world-class manufacturer of plastic components for appliance, automotive, office furniture, and other industries. Drake Products Corporation offers a complete line of processes, from design and engineering to production, decorating, and assembly. Computerization and robotics are integral parts of the total operations. State-of-the-art equipment, highly skilled people, and QS-9000 business philosophy keep customers satisfied.

Currently, two plant expansions are taking place. One is for 40,000 square feet and the other is for 64,000 square feet. Just recently, new corporate offices were opened in Grand Rapids, Michigan. The workforce of approximately 300 is dedicated to maintaining the double-digit growth rate. Drake Products Corporation has achieved Tier I status to the highly competitive automotive market. In large part, achieving QS-9000 registration has fostered Drake's team approach and problem-solving abilities.

COMMANDMENT 1: KNOW QS-9000 . . . NO OTHER SYSTEMS

One cannot expect to achieve QS-9000 registration without knowing the requirements. In practice, QS-9000 must be fully understood by all top and staff management. They must endorse it wholeheartedly and make it the business philosophy for the corporation. This endorsement must be effectively communicated to everyone. All employees throughout the organization will be touched by the implementation of QS-9000, no matter what department they work in. It is not just another quality program.

All employees throughout the organization will be touched by the implementation of QS-9000.

The old way of doing things must be carefully scrutinized. Almost all procedures and practices will need to be reviewed and rewritten. The scope of QS-9000 can best be described by rearranging the requirements so they make sense to any individual corporation. The following rearrangement was used at Drake Products Corporation:

A. Management Commitment
    1. Management responsibilty
    2. Quality system
B. Design Assurance
    3. Contract review
    4. Design review
C. Manufacturing Planning
    5. Document and data control
    6. Purchasing
    7. Production part approval process
    8. Manufacturing capabilities
D. Manufacturing Control
    9. Control of customer-supplied product
    10. Product identification and traceability
    11. Process control
    12. Inspection and testing
    13. Inspection, measuring, and test equipment
    14. Inspection and test status
    15. Control of nonconforming product
    16. Corrective and preventive actions
    17. Handling, storage, packaging, and delivery
    18. Control of quality records
    19. Servicing
E. Product Improvement
    20. Training
    21. Statistical techniques
    22. Continuous improvement
F. Audit
    23. ISO 9001 and QS-9000 system audits

The six categories are logical. Grouping the 23 elements in this fashion made the entire scope of the QS-9000 understandable to our employees. Briefly, a corporation must have management commitment for any sizable project. Next, to manufacture a new product, there should be some assurance that the product is designed correctly. This is followed by complete planning for manufacturing. Once in production, the manufacturing of the product must be controlled. The next phase, Product Improvement, has become a way of life in the industrial world; cost savings and quality improvements are demanded by customers. Finally, audits prove that the entire cycle is being followed.

In summary, QS-9000 ensures that the entire product life cycle is considered. It simply makes good common sense. Management would be wise to forget the old quality systems and incorporate all the elements of QS-9000. Rather than trying to defend the old quality assurance (QA) manual, it may be cost effective to establish a new system that follows the elements of QS-9000 element by element. The QA manual at Drake Products Corporation does that exactly. It makes for easy document review not only by the registrar but by any customer. Also, several additional sections were added to our QA manual since they were not formally called out by QS-9000 but are believed to be very important. These are as follows: quality costs; product liability and safety; customer satisfaction; and an appendix that cross-references our manual to seven other quality systems including Mil-Q-9858, GMP, 10CFR50, and the Malcolm Baldrige National Quality Award.

COMMANDMENT 2: DO NOT DO IN VAIN (AN EXCELLENT COST-SAVING PROGRAM)

There is no need to take QS-9000 registration in vain. It is an excellent cost-saving program. As with any business decision, you must spend corporate dollars where they will provide a favorable return on investment. This is true with the costs associated with achieving and maintaining QS-9000 registration. For a $50 to $100 million corporation, registration costs are believed to be approximately $180,000, while average annual savings are $130,000 less than a two-year payback. The data reflect that larger companies will experience a faster payback—approximately one year—while smaller companies (under $11 million in annual sales) will experience a three-year payback period.

At our corporation, the expenses were considerably less than average. We were fortunate to have an excellent registrar located within 50 miles of two of our manufacturing sites. This allowed considerable cost savings regarding travel and lodging expenses. Furthermore, all training was done by company personnel. There was zero expenditure for outside consultants and preaudits. Management trusted employees, which truly paid off. Employee awareness and involvement were fostered mainly through shift meetings. However, cross-functional QS-9000 teams were established at each plant undergoing registration. These teams were composed of a corporate technical director, a plant manager, a quality assurance manager, a buyer, a scheduler, and a shipping supervisor. Weekly meetings of the QS-9000 teams took place. This will be the topic of the next commandment.

COMMANDMENT 3: ESTABLISH A MEETING DAY . . . AND KEEP IT HOLY

In order to keep the QS-9000 registration on time and meet management deadlines, our plant QS-9000 teams established a weekly meeting day and kept it "holy." Typical of each of the three plants' QS-9000 schedules are the following weekly milestones:

1. Letter of intent to registrar.
2. Establishment of plant QS-9000 team.
3. Initial team meeting.
4. Review of corporate policies and standards.
5. Individual team member element assessment.
6. Assessment review and corrective actions.
7. Implementation of corrective actions.
8. Preparation of evidence files.
9. Plant QS-9000 team audit.
10. Team audit review and action plans.
11. Implementation of QS-9000 team action plan.
12. Management audit.
13. Implementation of corrective actions.
14. Registrar's initial assessment.

The weekly milestones were established after management commitment was secured and the corporate document review was completed. After the registrar's initial assessment, the following additional steps were scheduled. The length of each of these steps varied from one week to one month, depending on the corrective actions that had to be implemented.

1. Corrective actions for noncompliances.
2. Corrective actions documentation package to registrar.

3. Registrar's review of corrective actions.
4. Team assessment of plant's QS-9000 readiness.
5. Registrar's assessment audit.
6. Corrective actions for noncompliances.
7. Corrective actions documentation to registrar.
8. Review by registrar's board.
9. Final corrections and implementation.
10. Formal registration.

As can be seen from the two preceding lists, there are essentially three internal stages: individual team member assessment of specific elements, plant QS-9000 team audit, and corporate internal audit. These are followed by at least two audits carried out by the registrar: the initial assessment and the final QS-9000 assessment.

It is important to realize that the schedules must be flexible and are highly dependent on dedication and time availability of key personnel. Cooperation between departments and individuals is paramount for task completion. Weekly meetings of the QS-9000 plant team and adequate preparations must have high priority throughout the registration process.

COMMANDMENT 4: HONOR THE ORGANIZATION AND PAST ACHIEVEMENTS

In pursuing QS-9000 registration, the entire employee workforce, especially the QS-9000 team, must remember the past achievements of the corporation and take pride in its present position. Procedures and policies that have stood the test of time should not be abolished. Organization structure should not be radically changed. If the current organization is in proper standing with customers, the mood of operation should be business as usual. Gradual changes done with affected employees' knowledge will produce the improvements necessary to satisfy QS-9000 requirements.

Naturally, if the corporation is not doing well and has been on a downhill slide for an extended period of time, then indications demand that drastic steps be taken. Taking drastic measures is not the usual case, however, and extreme care must be exercised if that is the true situation. More harm than good may result by changing too much too fast.

The commandment to honor the organization presupposes that the duties of management and workers are defined and understood. Are job descriptions up-to-date and available for all employees? Regarding the QS-9000 team, is there a clearly defined charter? How much authority can the QS-9000 team or individual members exercise? Observing this commandment brings its reward. Respecting this commandment provides peace in daily operations and will make the journey toward QS-9000 registration go smoothly. Conversely, failure to observe it will bring great harm to the corporation and to individual employees.

Traveling toward QS-9000 registration, the corporation and all its employees (salaried as well as hourly) should learn to care and take responsibility for complete customer (external and internal) satisfaction. By doing so, new tasks and responsibilities may be defined. Proper authority must then be assigned and respected. Those who exercise authority should do so as a service. Obedience to those in authority should not be blind but rather completely understood. Employers have always had a responsibility for the education of their employees. It should be no different regarding QS-9000 requirements.

COMMANDMENT 5: DO NOT OVERKILL

Commandment 5 will be devoted to document control. Many surveys and published articles have claimed that document control is the most difficult area of QS-9000. The best advice for document control is simply this: DO NOT OVERKILL. Keep only those documents that are appropriate, relevant, simple, understandable, and consistent with the corporate operations in use. A guideline for any corporation seeking QS-9000 registration is, *"Document what you do and do what you document."* If it is not documented, it has not been done. Verification of document effectiveness should be done with extreme care to avoid establishing policies and procedures that are unnecessary or ineffective.

Policies, procedures, records, and other documents must be considered as the blood of life for the corporation regarding QS-9000. The legitimate defense of document control is not only "because it is a QS-9000 requirement" but also that it is a grave duty for the common good of the corporation. Preserving the common good of the corporation requires rendering policies and procedures unable to inflict harm. For this reason the corporation should establish legitimate authority to revise policies and procedures. The primary effect of changing documents must be to redress the disorder caused by the faulty policy or procedure.

Policies and procedures must be written and enforced to avoid scandal within the corporation. That is, policies and procedures must not promote an attitude or behavior that may lead to corporate harm by tempting an employee to misapplications. Respect for the health of the corporation can be shown by employees exercising temperance—that is, avoiding every kind of excess—when writing policies and procedures.

Document control should safeguard peace within the corporation. Peace is not merely the absence of conflict between individuals and departments. Nor is it limited to maintaining a balance of power. All employees are obliged to work for peace and to avoid conflict by following corporate rules; thus, document control is vital for the life of the corporation.

COMMANDMENT 6: COMMIT NO DEPARTMENTAL SIN; BE LOYAL

Each of the elements in QS-9000 must be treated as equal. The harmony of the quality system requirements depends on the complementary needs and mutual support among the elements. Specific elements of QS-9000 need to be assigned to corporate experts on the QS-9000 team to ensure that successful integration throughout the organization takes place. The alternative is clear: If one department dominates (e.g., purchasing), the other departments suffer.

Loyalty must be practiced by the QS-9000 team members. Within a corporation, loyalty involves a cultural effort, for there is an interdependence between departmental betterment and the total improvement of the corporation in becoming QS-9000 registered. Loyalty presupposes respect for the rights of the individual departments, in particular the right to receive and give information. Loyalty is expressed notably in friendly relationships with other departments.

All departments within a corporation must work in harmony for the continued growth and welfare of the corporation. Lack of cooperation among departments is dangerous because it introduces disorder into everyday operations. This disorder brings grave harm not only to the deserted department but also to any other department ments that have direct working relations with it. The concept of the "collaborative organization" is paramount for achieving QS-9000 registration. That is, responsible employees and departments must work together to achieve an agreed-upon goal: QS-9000 registration.

COMMANDMENT 7: DO NOT STEAL; ADAPT QS-9000 TO YOUR OPERATIONS

Many corporations think a simple way to achieve QS-9000 registration is to buy a ready-made QS-9000 manual and force employees to follow the stated procedures. Other corporations think that short-term consulting by experts is the way. Neither of these two ways seems to bring desired results. There is no quick, easy, inexpensive method by which to achieve QS-9000 registration. Only hard work by corporate employees who are dedicated to a collaborative cross-functional team will produce long-lasting results.

At Drake Products Corporation, no outside consultants were used, nor was there any massive attendance by employees at QS-9000 seminars and conferences. This does not imply that outside resources cannot help or reduce the time required. However, it does imply that many corporations have all the necessary resources at their current disposal; all they need is management trust and commitment.

The best information for achieving QS-9000 is the requirement itself. Careful reading by management is necessary. Roundtable discussion groups are very beneficial because they can focus line and staff management, as well as promote management involvement. Employees are to be entrusted with corporate resources. Through common stewardship, they must take care of them, master them by labor, and enjoy their fruits. The secret to success at Drake Products Corporation was to establish at each plant an empowered QS-9000 team whose members were organized, authorized, responsible, competent, and knowledgeable (or at least highly interested).

COMMANDMENT 8: DO NOT MISREPRESENT THE TRUTH

The eighth commandment forbids misrepresenting the truth in our relations with others. Offenses against the truth expressed by word or deed are a refusal to commit oneself, as well as the corporation, to moral uprightness. False words and deeds are fundamentally wrong and, in this sense, will undermine the good that can be accomplished through QS-9000 registration.

Lying is the most direct offense against the truth. To lie is to speak or act against the truth in order to lead into error someone who has the right to know the truth. Policies, procedures, and records are important aspects in QS-9000. They must contain truthful statements. Anything contrary to the truth in them must be avoided. Misrepresenting the facts must be stopped for the common good of the corporation.

Every offense committed against the truth entails the duty of reparation. Any employee, department, customer, registrar, or other party or entity who has suffered harm must be compensated. This can be accomplished by rewriting policies or procedures, allowing for return of faulty product, providing just compensation, and so on. In the language of QS-9000, corrective actions are mandated. Furthermore, verification of effectiveness for the corrective actions must be present before an injustice can be closed out. This duty of reparation also concerns offenses against the reputation of another (whether fellow employee, department, customer, registrar, auditor, etc.). The reparation must be evaluated in terms of the extent of the damage inflicted. It is helpful to think in terms of the "product" or "service" reputation being misrepresented.

The right to the communication of the truth is not unconditional. Charity and respect for the truth should dictate the response to every request for information or communication. The safety of others, respect for privacy (especially corporate financial figures), corporate strategic plans, protection of trade practices, and professional secrets are sufficient reasons for being silent. No one is bound to reveal the truth to someone who does not have the right to know it.

In pursuing QS-9000 registration, all employees of the corporation, especially the QS-9000 team members, must be constantly reminded that truth in writing policies and procedures, and in keeping records, is of vital importance.

COMMANDMENT 9: REMAIN PURE

Temptations to make the QS-9000 registration process complicated should be avoided. The corporation and all its employees should have purity of intention, which consists of seeking QS-9000 registration with simplicity. Exercise restraint when you are tempted to make things more complicated than necessary, especially in policies and procedures. If you state a process temperature of 100 degrees plus or minus 1 degree, you will be required to hold the 1 degree tolerance. Wouldn't it be better to say plus or minus 10 degrees if the product quality remains satisfactory?

> *Temptations to make the QS-9000 registration process complicated should be avoided.*

At Drake Products Corporation, the path to QS-9000 registration at three plant sites was governed by the following thoughts:

- Define QS-9000's value for the company.
- Obtain executive approval.
- Select "executive champion."
- Create steering committee.
- Conduct training.
- Develop strategy with realistic time line.
- Perform gap analysis and benchmark to QS-9000.
- Institute corrective actions.
- Conduct internal management audit.
- Carefully pick the registrar.
- Plan the formal assessment.
    - Document review.
    - Preassessment survey.
    - Assessment audit.

COMMANDMENT 10: DON'T COVET ANOTHER'S QS-9000 SYSTEMS

The 10th commandment unfolds and completes the 9th, which is concerned with internal corporate concupiscence. Commandment 10 forbids coveting the goods of another corporation, consultant, organization, club, and so on. In the true biblical sense, when the law says "You shall not covet," these words mean that you should banish your desire for whatever does not belong to you. It may seem that a corporation's thirst for another's QS-9000 system is immense, infinite, and never quenched, but envy must be banished from corporate comparisons of QS-9000 systems. However, it is not a violation of this commandment to desire to obtain things that belong to another, provided this is done by just means.

Envy is a capital sin and applies to the business world. It can refer to the sadness one feels at the sight of another's corporate QS-9000 system and the immoderate desire to acquire it even unjustly. Corporations should struggle against it by exercising goodwill and honest sharing of QS-9000 "tips for success."

THE FUTURE: LIFE ETERNAL

Drake Products Corporation achieved ISO 9001 registration along the road to becoming compliant to QS-9000. Governor John Engler of Michigan states the future well in his congratulatory letter:

> You should all be proud of what this exceptional honor says about the caliber of your work. Your successful efforts have proven that your company's quality standards, without a doubt, can match up with any other firm in the world.
>
> I am proud to acknowledge Drake Products as a representative of the type of business excellence we have come to expect here in Michigan. Keep up the outstanding work!

At Drake Products Corporation, we have learned that QS-9000 makes three demands: First, the corporation must document not only the quality system but also the entire business process in detail. Second, the corporation must ensure that each employee understands and follows the policies and procedures. And third, the documented QS-9000 system must be constantly monitored through internal and external audits, and changed or updated as necessary.

Continuous improvement has become a way of life at Drake Products Corporation, and all employees know and understand that it is the only assurance of continued growth and job security. Drake Products Corporation is truly a collaborative organization where responsible employees work together to accomplish agreed-upon goals. We are on a "quest to be the best."

This case study is contributed by John A. Paroff, Technical Director, Drake Products Corporation, Grand Rapids, Michigan.

CHAPTER 7

Journey to Manufacturing Excellence

J. B. Tool & Machine, Inc.

GENERAL

• *Headquarters*	: **Wapakoneta, Ohio, U.S.A.**
• *Year Founded*	: **1959**
• *Number of Employees*	: **400**

QS-9000 SPECIFIC

• *Registered Location(s)*	: **Wapakoneta, Ohio, U.S.A.**
• *Number of Employees*	: **400**
• *Registration Date*	: **February 9, 1995**
• *Product(s)*	: **Automotive, Trailer, Consumer Electronics**
• *Tier I, II, III Supplier*	: **Tier I and II**
• *Major Customer(s)*	: **Chrysler, Goodyear Tire, Freudenberg-NOK, Honda**
• *Annual Sales*	: **U.S. $50 Million**

INTRODUCTION

Our mission statement concludes with the following phrase: ". . . the forever commitment to the continuing pursuit of manufacturing excellence." J. B. Tool & Machine, Inc., thus has a mission statement that is forever a directed journey with conviction, but without a fixed destination. In this case study J. B. Tool & Machine, Inc., presents an armchair journey into the halls of understanding through the corridors of implementation, to the audits of maintenance to QS-9000.

J. B. Tool & Machine, Inc., took the journey to QS-9000 registration due to a belief that, if properly implemented and maintained, QS-9000 is the best overall quality system available today. Properly adhered to, it gives a solid base for business planning with measurements of performance.

Substance rather than image will be the focus of this journey. Life can only be understood backward, but it must be lived forward. The same is true for a journey. By sharing our journey, we hope that other organizations' QS-9000 journey will be an evolution rather than a revolution.

BACKGROUND

J. B. Tool & Machine, Inc., was founded in 1959 in Wapakoneta, Ohio, by Mr. William G. Petty, original co-founder and present owner and chief executive officer (CEO) of the company. Wapakoneta is best known as the hometown of another very distinguished pioneer who made a journey mankind dreamed of taking since the dawn of history. His name is Neil A. Armstrong; his journey was to the moon and back.

Through the 1960s, 70s, and 80s, Mr. Petty guided the growth of the company and solidified the customer base of automotive and consumer electronics. With a customer base of major international corporations in both of these fields, Mr. Petty could see that a change in business philosophy would be required for the 90s.

The start of the 90s required a complete refocusing and restructuring of the company to implement a business plan with the required management and manufacturing disciplines to compete in the new global marketplace. A new company president, Mr. Neil R. Yantis, was recruited by Mr. Petty. Mr. Yantis brought on board a staff of talented people in all facets of the business, putting in place the team required to compete globally.

J. B. Tool & Machine, Inc., started implementation of its internal total quality management (TQM) "Excellence" program in 1993 under the umbrella of ISO 9000. The appearance of QS-9000 the following year was a real treat. QS-9000 gave an already good system (ISO 9000) the added depth required to ensure an excellent system.

Today, J. B. Tool & Machine, Inc., is a state-of-the-art international designer and manufacturer of metal fabricated and robotically welded automotive bracketry, consumer electronics, and heavy truck and trailer components. Depending on the situation, J. B. Tool & Machine, Inc., is either a Tier I or Tier II supplier to its customer base. J. B. Tool & Machine, Inc., is the largest employer in Wapakoneta, Ohio, with three facilities and 400 employees. All facilities are registered to QS-9000 and ISO 9001 under both Raad voor de Certificate (RvC) presently Raad voor de Accreditatie (RvA) and Registrar Accreditation Board (RAB) accreditation.

J. B. Tool & Machine, Inc., enjoys a great customer base. Our customers are as follows:

American Matsushita Electronics Corporation

Bridgestone AMP Company

Chrysler Service and Parts Purchasing

Clevite Elastomers

Dawson Manufacturing Company

Freudenberg-NOK

Fruehauf Trailer Corporation

Gencorp Automotive

Goodyear Tire & Rubber Company

Honda of America Mfg. Inc.

LBT, Inc.

Paulstra CRC

Philips Display Components Company

Rauland Division

Standard Products (Canada) Limited

Thomson Consumer Electronics

Yale South Haven, Inc.

Yusa Corporation

Zenith Electronic Corporation

Our customers are placed at the top of our organization chart, with all employees including our owner and CEO reporting to them.

START OF JOURNEY

The start of the 90s definitely redirected the journeys of many companies. Sad to say, it also stopped the journeys of many others. The only thing consistent is change, and the business world entering the 90s accelerated change. Companies maintaining their status quo in the changing marketplace either shrank or went out of business. Others realized that the only way to meet change was with effective change.

J. B. Tool & Machine, Inc., got busy changing its organizational structure, culture, and managerial style to meet the requirements of the 21st century. J. B. Tool & Machine, Inc., believed QS-9000 was the best system available to guide such a change. Properly implemented and maintained, QS-9000 gives a solid base of business planning with measurables of performance through management involvement and reviews. It holds all employees as well as all management at all levels accountable for quality management of all the functions of an organization, not just the quality of a product produced.

We saw immediately that QS-9000 would be a license to be in business in the 90s. "QS-9000 is a management system, not a quality system" is our QS-9000 interpretation, one that continues to escape many in top management today.

The journey of a thousand miles starts with the first step. Step in the wrong direction, however, and you will have a two-thousand-mile journey just to return to your original starting point. Managers who view QS-9000 as a quality system with an objective to get a registration plaque to hang on the wall should seriously question their direction of travel. Visionaries who see QS-9000 as a management system are capable of designing and maintaining quality throughout all facets of an organization.

MILE MARKER 1: MANAGEMENT COMMITMENT

The word to focus on as we start hitting the mile markers of this journey is *process*. A reliable quality process produces a reliable quality result. Understanding, implementing, and maintaining QS-9000 is a process.

The first requirement and the most important item to obtain for the QS-9000 process implementation is management commitment. The top-ranking executive and the functional staff-level management must commit, in conviction and in writing with signatures, to a management statement. This statement must be posted, communicated, and understood throughout the organization.

We found that obtaining top-level management commitment in true substance is not easy. This is the first time top executive management has been required to be involved, knowledgeable, and subject to audit for a quality process. Quality systems of the past could be given to the quality department for implementation and maintenance. Successful implementation of QS-9000, however, requires vision and involved leadership of top management to provide the planning and resources for proper implementation. Without top management commitment it becomes impossible to create the cross-functional teams of cooperation and the continuous improvement environment required for a successful QS-9000 program.

Leaving mile marker 1 without a true management commitment is like starting a journey with an empty gas tank. You must fill up with a total understanding and commitment of QS-9000 so that you don't find yourself stranded along the roadside.

MILE MARKER 2: FORM STAFF STEERING GROUP AND SELECT MANAGEMENT REPRESENTATIVE

The second mile marker of the implementation process was forming our staff steering group. This was the same group of managers that committed and signed our management statement. Although the group was born at mile marker 1, it must now take its own form to start the training, communication, and commitment process of the organization. Training videos were shown to all company personnel. Individual instruction booklets were printed and disbursed. Off-site meetings were held by the company president with the entire organization for the purpose of presenting information and obtaining feedback on the QS-9000 status.

A management representative who has the desire, ability, tenacity, and time to devote to the implementation and maintenance of QS-9000 should then be selected. At J. B. Tool & Machine, Inc., the selection of the management representative was by top executive decision. Some companies allow the staff steering group the liberty of this selection. Whatever the selection process used, this is a vital point in the QS-9000 implementation process.

Cultures, structures, and management styles vary greatly from one company to another. It is unfair to ask someone such as a quality manager to be responsible as a management representative to change a company's culture, structure, and management style to accommodate QS-9000 implementation. Attempting to use an existing incapable organizational structure with diluted lines of authority and communication for the QS-9000 implementation process is also unfair. Many quality managers presently are caught in this situation of frustration while desperately attempting to keep their own quality department functioning.

Be guided by a focused vision in the selection of a management representative. This individual helps management weld together the doers and the thinkers of the organization. The management representative is the driver of the QS-9000 vehicle on this journey.

Be guided by a focused vision in the selection of a management representative.

After selection of the management representative, the staff steering group was ready to move on with a plan of action for total implementation of QS-9000. A communication plan for total employee involvement and buy-in was started, along with a quest for the company mission statement. J. B. Tool & Machine, Inc., is a nonunion company. In a unionized company this would be an opportune time to involve union leadership.

We obtained copies of the *Quality System Requirements QS-9000* and *Quality System Assessments (QSA)* for all members of our staff steering group. We also ordered the five manuals that go with QS-9000: *Advanced Product Quality Planning and Control Plan, Measurement Systems Analysis, Statistical Process Control, Production Part Approval Process*, and *Potential Failure Mode and Effects Analysis*. In addition, Section III of QS-9000 itself with original equipment manufacturers' specific requirements, EN45012 paragraph 18, and International Automotive Sector Group (IASG) Sanctioned QS-9000 Interpretations gave the staff steering group the foundation of documentation required to implement QS-9000.

MILE MARKER 3: DOCUMENT WHAT YOU DO

Obtaining buy-in of all employees of the organization through involvement and motivation is a key task of the newly formed staff steering group and the management representative. One of the easiest ways to accomplish this task is to ask all employees in the organization to document what they really do every day.

All organizations have a formal system that is normally documented. They also have an informal system that is not documented but is how the organization really functions. We found most employees eager to document what they really did every day. They also informed us why they didn't use the formal system. Being asked to assist in documenting a system that would work for them on a daily basis was a real inspiration.

Every functional area of the organization needs to document what it is really doing, right or wrong. Without the factual input of what the informal organization is doing, one cannot understand the changes required to qualify to the elements of QS-9000. We first make our habits, and then the habits make us. Companies run daily on the habits of people. People are the portals through which success is achieved. Let them speak. Their mistakes are the stepping-stones to opportunity and success if understood properly.

What is received as documentation of how the company is really being run can be a shock if the informal organization has been operating for a long time. One may find that there are five forms and six tags all performing the same function—but if this is the situation, it should be documented.

At J. B. Tool & Machine, Inc., developing trust and understanding between those documenting what they were doing and those reviewing the documentation was sometimes trying. A common purpose and mutual trust began to occur at this point as 100 percent of the total organization started documenting some of the silly things being done daily. Some documentation showed that people weren't performing their own function but rather someone else's. The emphasis here is that employee involvement is extremely important.

MILE MARKER 4: FORMALIZE DOCUMENTATION

Formalizing documentation can be an interesting and creative project. It is a fairly simple process of reviewing what is documented as being presently done against what should be done per QS-9000.

We measured each element of what we documented against what we would like to do and against what QS-9000 states we must do. We addressed every QS-9000 requirement in both the Level 1 quality manual and the Level 2 procedures. In Level 3 instructions, however, we addressed only those elements we felt must be more clearly defined.

Again, total employee involvement was required in the new documentation. If the employees help develop the process, it has a better chance of success. Either a manual or an electronically based system may be used as long as the people are involved in its development.

Generic software can reduce implementation time, especially with the Level 1 quality manual. J. B. Tool & Machine, Inc., however, felt that the Level 2 procedures and the Level 3 instructions should be completed for electronic input by the hands of people who must use them every day as their road map of activity. Flowcharts and well-documented directions in simple language guide an everyday user of the system—the same user that helped in the development of the documentation.

Documentation, whether manual or electronic, must be controlled. A form's design and control function needs to be established. This is vital to the design and content of the form as well as to the success of QS-9000 control. All documents, including all forms and tags, that require an initial design or a change must have the staff steering group and executive approval.

The shop floor documentation should not be forgotten. All tags, forms, process sheets, and so on that run the shop floor must conform to QS-9000 and show control.

Documentation should be kept simple. J. B. Tool & Machine's documentation (i.e., the Level 1 quality manual, Level 2 procedures, and Level 3 instructions) used to run our three facilities measures only three-quarters of an inch in thickness. We have less than a dozen tags.

MILE MARKER 5: DO WHAT YOU DOCUMENTED

It's now time to start practicing what we agreed to do in our formalized documentation. The documented system must now be put to the test to prove that it will work. Every element of QS-9000 will now be the focus for expansion of knowledge and for assessment of results obtained. In this case study we will not dwell on the individual elements of QS-9000, which are self-explanatory. Our focus will remain on the journey to and through registration.

Teamwork and process rather than the traditional individual tasks and efforts will be required during the stage of hands-on use of the new system. Problem solving and process improvements to make the new system work will happen effectively only through participative cross-functional management and teams. Training is essential to this stage of the effort. Employees must understand their role in the organization above and beyond the documented instruction. Everyone in the organization needs to understand how he or she personally influences the organization.

Quality personnel who previously inspected the product were trained to become quality auditors of the processes. Others were sent off-site to Automotive Industry Action Group (AIAG) training for QS-9000 related subjects. All levels of the organization were involved in one form of training or another during this stage of the process.

Every organization is unique in some way. There is no one right way to implement QS-9000 into an organization. *Flexible approach* is probably a good term for what we used at J. B. Tool & Machine, Inc. Our company president always says that a wise man changes his mind a thousand times but a fool won't change it once.

We have found it more beneficial to have a focused philosophy of implementation toward a common purpose rather than a fixed-in-concrete plan. As an example, our focused philosophy was to have an operator-based inspection to prevent mistakes rather than a detection-based system to find them. We allowed the plan to float to the foundation of philosophy. The road to implementation can be a difficult one. Natural resistance to change as well as unequal levels of enthusiasm occur in all organizations. These barriers challenge the patience of many.

Training wheels may be required for some during this period. Our philosophy includes assisting those who have difficulty doing what has been documented to do. There must be a desire and effort on everyone's part to make this documented system a new way of life, a new set of habits.

MILE MARKER 6: ASSESS WHAT YOU'RE DOING

When we put the documented system to work, some of us began to think we knew what we were doing, while others thought we had no idea what we were doing. After a few internal audits were conducted, some thought we were much better than the audits revealed while others thought we were much worse.

In our journey, just prior to selecting our registrar, we interviewed and contracted a local consultant to assist in the final phases of our implementation and internal audits. This was a very rewarding experience and gave a great lift to the momentum of our implementation. This consultant not only put us over the edge for the registration but also trained our audit team internally.

Our consultant traveled to our vendors with our purchasing and quality group for outsource audits. Our consultant helped us in the selection of a third-party registrar and stayed with us through the audit and registration process. Enough cannot be said about using a qualified consultant to assist an organization through the QS-9000 process. In our case, it was not a cost but a cost *savings* to have contracted one.

There are presently many well-intentioned but very inexperienced practitioners in the marketplace. An organization should be selective and should obtain references prior to using any outside practitioner.

MILE MARKER 7: REGISTRAR SELECTION

After our internal assessment, we thought that at this point in the journey we were good enough to obtain registration. Although our consultant assisted in our selection of a registrar, it took a lot of reference checking of experience and background. We did a reference check of our registrar much the same as we would have done an employee reference check.

Contacting companies in the same line of manufacturing that had used or were presently using a registrar proved to be an effective method in the selection process. Based on our experience, some registrars are better suited than others to certain types of products and industries.

MILE MARKER 8: AUDIT

With our registrar selected, we submitted our Level 1 quality manual and our Level 2 procedures for a desktop audit. Having obtained approval of both of these and having operated under our quality system for three to six months, we felt ready to take a shot at an audit for registration.

However, our internal audits indicated that we were ready for registration when in fact we weren't even close! We would audit one week and find that we had 40 nonconformances; the next week we might have half as many. We decided to postpone the formal assessment until the next year because our system was so inconsistent.

We completed our assessment at last in January 1995. We had 21 nonconformances across our three facilities, which was enough to require our registrar to return the following month, after action taken to correct the nonconformances was complete. We noted that a majority of our nonconformances were in process control and document control. We received our registration in February 1995.

MILE MARKER 9: SURVEILLANCE AUDIT

Six-month surveillance by our registrar continues to improve the performance of QS-9000 effectiveness. Selective elements are chosen for each surveillance; the following, however, are required to be audited each visit:

- Internal audit.
- Customer complaints.
- Corrective action.
- Management review.
- Continuous improvement.
- System changes.

Our registrar rotates lead assessors at each surveillance and assures that we have no new lead assessor we have not met. Lead assessors also must have been part of a previous assessment at our company, which helps to ensure continuity.

RECAPPING THE JOURNEY

Our journey at J. B. Tool & Machine, Inc., is continuing into the 21st century with the implementation of ISO 14001, Environmental Management Systems, and ISO 10303, Product Data Development. Our commitment to the continuing pursuit of manufacturing excellence will forever hold us in a future-driven journey.

Reflecting back on our QS-9000 journey, we can say that it was definitely worthwhile. Our facilities are operating 24 hours a day, seven days a week, with our customers requesting added capacity.

The road we traveled to registration would most probably be the same one we would take today.

The frustrations of the journey are outweighed by the rewards—not just the monetary rewards of added business base but also the rewards of observing the growth of people and departments in the organization. The bonding of the customer and vendor base as well as local, state, and national communities is very rewarding.

For being a QS-9000 pioneer, J. B. Tool & Machine, Inc., has received appreciation letters and rewards from many local, state, and national leaders, among whom are the following:

- Ronald Reagan, former U.S. president.
- Neil A. Armstrong, former U.S. astronaut.
- John Glenn, U.S. senator.
- Michael G. Oxley, U.S. congressman.
- George M. White, architect of the Capitol.
- George V. Voinovich, governor of Ohio.
- Donald R. Wittwer, mayor of Wapakoneta, Ohio.

Our area newspapers and television stations shared our registration success with the public. Although we appreciate the publicity, we at J. B. Tool & Machine, Inc., know and understand that this must be now and forever a journey of substance, not image, if we are to survive in the new global marketplace.

This case study is contributed by Richard H. Busch II, TQM Manager and Excellence Facilitator, J. B. Tool & Machine, Inc., Wapakoneta, Ohio.

CHAPTER 8

The "Just Read It and Do It" Approach to QS-9000

Jamestown Container Companies

GENERAL

- *Headquarters* : **Falconer, New York, U.S.A.**
- *Year Founded* : **1956**
- *Number of Employees* : **252**

QS-9000 SPECIFIC

- *Registered Location(s)* : **Jamestown, New York, U.S.A.**
- *Number of Employees* : **95**
- *Registration Date* : **June 25, 1995**
- *Product(s)* : **Corrugated and Related Packaging Products**
- *Tier I, II, III Supplier* : **Tier I**
- *Major Customer(s)* : **General Motors, Eastman Kodak**
- *Annual Sales* : **U.S. $40 Million**

INTRODUCTION

The purpose of this case study is to share our experience with other manufacturers, particularly smaller manufacturers that either choose to or are being required to become QS-9000 registered.

It is important to realize that registration can be achieved with limited resources and without having to spend large amounts of money with outside consultants. If a small corrugated box plant like Jamestown Container can first achieve ISO 9001 and then QS-9000, so can other manufacturers. All it takes is the desire and fortitude to accomplish the task.

Jamestown Container decided in January 1995 to pursue QS-9000 registration at its surveillance audit scheduled for March 2–3, 1995. This gave Jamestown Container approximately seven and a half weeks to document, implement, and make effective the additional requirements of QS-9000; to incorporate those requirements into its existing ISO 9001 quality system; and to audit the system for effectiveness.

QS-9000 registration is important to Jamestown Container because it is a Tier I supplier to the automotive industry and registration would have eventually been required.

BACKGROUND

The Jamestown Container Companies manufacture corrugated packaging and related products and operate manufacturing facilities in Jamestown, Lockport, Medina, and Rochester, all in New York state. The company is privately owned, has sales in excess of $40 million and employs over 250 people. Jamestown Container is also a partner in a 100 percent recycled paper mill located near Syracuse, New York.

Since its founding in 1956, the company has grown by acquiring corrugated manufacturers in contiguous markets and integrating and expanding its product lines. In addition to its traditional corrugated business, Jamestown's four factories make plastic reusable cartons, foam packaging, and point-of-purchase displays. The company also offers its customers packaging and fulfillment services, "full loop" recycling, and access to its internationally accredited packaging laboratory.

Jamestown Container's customers are predominantly manufacturing firms located in New York, Pennsylvania, and Ohio, and Southern Ontario, Canada. These firms represent a wide range of industries with large concentrations in automotive, furniture, plastics, and tool and die.

Jamestown Container is a Tier I supplier to two General Motors facilities and also makes packaging for numerous Tier II and III suppliers of Chrysler, Ford, and General Motors.

THE DEMING PHILOSOPHY AND QS-9000

The Jamestown Container Companies have been practicing Dr. W. Edwards Deming's philosophy of management for continuous improvement since 1988. The Deming philosophy focuses on management leadership and cultural change in order to create never-ending improvement of all processes, products, and services. Jamestown's management believes that this philosophy has been the driving force behind the company's success over the last several years. The company has included its ISO 9001 and QS-9000 registrations as part of this continuous improvement effort.

Jamestown's Falconer, New York, manufacturing plant received its ISO 9001 registration in August 1994 and was the first corrugated packaging manufacturer in the world to earn QS-9000 registration. Jamestown Container's other three manufacturing facilities are in the process of obtaining their ISO 9001 and QS-9000 registrations.

Meeting the ISO 9001 standard and QS-9000 quality system requirements has significantly benefited Jamestown Container. Adopting the requirements forced the company to recognize and address previous weaknesses in its quality system. It led to the creation of a quality system that is well documented, well implemented, and effective. Jamestown Container's customers appreciate the fact that the company's quality system is audited by an independent authority and that it meets internationally recognized criteria.

REGISTRAR SELECTION

Jamestown Container selected a registrar based on its location and reputation. The registrar's North American central offices are located in Jamestown, only a few miles from the company's Falconer facility. This proximity greatly reduced travel expenses.

From the beginning, which involved a "grilling" preassessment in April 1994, Jamestown Container remained confident that it made the right choice in registrar selection. The corporation's experience with the registrar during both its ISO 9001 registration in August 1994 and the ongoing surveillance audits has proved to be very positive.

USE OF CONSULTANTS

Jamestown Container did not receive any consultation services during the implementation of ISO 9001 and had no intention of using consultants for QS-9000. The requirements were simply read, reread, and then interpreted by the corporate quality director and packaging engineer. If a confusing or conflicting situation arose, clarification was sought with the registrar.

Between the corporate quality director, the director of manufacturing, and the packaging engineer, 90 percent of the company's processes were well understood. The key to success is understanding these processes because many of the requirements in QS-9000 were already being done but just had to be recognized, documented, and verified as to their effectiveness.

Part of the learning process was making mistakes in interpreting QS-9000. From these mistakes, each area, as well as each requirement, was better understood. In retrospect, this was the best option because the employees implementing the system became experts in specific sections of QS-9000—and these employees still work for the company, unlike consultants who take the knowledge with them after they leave.

THE SITUATION

The quality manager and packaging engineer were the point people for the implementation process of QS-9000. It was their responsibility to assign what needed to be done, to review progress, and ensure that the steps taken would satisfy the quality system requirements of QS-9000. The work was divided up between the quality manager, packaging engineer, plant manager, director of manufacturing, and the chief financial officer.

The game plan was to have the additional QS-9000 requirements documented within five weeks. This gave Jamestown Container the sixth week to implement the new requirements and see how they would work. An internal audit was scheduled for the seventh week. After the completion of the internal audit, the first three days of the audit week would be available to fine-tune the system and make any necessary changes. The approaches used are described in the following sections.

THE NINA

NINA stands for the "new item/new account" meeting. This meeting and corresponding form were developed to satisfy the following requirements: organizational interfaces, advanced product quality planning (APQP), special characteristics, use of cross-functional teams, process failure mode and effects analysis (FMEA), and the control plan.

The NINA is a cross-functional team made up of representatives from various departments. This team assembles to review the requirements of all new accounts and items. During the meeting, all customer requirements are reviewed and documented. If additional requirements such as FMEAs or new control plans are required, they are assigned to someone during this meeting.

Due to the nature of Jamestown Container's product (corrugated packaging), special characteristics or anything relating to special characteristics did not apply. This is because the product does not directly impact the performance of a vehicle nor is it a component part of the vehicle.

DOCUMENT AND DATA CONTROL

The document and data control system at Jamestown Container is a manual system that consists of most documents and data being distributed to designated employees as a hard copy on blue paper. The blue paper indicates to the employees that the document is controlled and that they are accountable for the proper maintenance and handling of the document until it is revised or obsolete. A manual system was adopted because, at the time, no corporate computer system was available that was common to all employees.

The document control officer is responsible for the control of all documents, data, and forms in the building. The current number of controlled documents totals about 100. Future plans and computer upgrades will transform this manual system into an electronic system.

During the implementation of QS-9000, only a few modifications consisting of additional statements had to be made to the document and data control, design control, and contract review procedures to cover the additional requirements. Document identification for special characteristics was not a major issue because there were no customer-identified significant characteristics on the parts manufactured.

PROCESS CONTROL

The process control requirement turned out to be one of the easiest because the following were already in place:

1. A process to ensure compliance with all applicable government safety and environmental regulations.
2. Preventative maintenance.
3. Process monitoring and operator instructions.

4. Verification of job setups.

5. Process changes.

Jamestown Container had only to ensure through the use of internal quality audits that these requirements were documented, implemented, and effective.

INTERNAL QUALITY AUDITS

Auditing is one of the best tools available to determine the overall effectiveness of the quality system. The "ideal" quality system is dynamic; that is, it is constantly improving and evolving. A system that is static is a system that is not used or understood. If the system is working as it should and the audit is taken seriously, the task of auditing is monumental. The auditors should be finding nonconformities.

The greatest challenge of internal auditing is finding the time to do it. Each requirement of QS-9000 must be audited at least once a year. Given that there are 20 elements in QS-9000, plus the production part approval process, continuous improvement, manufacturing capabilities, and customer-specific requirements, two elements could be audited each month.

Jamestown Container decided that the best use of time would be to do a full system audit (every element) twice a year. These audits, combined with the registrar's surveillance audits, ensure that the system is audited at least quarterly. The full system audit takes two auditors a minimum of five working days. These five days break down as follows:

Day 1: Review all documents, such as procedures and work instructions, and develop the audit plan.

Day 2: Conduct the opening meeting with management, begin the actual audit, and write up any nonconformities at the end of the day.

Day 3: Conduct the actual audit and write up any nonconformities at the end of the day.

Day 4: Conduct the audit, write up any nonconformities, and present all nonconformities to management during the closing meeting.

Day 5: Begin writing the audit report detailing the findings of the audit and the overall effectiveness of the quality system.

The auditors will spend the next several weeks reviewing the corrective action(s) taken to address all the nonconformities found during the course of the audit. Each corrective action must be analyzed by the audit team for short-term solution, long-term solution, implementation, and effectiveness. If the corrective action is acceptable and deemed implemented and effective by the audit team, that nonconformity will be closed out.

CONTINUOUS IMPROVEMENT

As mentioned before, Jamestown Container began implementing the Deming philosophy of continuous improvement in 1988. This philosophy was and still is the foundation for all ISO 9001– and QS-9000–related activity. It begins with senior management, or what is known as the functional management team (FMT). The FMT meets at least twice a month and consists of the following members:

- Chief operating officer (team leader).
- Chief financial officer.
- Corporate controller.
- Corporate marketing manager.
- Director of manufacturing.
- Plant manager.
- Sales manager.
- Materials manager.

The purpose of the FMT is to review the effectiveness of the quality system by working on and improving the company's quality core objectives. These core objectives were determined by interviewing the company's customers, suppliers, employees, former customers, bankers, accountants, and so on. From these interviews five core objectives and associated measurements were determined. The five core objectives are as follows:

- Customer satisfaction.
- Positive environment.
- Resource optimization.
- Continuous improvement.
- Long-term growth.

Funneling down from the FMT are process management teams (PMTs). These teams are led by a member of the FMT in their own individual functional area. For example, the plant manager will lead a PMT consisting of all supervisors in the plant.

The cycle of PMTs is repeated down to the next level in the organization. For example, the printing supervisor will lead a team consisting of all the employees in his area who work for him.

In both cases the meetings began with the review of all data and measurements associated with the core objectives. Both teams have the same five core objectives, except that the associated measurements for each objective will be specific to the team's area of responsibility. Action plans are developed to improve any area that has become stagnant or is not showing continuous improvement. Also, during these meetings, the results of any internal audits are examined, as well as all customer complaints.

By having this foundation of continuous improvement firmly in place, Jamestown Container was able to integrate the QS-9000 into its already existing organizational structure. This meant that no additional meetings or structure had to be created to achieve registration. The FMT and PMT concept ensures that every employee is involved in the creation and review of the quality system.

CONTROL OF INSPECTION, MEASURING, AND TEST EQUIPMENT

Prior to the implementation of ISO 9001 and QS-9000, most of Jamestown Container's measuring devices and test equipment were not routinely calibrated to nationally recognized standards. Calibration proved to be quite a challenge, until the acquisition of the company's fourth manufacturing plant. Test equipment included with the purchased plant was calibrated to nationally recognized standards by one calibration company. Jamestown Container contracted with that supplier to calibrate all of its plants' testing equipment on a fixed schedule. This would ensure that all the company's inspection, measuring, and test equipment would be periodically calibrated per ISO 9001 and QS-9000, with the exception of tape measures.

The calibration of employee-owned tape measures was accomplished by having several steel bars mounted throughout the plant, manufactured to an exact length and traceable to a nationally recognized standard. Each department manager routinely checks and documents the calibration status of his employees' tape measures. If a problem arises, the tape measure is either fixed or replaced and recalibrated. People tend to downplay the need for tape-measure calibration, but actually it is critical to ensure that a piece of equipment is not damaged or misreading. One drop of the tape on a concrete floor could affect the reading and cause a machine to be set up improperly. As customers' tolerances get ever tighter, the importance of this check becomes clearly obvious.

Records of the calibration and verification activities on all gauges, measuring, and test equipment, including employee-owned gauges, was never an issue due to the record system already in place. Gauge repeatability and reproducibility (R&R) studies had to be performed in specific areas, however; many of the nationally published test procedures that were followed referenced their own R&R studies.

EMPLOYEE AWARENESS AND INVOLVEMENT

Employee involvement in the implementation of QS-9000 at Jamestown Container was typical of any new program being introduced into an organization—employees tended to look the other way and hope no one would call on them. This was not true of all employees, but many resisted the change.

Fortunately for Jamestown Container, the need to adopt ISO 9001 and QS-9000 initially came, and continued to come throughout the entire process, from upper management. Upper management was committed to achieving these goals, and this approach ensured that all midlevel managers and their employees would be involved and committed to the implementation of ISO 9001 and QS-9000.

Employee involvement varied; the new processes ranged from requiring little or no change in the way workers did their jobs, to nearly doubling the time it used to take to do their jobs. During the implementation process, employees were very aware of the changes being made; some questioned "Why are we doing this?" The general thought was that the company was abandoning Dr. Deming's philosophy of continuous improvement in favor of ISO 9001 and QS-9000. People felt that in a few years ISO 9001 and QS-9000 would only be a memory: "Why, then, since we had been committed to 'doing Deming' since 1988, would we stop doing it, when we know that it works?" they would ask. It therefore became the responsibility of management to convey the message that the company was not giving up on Deming, but rather using Deming as a foundation and strengthening that foundation with ISO 9001 and QS-9000 registration.

Regardless, some employees took the attitude of "OK, let's do this, get the plaque on the wall, and it will all be over." Of course, this was not the case. Continual internal audits and surveillance audits being conducted every three months, as well as corrective actions being issued over and over for not maintaining the new system, reinforced in people that Jamestown Container was committed to maintaining its ISO 9001 and QS-9000 registration.

Without employee cooperation QS-9000 could not have been possible.

In due time, resistance turned to cooperation, and without employee cooperation QS-9000 could not have been possible. It was due to this group effort that Jamestown Container was able to become registered in a minimal amount of time.

SUMMARY

It is relatively easy to obtain QS-9000 registration; it just takes focus, commitment, and time. Any company can achieve it. Each individual company has to determine whether a consultant would or would not be helpful. Jamestown Container decided to "just read it and do it." No additional people were hired to help with the implementation. Everyone just pitched in and did it!

As mentioned earlier, a good quality system is dynamic. The quality system must keep changing and evolving in order to serve the organization. After registration has been achieved, it becomes difficult to maintain the focus and drive that allowed the organization to become registered in the first place. The real challenge of ISO 9001 and QS-9000 begins once you have the certificate on the wall. The quality system that was created now needs to be nurtured and maintained by everyone in the organization.

This case study is contributed jointly by Joseph M. Palmeri, Corporate Quality Director; Brian H. Storms, Packaging Engineer; and Bruce G. Janowsky, Chief Financial Officer with Jamestown Container Companies, Falconer, New York.

CHAPTER 9

A Small Company Meeting Big Requirements

Laser Specialists, Inc.

GENERAL

- *Headquarters* : **Fraser, Michigan, U.S.A.**
- *Year Founded* : **1985**
- *Number of Employees* : **23**

QS-9000 SPECIFIC

- *Registered Location(s)* : **Fraser, Michigan, U.S.A.**
- *Number of Employees* : **23**
- *Registration Date* : **July 25, 1995**
- *Product(s)* : **2-D and 3-D Laser Cutting**
- *Tier I, II, III Supplier* : **Tier I and II**
- *Major Customer(s)* : **Chrysler, Ford, General Motors**
- *Annual Sales* : **U.S. $3 Million**

INTRODUCTION

For companies contemplating whether or not to seek QS-9000 registration, their size, resources, staff, and experience will play a significant part in a weighty decision. When a small company assesses its chances of achieving QS-9000, it may view that commitment and the involved process as terrifying.

The accomplishment of Laser Specialists, Inc. (LSI), is proof positive that with vision, leadership, commitment, and hard work on the part of each employee, a small company can achieve the paragon standard of quality. LSI took the risk. The company's sweat, fortitude, and dedication paid off in July 1995. We are proud to be a pioneer in the QS-9000 registration process. This is the story of that vision and the long road to QS-9000 registration.

Our case study will attempt to demonstrate several important points for an organization to remember as it embarks on the QS-9000 registration process:

- QS-9000 registration is a significant quality system attainable by small companies with limited financial resources and with personnel who have not previously been trained in QS-9000. Corporate personnel should be simultaneously acquiring QS-9000 training in these procedures.
- Once understood and implemented, QS-9000 makes good common business sense. It is more than just additional paperwork; it is a change in the culture of manufacturing from getting the job done to adopting and conforming to an objective quality standard in which all jobs are now done.
- The customers get what they want: products and services produced to their job specifications and tolerances, with on-time deliveries.
- The purchasing public acquires end-assembled products containing inherently better manufacturing quality, both in the component parts and in the final assembly.

BACKGROUND

Founded in 1985, LSI is a privately owned corporation located in suburban Detroit, Michigan. It is a small company among automobile suppliers, with 23 employees and sales in the $3 million range. It provides laser machine cutting services to automotive and nonautomotive customers. LSI utilizes carbon dioxide gas lasers to cut customer parts to specifications within 0.001" tolerances, the size of a human hair. It presently occupies a single manufacturing facility of 26,500 square feet. LSI effectively introduced practical applications of three-dimensional laser cutting to the metropolitan Detroit prototype manufacturing industry. This was done through the introduction of six-axis laser-cutting applications to preformed stamped parts, along with more conventional applications of two-dimensional flat material laser cutting. LSI became one of the few job shops located in the metropolitan Detroit market exclusively dedicated to the sale of laser-cutting services.

Originally started in 1985, the LSI of today hardly resembles the start-up company. The original majority shareholder was accidently killed in June 1993; his business partner and minority shareholder also died unexpectedly (from a heart attack) in January 1993. The surviving member of the board of directors and vice president assumed the position of chief executive officer (CEO) in mid-1993 and continues today as president and CEO. The ownership of LSI, now technically held by two estates, is in transition. Plans are that the current president will continue as CEO and that ownership will eventually be transferred to the company's key employees.

LSI's laser-cutting operations are supported by integrated computer manufacturing software, as well as by its own developed and copyrighted software programs. LSI's software permits it to make engineering changes in six-axis programming in a matter of minutes, while the company's competitors, even using the same laser equipment, wrestle for hours with similar changes in their programs.

LSI's long-standing reputation for fair pricing and competent programming, coupled with its implementation of QS-9000 and on-time delivery, has secured for it a significant number of loyal, satisfied customers. LSI provides laser-cutting services for divisions of Chrysler Corporation, Ford Motor Company, and General Motors Corporation, as well as for many automotive original equipment manufacturers (OEMs), Tier I suppliers, and Fortune 500 companies. Laser Specialists, Inc., also provides laser-cutting services to the appliance, furniture manufacturing, and aerospace industries. LSI is one of three qualified laser-cutting suppliers to Rolls-Royce Jet Engines of North America.

A NEW GOAL: QS-9000 REGISTRATION

If LSI's intent was to stay in the parts production manufacturing business on a long-term basis, then QS-9000 registration was a foregone conclusion. But more important, LSI saw that conformity to QS-9000 created objective performance standards against which both management and manufacturing could benchmark their efficiencies in operation. LSI identified its need to conform to the known standard of ISO 9000, then a forerunner to the as-yet-to-be-created QS-9000. Legal counsel for the corporation first brought ISO 9000 quality standards to the attention of LSI's president in 1989.

ISO 9000's invasion into U.S. manufacturing was seen as inevitable. With the North American Free Trade Agreement (NAFTA), the Canadian/U.S./Mexican–Western hemisphere trade coalition agreement adopted the ISO 9000 series as its quality manufacturing standard in 1991.

The handwriting was on the wall; LSI got started immediately in late 1991 to conform its skilled laser-cutting process and production part management program to these objective quality standards. LSI wrote its first quality procedures manual premised upon the 1987 ISO 9000 standards and initiated a Q-90 standards (the United Kingdom's version of ISO 9000 standards) audit of its manual in 1993, to verify its conformity. LSI passed this registration audit. However, LSI did not receive its ISO 9002 formal registration until it simultaneously passed its QS-9000 registration audit.

LSI's QS-9000 registration, when coupled to its defined niche market using 3-D carbon dioxide lasers for production parts processing, became its goal. QS-9000 registration would move LSI more effectively than any other known accomplishment, or additional equipment purchase, from the ranks of prototype shop to production manufacturer. After all, QS-9000 registration compliance initially was mandated by the U.S. automobile manufacturers for their production parts and service suppliers and not their prototype parts developers. What better way for LSI to make itself known in the automobile manufacturing market as a production laser-cutting service than to conform its quality operations to the standards applicable to all production parts suppliers?

The journey toward QS-9000 registration was a perilous one, taken alone and often in the dark. The process of implementation was made more hazardous than it ever needed to have been by unscrupulous consultants essentially intent on milking the opportunity. LSI expended far more money on consulting advice than it should have, and at least once was almost derailed by a consultant's misdirected advice.

From the 1991 beginning through the October 1993 Q-90 audit, LSI was also overcoming the unfortunate accidental death of its owner and president, who had acted as the initial catalyst in this undertaking. The company faced some overpowering decisions after this tragedy: where to turn for help, how to proceed, and how to secure the targeted results in a totally unfamiliar terrain. LSI's successor management could have abandoned the process of QS-9000 registration given the magnitude of these problems, not to mention the one of filling the leadership void left by the owner's death. Instead, the new president, the former general legal counsel, dug in, pulled the key employees together, and utilized some old-fashioned American ingenuity, willpower, and sleeves-rolled-up hard work to get these important goals back on track. The current president had to overcome a massively imposing learning curve. He began by immersing himself in the known QS-9000 commentary literature, reorganized the workforce, and began to develop an all-employee esprit de corps focused on grabbing the brass ring on the first try at QS-9000 registration.

THE INITIAL ATTEMPT AT QUALITY STANDARDIZATION
A False Start

An outside consultant was engaged in 1992 to establish a quality program. This was done in isolation from actual job processing analysis and intervening events taking place at LSI. Even though several prequality planning meetings were held and documented with minutes, there still seemed to be a recurring wide gap between the first written draft of the quality control procedures and actual LSI operations. A review of the 1992 quality team minutes disclosed that although a quality control manual was completed in 1992, its procedures were rubber-stamped into existence by the former general manager. They were never consistently implemented in daily operations. The major problems of scrap, misdeliveries, and poor workmanship continued, although their occurrence frequency was reduced. There was little, if any, link between this first procedure manual and a comprehensive coordination with actual operations. Everyone euphorically believed that if there were no customer complaints, then all was well. Despite recurring manufacturing problems, 1991 and 1992 also produced some long-running laser-cutting production jobs that paid handsomely. Thus, strong gross sales figures masked recurring, underlying quality verification problems; LSI succeeded in spite of itself.

Artificial Success

Now that LSI has obtained QS-9000 registration, much of the early frustrations, confusion, misdirected efforts, and misspent consulting funds can be easily forgotten. However, memories of those early struggles should not be blocked. They reveal how easy it was to get off track and fool ourselves. Just because there was a quality procedures manual authored for LSI, it meant nothing without an across-the-board commitment, top to bottom, to understand and live by the new standards. Implementation of QS-9000 cannot be just a marketing and sales tool; it has to be an ongoing commitment and pledge to an entirely new method of process manufacturing. Registration is a lifelong pledge to measure continuous improvement in the QS-9000 conforming quality system implemented by the company, and not an end unto itself.

Commitment in Earnest

LSI's first quality management program began in earnest in October 1992. A time line for completion of a quality control manual was established. Target dates were established to begin employee instruction during the first week of February 1993. The quality control manual was written and completed by the outside consultant and accepted without challenge or question by the general manager. Meetings were held during lunchtime, at two-week intervals. Initially, more discussion was given to launching the new quality program as a marketing tool than to working on writing meaningful quality procedures. By mid-November 1992, an organizational chart had been drafted.

Organization Is the Key

The initial organizational chart was constructed along four responsibility lines: engineering, production, purchasing, and quality control. These targets then became the focus of the initial quality manual, written and ready for a quality audit by June 1993, according to the consultant.

Preliminary Audit

A Q-90 series audit was conducted by an outside auditor, joined by LSI's consultant, in October 1993. Its results were not objective because LSI's consultant also acted as an auditor. Even with the consultant's opportunity to steer the results of the audit, the audit revealed an overwhelming lack of implementation of the written quality procedures. Close scrutiny of this first manual revealed that it was a copycat version of Ford Motor Company's Q-101 quality system standards and had not been customized to reflect LSI's laser-cutting processes, practices, or procedures. It also remained foreign to most LSI employees. LSI passed this Q-90 audit, but just barely. The consultant said much more effort was needed; he could not explain how LSI missed the mark so badly, just getting by after one year's work.

Although the first LSI quality manual touched on the applicable points of ISO 9002, there was little integration of these points as quality procedures into LSI's manufacturing processes. The quality manual and the laser-cutting work ran independent of each other.

Implementation of Quality Procedures

Beginning in January 1993, with the pro forma procedure manual in hand, LSI focused its first implementation attention on four areas:

1. Establish materials receiving inspection.
2. Calibrate all gauges utilized in quality checking.
3. Provide statistical process control training to employees.
4. Set up a dock audit for incoming and outgoing material.

LSI set for itself a completion date of April 1993 for implementing these tasks.

Quality Control Training

Beginning in February 1993, LSI brought in a certified quality engineer and commenced in-house statistical process control (SPC) employee training. LSI held its first quality planning team meeting on March 10, 1993. The outside consultant directed the meetings, set the agenda in advance, and documented the minute book following each meeting. The first quality planning team meeting consisted of management, quality assurance, engineering, purchasing, and sales. The consultant announced that a quality planning team would be utilized to review new customer contracts and customer job requirements and to assess feasibility to meet all programming objectives. The consultant also stated that the quality planning team would be used to establish analytical techniques to help identify causes of variability. The ongoing agenda for future quality planning team meetings would focus on (*a*) purchase order control, (*b*) subcontractor control, and (*c*) designation of responsibility. Attendees started with preassigned projects.

Setbacks

Despite the appearance of implementation through these ongoing quality planning team meetings, in reality the company reverted to its traditional method of problem-solving; putting out the fires of current customer complaints. Masked throughout 1992 and into 1993, even after formation of the quality planning team and the setting of its agenda, was the fact that LSI still was driven by its salespersons' unpredictable responsiveness to individual customer demands and complaints. The quality planning team minutes, when addressing problem-solving, were documenting sales-identified problems and solutions. Corrective action procedures, which would prevent future recurrences, were not being developed. Again, in reality, quality manual procedures were ignored and sacrificed for individual salespersons' needs.

MANAGEMENT RESPONSIBILITIES: A SECOND OPPORTUNITY FOR COMMITMENT

The Q-90 series audit experience was a litmus test of LSI's effective implementation of an objective quality standard manual. Even though LSI tested positive and passed that audit, it had been done without real commitment to a working quality control system. At best, it represented a superficial success. The successor to the deceased company founder knew no truly successful quality control program could be lastingly established at LSI without the following:

- A companywide commitment to a quality control program, from top to bottom.
- Active involvement by every employee in the design, development, and implementation of each quality procedure necessary to make QS-9000 operational in every aspect of LSI's workplace.
- A substantial commitment of work time, overtime, and employee personnel free time. To reach this level of participation involved an unwavering commitment of every worker, crew leader, shift foreman, manufacturing

manager, general manager, salesperson, and comptroller, as well as the president.

- A realistic time line against which LSI could measure both its progress and the extent to which its employees absorbed the changes and implemented them as second nature.
- A business plan by top management and a quality control budget to ensure sufficient funds for undertaking such a project.

LSI's budget allocated both internal time dedicated to the implementation of QS-9000 procedures and real dollars for training and outside consultants. Management then directed persons who were going to take responsibility for defined aspects of this project and authored a mechanism for tracking and reporting results.

Commitment Begins at the Top

At the first top leadership meeting it was agreed that objective quality standardization conformity was going to become manufacturing's new way of life. Conclusions drawn from that meeting were primarily that management needed lots of help in defining an implementation plan to achieve the short-term and long-term goals of the corporation beyond taking day-to-day work, quoting, selling, producing parts, and completing delivery. A second consultant with strong financial planning skills (and thus able to focus LSI specifically on realistic projected costs and income) was engaged to facilitate the preparation of a business plan, defining company short-term (12 months) and long-term (5 years) goals and setting a comprehensive corporate budget, inclusive of quality control. A new organizational chart was drawn, and job descriptions were written first by the employees who would be affected by them. These job descriptions were then negotiated with upper management to expand or contract each job description to include, among other points, the employee's defined responsibility in the overall quality procedure process.

Living the Quality Control Procedures

Once adopted, the ISO 9000 "20 elements" compliance program was analyzed by the newly reconstituted quality planning team, which now included the president as a regular attending member. The actual text of ISO-9002 requirements became the basis for a thorough internal dialogue within the quality planning team meetings following the Q-90 series audit fiasco. Extensive revision of the quality procedures manual was undertaken, first by the quality consultant, who was directed by the newly appointed general manager so that this time there would be no rubber-stamping implementation. This time, final buy-off was to be by the president, after substantive review, challenge and revision, and then ultimate adoption. Rewrite of the LSI quality procedures manual, with concurrent section-by-section reimplementation, occurred from January through June of 1994.

Staying Focused

Implementation progress was periodically tested during these same six months. The president's office became a war room with agendas, schedules, checklists, and other flowcharts adorning the walls, all to drive the agenda toward completion of the quality system. It was during this process that LSI became aware of the forthcoming August 1994 draft of *QS-9000*. LSI finalized its rewritten procedures before the *QS-9000* draft was issued.

The company underwent a QS-9000 preregistration audit in September 1994 that was conducted over three days, by three auditors. The written report indicated major nonconformities; most criticisms were of upper management's lack of detailed knowledge of the quality control procedures and their implementation. LSI was given 30 days to correct all points of criticism and to demonstrate those corrections. The correction was done on time.

IMPORTANCE OF THE BUSINESS PLAN AND QUALITY CONTROL BUDGETING

QS-9000 elements require management participation. Management's real responsibility is one of leadership, which includes prioritizing the company's business on meeting QS-9000 and directing the socioeconomic and personnel goals to make sure that sufficient time is given to the company's personnel. Time must be allowed for total assimilation of this entirely new corporate culture at less than warp speed. To reimplement the daily agenda along these lines, and to expect it all to run smoothly as well, is, realistically, asking too much from a workforce already stretched by flexible work assignments, continual machine skill cross-training, and simultaneous training in quality implementation. Before getting in too deep, management must ask, At what price does QS-9000 implementation become too expensive for a small company? This analysis and

> *Management must ask, At what price does QS-9000 implementation become too expensive for a small company?*

its answers were not immediately apparent, but they became a major byproduct of a well-reasoned total business plan.

EMPLOYEE AWARENESS AND INVOLVEMENT

Without enthusiastic employee participation from the outset through final assessment, the registration process is doomed. Thus, the first "selling" of QS-9000 was not to company customers but to all employees. The employees learned what the procedures were, how to implement them, how to explain what they were doing, and why they were doing it. Employees were asked to explain all of this to an inquiring auditor or an inquiring customer. To achieve this level of enthusiasm and quality procedural know-how, employees came to believe that QS-9000 registration held benefits for them personally as well as for the company.

> *Employees came to believe that QS-9000 registration held benefits for them personally.*

Involvement became much more than general awareness prior to implementation and learning the quality procedures upon the manual's distribution. Employees were encouraged to fully participate throughout the quality manual writing process—such as in writing their own job descriptions and prioritizing their daily duties—and were invited to describe how they check quality during the laser-cutting process. Even though the final written quality procedures often varied widely from an employee's first conception, that difference, when explained, helped the employee's quality procedures grow and strengthened the employee's overall understanding. Developing a growth line such as this is an important step to bringing a laser operator, a forklift driver, and an accounting manager along the QS-9000 quality control system path. Human adaptation to changing quality procedures in the workplace takes time. At LSI, time was allocated to allow this to happen before any registration assessment was undertaken.

PROCESS CONTROL

The quality process control at LSI is accomplished through a combination of written documentation, employee input, and cross-checking a machine operator's quality verification of parts being laser cut. The cross-checking is done first by that operator's immediate supervisor and again by the quality control department manager at the job's commencement and conclusion, as well as hourly. Each inspection is logged and acknowledged in writing by the inspector on both the quality control inspection report and on the "job traveler." One of the problems associated with written documentation is finding the right forms and making sure all steps are completed accurately and on time. These problems have been reduced or eliminated by using one main job control document that details all of the steps in the job process, and making the person who is responsible for each step sign and date that step. Each quality control step must be owned by its performer.

LSI uses its job traveler form to outline the details of the process control it employs. The process control starts with the operation's manufacturing manager, who has the final approval of all scheduling and determines that a job is ready for laser cutting. The job is not cut until the materials have been received and verified, the program has been verified by quality control against customer prints, and a sample has been cut and approved by the customer. The job will now be assigned a quality control sheet and is ready for production. The flowchart of the LSI quality operating system (QOS) through its manufacturing processes is shown in Figure 9–1.

The job will now run according to statistical process control and the customer's specific work instructions, if so requested by the customer in writing at the outset of LSI's quotation process. These procedures are used to verify the continued accuracy in quality of each part. When completed, the job will be submitted to quality control for final inspection. The finished parts will be packaged and transferred to the shipping department for pickup by the customer or delivery by LSI.

Flowchart of LSI's Quality Operating System (the Job Traveler)
through Its Manufacturing Processes

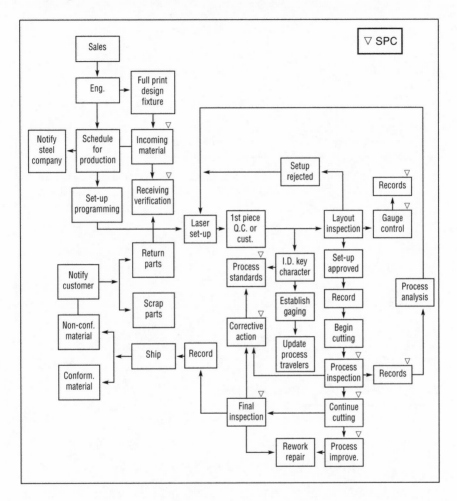

Figure 9–2 shows the flowchart of the LSI quality operating
system (QOS) through its shipping and receiving department. Each
step in this process is documented on the job traveler form, which
assures that all steps in the process have been completed. Particular
emphasis is paid to written customer approval of the first sample
part, which has helped significantly to reduce nonconforming parts
and scrap, and has significantly increased the quality of all parts
delivered.

Flowchart of LSI's Quality Operating System through Its
Shipping and Receiving Department

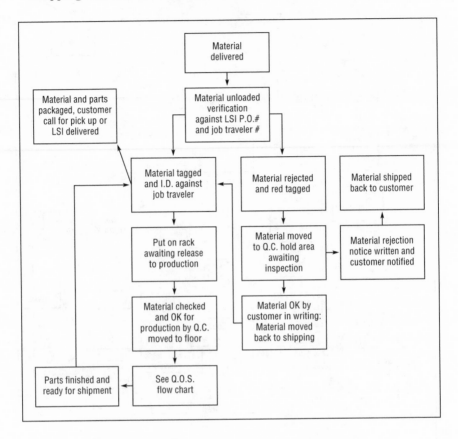

TRAINING AND EDUCATION

LSI has always believed that its strength is in its people. It empha-
sizes training and education to strengthen its human resources
component. One area of training, with semiannual classroom and
laboratory reinforcement, is statistical process control (SPC). LSI
utilizes SPC to monitor laser-cutting parts' primary characteristics,
perimeters, dimensions, gauge openings, and symmetry of overall
dimension during the cutting process. When technical training is
the subject, LSI has found it most effective to have one key employee attend an off-site specialized training seminar program and
then to disseminate that training in-house with similarly affected
employees through the seminar attendee.

LSI's training and education program involves all employees from the shop floor through senior management. Operator training tends to be specific to machine and parts quality, so that employees can improve their performance during machine operations. The machine training is specifically provided by the OEMs. Parts manufacturing training combines machine operating skills with how machine operations affect quality. Trainers seek input from employees on how they can enhance quality production techniques during the manufacturing process.

Midlevel and upper managers participate in continuous QS-9000 updating through attendance at industry trade associations' quality programs and off-site quality seminars. The emphasis on training from top to bottom ensures that the total organization adopts the uniform QS-9000 quality system and is actively involved in its pursuit rather than deferring continued knowledge and skills growth to the "quality control department."

As mentioned earlier, LSI has only 23 employees, over half of whom are hourly manufacturing workers. Their quality training is ongoing as they perform their daily work assignments under the supervision of the quality control department manager and their direct supervisors. Additionally, they receive semiannual statistical process control and document control in-house training. The remaining LSI employees, consisting of clerical, sales, accounting, computer programming, shipping and receiving, and the president, receive quality control reinforcement training through utilization of consultants, conferences, and QS-9000 related programs.

INTERNAL QUALITY AUDITS

QS-9000 requires independent internal quality audits. In the past, internal auditing was conducted by the president, general manager, and quality control manager. There was a logic to assigning this task to a three-part team not dominated by the quality control person, since top management is fully responsible for the quality control system operation. However, the quality control manager's participation does not satisfy the total independent requirement for QS-9000. Thus, LSI realigned its internal audit committee to consist of an executive management representative, an operations supervisor not affected by the section audit to be conducted, and a knowledgeable outside person. This demonstrated upper management's commitment to an independent audit and gave managers both insight into operational problems and a better hands-on understanding of the quality system and its supervision. Internal audits are scheduled every three months and are conducted in a manner similar to the original registrar's assessment. This system is combined with extensive note taking by the audit team so that areas of improvement are identified, corrective or improvement action plans developed, and quality control implementation enhanced. A final report is written that includes recommendations for changes in operations procedures, forms, and training, as well as any other changes to the present quality control system that would be consistent with QS-9000.

DOCUMENT AND DATA CONTROL

Record Retention

Tracing quality control documentation through the job process, start to finish, is a straightforward QS-9000 requirement. Auditors and registrars need access to the company files that demonstrate quality procedure implementation. The company itself needs access to completed job documents to review its own performance, answer customer inquiries, or respond to requests from anyone for replacement of misplaced data sheets. QS-9000 requires record retention for at least one year following completion of a job.

Record Retrieval

Master indexing is driven by an assigned job number from a permanent master list. The authorized operating forms set forth in the quality procedures manual are the only forms being used by LSI. Completed forms are placed in binders and kept under the control of the quality manager. These quality subject-matter binders are internally organized by job number. Quality control functions are addressed by captioned subject-matter binders.

The original job traveler becomes a part of the permanent completed job folder. Copies are filed in ascending job number order, a calendar year's worth to each binder. All other company forms are filed by customer name and assigned job number. There is a binder for each quality procedures function into which the subject form is placed. These records are retained by the quality manager, unless otherwise noted. Contract review minutes are maintained by calendar date of the meeting. Quality meetings that require any follow-up action are reported in a separate follow-up calendar-dated document. This report is generated intermittently as needed and distributed to management and all affected employees. Any prior week's follow-up action not yet completed appears in all subsequent reports. Actions to be completed will continue to appear until the specified action has been completed. Follow-up reports are maintained as a subsection of contract review reports in the president's office. Purchasing requests, once approved, are retained by receiving until the purchased item has arrived and been verified by receiving; thereafter, the written purchase order is sent to the comptroller for payment and record retention.

A customer may request engineering changes only in writing. LSI provides an engineering change notice form, the use of which is nonmandatory so long as the customer has made the request in writing. These documents become a part of the permanent job folder. Engineering change notices (ECNs) are acted on as soon as they are received and accepted in writing by the manufacturing manager.

The quality manual indexes a master copy of approved forms used at LSI in its companywide quality implementation, and no other form use is authorized unless specifically stated in the quality control procedure applicable to the quality procedure designating its use. Each LSI form is numbered, dated as to its date of implementation, and referenced to the latest revision letter applicable. Obsolete forms are purged from all quality control manuals immediately upon replacement. A form removed from the quality control manual is retained elsewhere as a discontinued form by an appropriate corporate representative.

CONTRACT REVIEW AND QUALITY PLANNING

Sales, manufacturing, quality control, and shipping and receiving meet daily to set the recommended manufacturing schedule. This schedule is subject to the manufacturing manager's approval. Laser-cutting work is scheduled from customers who have already accepted LSI's written quotation.

All customer-specific job characteristics and LSI's quality control special criteria to watch for during cutting are stated on the job traveler before a job is sent to manufacturing. Job scheduling is critical in meeting intermittent weekly and monthly customer part deliveries, avoiding downtime that can occur while waiting for customer material to commence a cutting schedule, and keeping all other jobs on time in their deliveries.

The contract review committee includes the manufacturing manager, president, comptroller, and quality control manager. To analyze the feasibility of undertaking a job, they examine purchasing requirements, manufacturing components, quality inspection, and laser machine staffing. In advance of LSI's quotation, all critical data are requested of the customer, and the company quotation incorporates the customer criteria. Thus, if the criteria change after quotation, another LSI bid is required before a customer purchase order, or amendment, is accepted by LSI.

LSI's strict adherence to its contract review procedures has prevented acceptance of quotations for some mouthwatering production volume jobs that, had the company accepted them, would have ultimately resulted in a project failure. Contract review analysis has allowed the company to take on new production jobs within its capabilities and deliver them to the customer's complete satisfaction.

CONTINUOUS IMPROVEMENT

Continuous improvement is an ever-occurring event. Ideas are encouraged and solicited from every employee monthly. Semiannually, a cross-functional committee appointed by the general manager reviews all operations and chronicles items, procedures, operations, and so on, that should be reexamined. The committee also estimates time for completion.

Each approved implemented change is measured to determine its effectiveness on quality, manufacturing, processing, marketing, safety and overall success and performance of LSI. This information is retained in the continuous improvement committee records. The effectiveness of continuous improvement action is also documented and retained. These documents are under the control of the quality manager and are made available upon request to employees, customers, and quality auditors for review.

REGISTRAR SELECTION AND QS-9000 ASSESSMENT

A preregistration audit is essential. LSI engaged a locally based QS-9000 qualified consultant to review its quality control systems and written procedures manual in September 1994. The preregistration audit was rigorous and critical; its assessment originally produced numerous nonconformities, any one of which would have been enough to deny the company QS-9000 registration. The audit, conducted by three auditors over two days, was expensive. Each critical point was thoroughly examined by LSI's quality planning team, and each resulted in a quality control procedure revision. All criticisms, nonconformities, and observations were corrected within 30 days following the audit, and these corrections were evidenced to the preregistration auditors and approved by them.

Upon issuance of the February 1995 *Quality System Requirements QS-9000,* upper management reviewed the requirements and again rewrote the quality control procedures manual. A QS-9000 registrar was selected based on its reputation. LSI also looked at registrar availability and reasonableness of costs. The final assessment audit was conducted in June and July 1995. The quality control procedures manual and quality policy manual were submitted to the auditor three weeks before the June audit. Written comments on the quality procedures manual were submitted to LSI at the time of the June 1995 auditors' on-site inspection and were thoroughly discussed with management and quality control at that time. There were no major or minor nonconformities stated.

When the auditors returned in July 1995, all observations and comments had been thoroughly addressed to the full satisfaction of the auditors. Registration occurred July 25, 1995. Passage on the first attempt could never have happened without the preregistration audit and the years of focused work that preceded it.

Employee awareness and involvement before, during, and after the registration audit is now the norm. Employees now refocus on continuous improvement and have the additional professional and personal pride of being part of that registration and ongoing compliance process.

CUSTOMER SATISFACTION

Customer satisfaction is what it's all about; it is the essence of the entire ongoing process. A strong quality control system objectively measures that each job has been completed to the customer's specifications and delivered on time. A strong quality control system also creates for management a dependable objective gauge for measuring the company's overall business performance.

LSI has realized some concrete direct benefits from its concerted three-year commitment to implementing its manufacturing quality control program systems:

- More production contract work awarded.
- Increased collection of receivables.
- Greater efficiencies in the manufacturing process.
- Increased repeat business from its Tier I and original equipment manufacturer customers
- Increased profitability.

SUMMARY

Obtaining QS-9000 registration is not the end but the beginning of an ongoing, evolving process that requires both vision and constant vigilance. Compliance with QS-9000 is verified by periodic independent audits. The future includes increased cross-training of employees in the quality systems, implementation methods, and greater interaction with customers to assure their continued satisfaction. The future holds a move toward a reduction in hard copy and an increase in computerization of documentation data storage and preparation. The lessons learned by LSI in the QS-9000 registration process include the following:

- Invest time and resources now for an important dividend later. The initial costs may seem ill advised at first, but LSI believes this investment will be returned if the system is followed.
- Involve each employee in the process. Without fully committed employee participation in the quality planning and implementing system, the program is doomed to failure.
- Utilize existing quality procedures and company strengths. Many business practices already satisfy a major portion of QS-9000.
- Integrate QS-9000 into the entire company process.

QS-9000 registration sets a company apart from its competitors. It states to the world a commitment to quality.

This case study is contributed by Daniel J. Henry, Jr., President and CEO of Laser Specialists, Inc., Fraser, Michigan.

CHAPTER 10

The Evolution of a
QS-9000 Quality Culture

MascoTech Inc.

GENERAL

- *Headquarters*   : **Auburn Hills, Michigan, U.S.A.**
- *Year Founded*   : **1955**
- *Number of Employees*   : **12,400**

QS-9000 SPECIFIC

- *Registered Location(s)*   : **Brighton, Michigan, U.S.A.**
- *Number of Employees*   : **150**
- *Registration Date*   : **January 18, 1995**
- *Product(s)*   : **Truck Cabs and Sleepers, Specialty Vehicles**
- *Tier I, II, III Supplier*   : **Tier I**
- *Major Customer(s)*   : **Chrysler, Ford, Mack Trucks, General Motors, Volvo-GM Heavy Truck**
- *Annual Sales*   : **U.S. $50 Million**

INTRODUCTION

MascoTech Automotive Systems Group (MASG) is part of the $1.6 billion MascoTech Inc. family of suppliers of world-class transportation products. MascoTech Body Systems & Assembly (BS&A), one of MASG's units, is not only the first MascoTech division to be registered to QS-9000 but also one of the first suppliers in the world to be registered, having been approved on January 18, 1995.

QS-9000 was regarded by our company as a logical next step to the ISO 9001 registration we obtained in May 1993. Moreover, QS-9000 complements all of our different client quality programs with a general quality system with which to manage and operate the business.

Of particular note, ISO and QS-9000 registrations have contributed to MascoTech's ability to secure new business, as many of our clients and best prospects come from industries where global influences have contributed to a growing awareness of international quality standards. In many cases, our prospects' first words have been, "Are you QS-9000 or ISO registered?" Saying yes is certainly not only a desirable response but now also a matter of survival.

The purpose of this case study is twofold: (1) to facilitate the reader's understanding of the steps involved in building a QS-9000 organization, and (2) to share in the strategies of preparing for and surviving a challenging five-day on-site registration.

BACKGROUND

MascoTech Automotive Systems Group traces its roots to the original Creative Industries Group, a company formed in the 1950s to provide technical services to the automotive industry. Creative was acquired by the formerly named Masco Industries family of automotive suppliers. In 1991, another Masco-owned company—Cars & Concepts, Inc.—was merged into Creative along with several other companies, after which the organization was renamed MascoTech Automotive Systems Group.

The origins of MascoTech's Body Systems & Assembly Division date back to 1976, when Dick Chrysler founded Cars & Concepts, a Brighton, Michigan, company whose purpose was to conceive innovative design solutions and develop products for original equipment manufacturers (OEMs). Cars & Concepts is generally credited with playing a major role in the rebirth of the domestic convertible; in 1982 the company joined forces with the Chrysler Corporation to launch the K-car convertible. Cars & Concepts would also go on to build over 277,000 Mustang convertibles for Ford Motor Company.

Today, BS&A's focus is to develop and integrate high-quality components into subassemblies and modules that satisfy customer expectations for value, delivery, and performance. Products and services include truck cabs and sleeper-cabs, specialty vehicles, systems assembly, and related sequencing into OEM plants. Major customers include Chrysler, Ford, General Motors, Mack Trucks, Inc., and Volvo-GM Heavy Truck Corporation.

BUILDUP OF QUALITY IN EIGHT STAGES

BS&A's successful journey toward QS-9000 registration was born of an evolutionary buildup of quality composed of eight stages, which to a large degree paralleled our OEM clients' experiences. This buildup is reflected in Figure 10–1.

In Stage 1, products were contained by way of inspections, audits, and conventional problem solving. In Stage 2, process control became the focus vis-á-vis statistical process control (SPC), although this approach initially suffered from being too narrow in scope and application insofar as company personnel were neither properly introduced to the process nor adequately trained.

F I G U R E   10–1

Eight-Stage Buildup of Quality

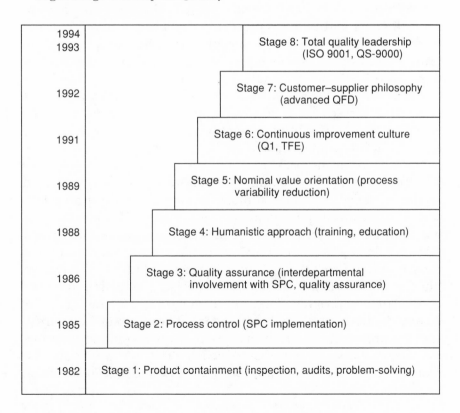

Stage 3 reflected an attempt by management to introduce quality assurance to the business through a cross-functional departmental approach to SPC, although in our case the focus mistakenly shifted to management personnel rather than to the actual performers of the jobs. As a result, SPC was only marginally effective in the plants where its application was required. Then in Stage 4 the emphasis began to shift to a more humanistic approach as the company sought to train and educate all employees. The company, quite simply, set aside the funds required to train up to 15 employees at a time in a classroom that was formerly an executive parking garage. All employees were exposed to two 40-hour sessions dubbed "core training," which in fact lasted one whole week each. Ultimately, this stage would pave the way for the successful transition from Stage 5 through Stage 8.

The company finally made SPC work when process variability reduction (PVR) was adopted. PVR puts SPC into a systematic customer-driven process, which seeks to reduce variation in the process, which in turn contributes to a stronger orientation and passion for the nominal value of a given process.

The company was now equipped with the right "tool box" to enter the next and perhaps most important phase of our cultural maturation, where continuous improvement became the company's primary motivator. The vehicles used to transform the company were Ford's Q1 for Assembly program and, shortly thereafter, General Motors' Targets for Excellence (TFE). It was during this phase that MascoTech officially became the first supplier in the world to earn Ford's Q1 for Assembly award, due in large measure to our "lead-dog" mindset (*lead-dog*, in this context, means the same as the "leader of the pack").

The lead-dog mindset cannot be fabricated, nor can it be forced on the organization; rather, it must develop naturally as an extension of the cultural personality of the company. In our case, the breakthrough occurred when a team of salary, hourly, and United Auto Workers (UAW) personnel were the first "outsiders" invited to visit Ford's first Q1 for Assembly plant in St. Paul, Minnesota (the Twin Cities Plant), as MascoTech was participating in Ford's internal quality program. Here our team heard their battle cry, "We want to be the lead-dog assembly plant at Ford Motor Company," and the phrase stuck. From that point on, we would strive to be the lead-dog operation at MascoTech. To this end, we adopted a more Marine Corps–like approach to ISO and QS-9000, which manifested itself in a process orientation and willingness to improvise as opposed to a more bureaucratic and procedural approach.

Our lead-dog phase also gave rise to Stage 6 and a customer–supplier philosophy (Figure 10–2) whereby each associate in the plant recognized his or her impact on the process and subsequent customer–supplier relationships up and down the assembly line. Our employees then institutionalized this philosophy through an iteration in the application of quality function deployment (QFD) featuring a new "house" designed to quantify the impact of these relationships.

Stage 8 was especially crucial to our evolution when it became evident that, for as much as MascoTech had accomplished, there was an unavoidable drop in intensity in the organization when the Mustang convertible program ended. Moreover, there was no real mechanism in place to reinvigorate either the Q1 or TFE efforts, as neither program required a follow-up surveillance or reregistration.

F I G U R E   10–2

Customer–Supplier Philosophy in QFD Form

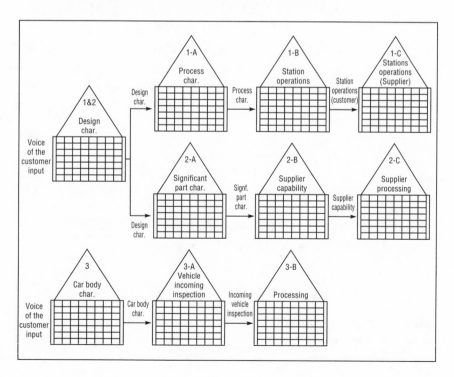

So BS&A's management jump-started the quality process by introducing total quality leadership (TQL) to the operation. TQL was in fact an extension of our lead-dog mindset, but it was larger in scope, with ISO 9001 and QS-9000 registrations as the goals. In addition, two of our largest clients, Mack and Volvo, decided to mandate ISO 9000 compliance for their suppliers, thus giving our organization a sense of urgency in starting the process.

"Any organization can learn from this evolution," says the Brighton operation's plant manager. "It takes the esoteric aspect of quality and puts it into a real game plan." Of equal importance are the lessons learned, for there is no law that mandates a long time frame or sequence for the evolution toward QS-9000 registration. Rather, companies should integrate the building blocks of quality at their own pace with an eye toward accelerating the process.

BS&A set its sights on ISO 9001, and in May 1993 became the first division in MascoTech to be registered, thus becoming the lead-dog yet again. Then in January 1995, the operation was registered to QS-9000. How we did it follows.

MANAGEMENT COMMITMENT: IT MAKES A DIFFERENCE

BS&A's president, Oddie Leopando, was a driving force behind the organization's early focus on quality. "I am extremely proud of all of our employees and their commitment," says Leopando. "Their efforts have made us one of the first automotive suppliers to achieve QS-9000 registration."

Indeed, management commitment is crucial to the QS-9000 registration process. After all, management's fundamental responsibility is to provide the leadership, direction, support, and tools required to enable the team to realize its goals. The management team must sustain the organization's evolution, whether in controlled stages or by way of breakthroughs where speed is the focus. One of the first tasks is to establish a quality vision.

QUALITY VISION: WHERE IT ALL BEGINS

All companies need a quality vision upon which to focus the business, and this vision must cascade throughout the organization to give it a strong customer focus (Figure 10–3).

MascoTech's Quality Vision

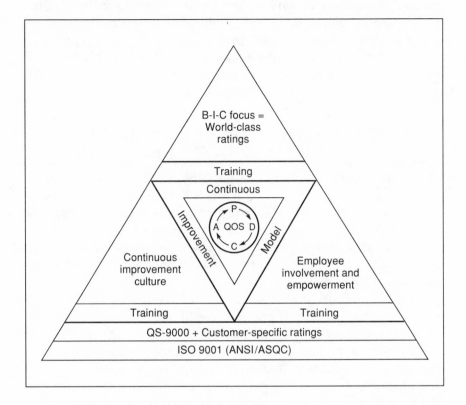

MascoTech's quality vision was derived through a cross-functional team effort to gather up, interpret, and package a meaningful and practical quality solution for our business. Our vision therefore has as its primary foundation the ANSI/ASQC Standard Q9001-1994, and as a secondary foundation the Automotive Industry Action Group (AIAG)–sponsored QS-9000 with "customer-specific ratings." At the core of the vision is a continuous improvement model driven by our quality operating system (QOS) and the Deming cycle of plan-do-check-act or P-D-C-A. This model, which acts as the engine in our system, has three gears:

1. Continuous improvement culture.
2. Employee involvement and empowerment.
3. Best-in-class focus (resulting in world-class ratings).

The fuel in the engine is training, as the total system still needs a human driver. Indeed, the entire process begins and ends with people. This quality vision in its earliest form served as the impetus behind the development of our quality policy, a fundamental requirement in both the ISO and QS-9000 programs. This policy was developed by all of our employees, signed off, and published well before the organization even began its effort to pursue ISO 9001.

GETTING STARTED: FINDING THE RIGHT "PARTNERS"

Finding the right consultant is especially important for companies that have little or no experience with ISO or QS-9000. If a company chooses to pursue QS-9000 first rather than ISO, then a consultant is almost surely needed unless the company hires an expert to remain on staff and lead the team. Therefore, consultants should be evaluated and screened in the same manner as an applicant for a key executive position.

At a minimum, the consultant should provide training to the management team and, if possible, to the entire operation; otherwise, the company may elect to do some or all of its own internal training (as was the case with MascoTech when we trained our own associates). In addition, the consultant should guide the initial development of the quality policy manual (the Level 1 document) and selected Level 2 documents, as required. He or she should also provide counsel to management with respect to choosing a registrar, an extremely important task given the long-term nature of the company's relationship with the registrar.

MascoTech hired a consulting firm in late 1992 to support our ISO effort. Personnel from the firm then helped MascoTech organize and develop the initial workplan and early drafts of Level 1 and Level 2 documents, and assisted in the selection of our registrar.

The consulting firm introduced MascoTech to a seven-step process for achieving ISO 9001, as reflected in Figure 10–4. The same approach (with a few adjustments) was employed for QS-9000, although in our case we had to focus only on the new QS-9000 requirements as opposed to starting the whole process over.

Selecting a qualified and reputable registrar is crucial for at least three reasons:

The Climb to Registration

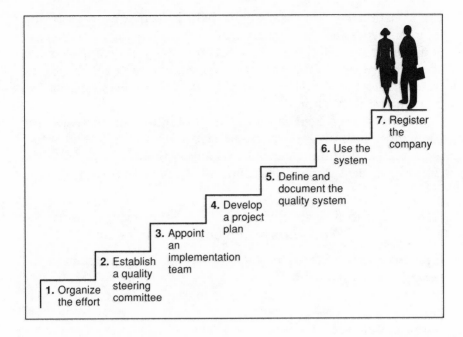

1. **A registrar will become** as much a partner as a third-party auditor, as the business relationship will be ongoing for at least three years.
2. **The registrar's credibility** and status will impact the credibility and marketing value associated with the actual registration.
3. **The registrar may be** expensive, so the company should perform a cost-benefit analysis (either formally or informally) before choosing one. Moreover, the company should expect a good return for its investment in the registrar (i.e., a favorable experience).

It is especially important for the company to identify and select, through its registrar, the right accreditation body. These choices should be based on (1) the country and markets in which the company will do business and (2) the implied status in being affiliated with a certain accreditation body.

THE CLIMB TO REGISTRATION AND BEYOND

Step 1: Organize the Effort

Our consultant's first task was to help MascoTech organize the effort and educate our management in regard to ISO requirements and basic responsibilities, the most fundamental of which is the appointment of a management representative to guide the effort. BS&A's director of quality was given the task of leading both the ISO and QS-9000 efforts.

Getting organized is crucial at this time. The management team must be fully prepared and supportive of the total effort required. In addition, great care and attention must be given to the next two critical steps in the climb to registration.

Steps 2 and 3: Establish a Quality Steering Committee and Appoint an Implementation Team

It is important to note that companies have many different experiences when organizing their teams. Our experience would suggest that it is desirable to obtain active participation from all team members regardless of whether they are executives or shop associates, as opposed to a structurally layered approach where there are too many managers. To this end, BS&A's approach may differ somewhat from the more conventional top-down approach advocated by some consultants.

MascoTech's core team was composed of salary and hourly personnel. The salary side of the core team included the director of quality, plant quality manager, director of business development, a manufacturing engineer, and a supplier quality engineer. These individuals, along with the plant manager and president (also the two co-sponsors), formed the quality steering committee. A mix of salary and hourly personnel formed the implementation team, which essentially functioned as an extension of the quality steering committee. The core team thus extended deep into the organization with a broad mix of participants in the process.

Whether pursuing ISO or QS-9000, the core team must be operations based, highly experienced as a unit, and composed of individuals who provide specific expertise. The team must also be completely empowered by senior management to get the job done. There should be no overlap in roles and responsibilities on the team and, in fact, each team member should be assigned to a manageable number of ISO or QS-9000 elements that fit his or her respective skill sets.

In selecting and recruiting team members, the individual's track record and work ethic must be considered, as the team will be faced with many challenges and heavier-than-normal workloads, which might otherwise discourage a marginal performer.

As mentioned under management commitment, the goal of senior management is to sustain both the team and the organization in general in order to foster a homogeneous quality mindset at the operations level. There can be no "chimneys" to contend with, nor any external interference such as an executive committee whose only role is to entertain "report-outs" by the core team. Indeed, the organization must strive to minimize the number of channels in the process to keep the effort as lean and focused as possible.

Step 4: Develop a Project Plan

The core team's first assignment is to develop the project plan inclusive of all the activities and milestones in the process. In addition, a budget should be established in support of the plan. A formally approved budget is probably more important than most companies realize, as the team without a budget may be forced to defend its financial needs at the expense of valuable time and energy that should be directed toward the actual registration process.

Prior to deploying a detailed project plan, the team will be well advised to develop a simple macro version so that all associates understand the major milestones and general timing. MascoTech's macro plan included the following 20 items:

1. Conduct ISO 9001 training (orientation).
2. Appoint a management representative.
3. Form a steering committee.
4. Form an implementation team.
5. Perform first gap assessment.
6. Develop and implement a corrective action plan (1).
7. Establish and communicate the quality policy.
8. Establish and communicate organizational responsibility and authority for quality.

9. Develop a quality policy manual.
10. Develop and update quality procedure manual.
11. Conduct training for items 7 to 10.
12. Perform second gap assessment.
13. Develop and implement a corrective action plan (2).
14. Schedule registration.
15. Organize and prepare for preregistration audit.
16. Conduct preregistration audit.
17. Develop and implement a corrective action plan (3).
18. Verify final corrective actions.
19. Finalize assessment logistics.
20. Conduct assessment.

One of our first tasks was to perform a "gap assessment" to identify areas of noncompliance to ISO 9000 and QS-9000 as well as other shortcomings. The gap assessment may be performed by internal qualified auditors who will record any nonconformities on a controlled document. (In this context, *qualified* means that auditors have been officially trained by a third party who has been appropriately certified.) Nonconformities should then be forwarded to appropriate personnel for disposition and resolution, after which a second (and third if needed) gap assessment must be performed to verify closure. In MascoTech's case, gap assessments were performed at the same time we developed the detailed project plan in order to speed up the process, as these findings (good or bad) may very well dictate the scope and pace of the effort.

In most organizations, several areas will likely surface as either deficient and/or in need of more objective evidence in support of the system's actual use, namely, the communication side of management responsibility, contract review, design control, document and data control, process control, inspection and test status, corrective and preventive actions (with an emphasis on the preventive aspect), handling, storage, packaging, preservation and delivery, internal quality audits, and the new production part approval process (PPAP). In addition, the organization must deploy the Chrysler, Ford, and General Motors' *Advanced Product Quality Planning Manual*, as these requirements will overlap and support many of the systems required in QS-9000.

Step 5: Define and Document the Quality System

The next major phase is to define and document the quality system. Here, the so-called hierarchy of documentation must be addressed, that is the company's quality policies (i.e., Level 1), procedures (Level 2), and work instructions (Level 3). The first step is to prepare the quality policy manual, a single document required to describe the organization's quality system and the elements which support ISO 9000 and QS-9000 compliance. As a rule of thumb, this manual should be started as early as possible given all of the iterations that are likely to occur.

The quality policy manual may be standardized to a point in larger organizations where multiple locations need to be registered. However, each operation or location will have slightly different needs, most of which are driven by the client, thus precipitating a certain level of variation in Level 2 and 3 documentation. It is estimated that, on average, at least 25 percent of the total quality package may be unique from one operation to the next. Recognition of this uniqueness may be reflected in the quality policy manual in either an addendum or by the simple stamp, DOES NOT APPLY (to the operation in question).

Most organizations already possess and maintain specific procedures. If not, procedures will have to be created. The team should then combine applicable procedures to form a common manual designed to address all of ISO 9000 and QS-9000 requirements. In this case, there can be no exceptions: Either the operation's procedures comply in their current or revised forms or they do not, in which case corrective actions are mandatory. Not having a system in place is grounds for a major nonconformity and therefore cause for serious alarm.

Step 6: Use the Quality System

The operation must also use the quality system to verify that it works and that the people using it understand it. This enables the team to retrieve objective evidence in support of compliance with a particular standard as opposed to being compelled to fabricate evidence for the sake of a "sales presentation" to the registrar (a dangerous strategy, to be sure). For example, the operation must not only have the systems in place to ensure process control but also provide statistical evidence to verify that the systems are actually producing the desired results.

Step 7: Register the Company

Once all of the six major steps in the climb to registration are put into motion and the major milestones are achieved, it is time to register the company with the registrar of choice. Much preparation is required to assure a successful registration. In MascoTech's case, our core team actually simulated the assessment during numerous pre-audits, wherein team members challenged each other to present their systems and evidence that supported actual use in the operation (as required in our project plan). In many cases, we found this process to be more challenging than portions of the formal on-site assessment.

According to our director of quality, "The original ISO assessment was very intimidating. I thought it would be the longest week of my life. But a funny thing happened by the second day. All that hard work and planning made Day 2 go a lot easier, once it became clear to the registrars that we really had done our homework."

In fact, five minor nonconformities were discovered on that first day, and the team stayed up until nearly 11:00 P.M. to correct the shortcomings. Several procedures were revised, and documents were also modified. By the following morning, all of the nonconformities were corrected and closed. And therein lies one of our secrets: address and close all open issues immediately in order to keep up with the assessment.

Address and close all open issues immediately in order to keep up with the assessment.

Over the next four days, BS&A was flagged for only four more minor nonconformities, giving us a total of nine, which at that time (1993) ranked among our registrar's best first-time performances. There were no major nonconformities cited. In addition, BS&A's registration process, from start to finish, ranked among the fastest ever, according to our registrar and consulting firm, due in large measure to our quality evolution and culture.

Since then, BS&A has successfully completed four more ISO surveillances and two QS-9000 surveillances as well. The first QS-9000 audit conducted by the registrar in January 1995 represented an "expansion of scope" of the ISO standard to QS-9000 and that meant yet another grueling but successful five-day audit.

The core team approached the QS-9000 registration with the same intensity as the ISO effort, except that this time we clearly benefited from our earlier experiences. Only five minor nonconformities were found, a significant improvement over our ISO effort, to be sure. As such, we may present several tips:

- Make sure that the company's advanced product quality planning (APQP) process is in effect as far ahead of the registration as possible. APQP is the bible of quality planning in the operation and therefore *must* be used whenever possible.
- Gather up and organize as much evidence as possible and sequence it to the questions posed by the registrar. (Note: These questions are forwarded to the team in advance, so there will be enough time to retrieve, but not create, the appropriate evidence.)
- Be confident when presenting a system during the assessment. Involve as many people in the effort as practical to validate the presentation. Invite the registrar to talk with anyone in the operation. Be advised that not everyone will share in the enthusiasm and plan-of-attack for the assessment; there is no such thing as a perfect operation. Nevertheless, the team should expect that the majority of participants will be an asset to the process.
- Stick with the topics and issues in question, and avoid irrelevant small talk or ego thumping. However, be friendly and even humorous, if the situation warrants. The bottom line here is to establish a good working relationship with the registrar.
- As indicated, address any and all open issues discovered during the registration on the same day they are discovered. While this strategy may or may not impress the registrar (it likely won't), it will keep the process moving forward in a more constructive manner.

THE PITFALLS OF QS-9000: POINTS TO CONSIDER

While there are many dos in the QS-9000 process (as highlighted throughout this case study), there are several key don'ts normally learned from firsthand experience. Our top 10 list is as follows:

1. Don't assign the role of management representative to any person not totally familiar with ISO 9000 and QS-9000 and, if at all possible, the audit process to be employed by the registrar.

2. Don't assign the role of management representative to a corporate executive whose time is thoroughly consumed by running his or her functional area and who will therefore not be able to participate in gap assessments, preaudits, and actual audits.

3. Don't put a team together where team members' roles and responsibilities overlap or in cases where egos may clash.

4. Don't put a corporate steering committee together whose only purpose is to hear a report-out by the core team. This is wasteful, nonproductive, and potentially an obstacle to getting things done on time.

5. Don't expect the core team to do everything; rather, form support teams with as much hourly support as possible to focus on specific elements in the process. Plant participation and support are the keys to success.

6. Don't confuse a policy with a procedure in preparing Level 1 and Level 2 documents. Treat a policy as an executive summary that cross-references one or more supporting procedures.

7. Don't wait until the last minute to organize files or presentations required during the registration. The registrar will almost certainly see through a marginal explanation and lack of evidence. There is no substitution for good preparation, and bluffing is a bad idea.

8. Don't patronize the registrar or seek advice from him or her during the registration (you won't get it); rather, learn how to listen and to be quiet when appropriate. (Hint: "Point well taken" is always a good response.)

9. Don't be overly discouraged by the number of minor nonconformities cited; rather, close any and all issues before the registrar leaves. (Again, fix the nonconformity on the same day it is discovered.)

10. Don't get hung up making everything perfect. Focus on the weaknesses first, and the rest will follow.

NEXT STEPS: BEYOND QS-9000

According to our director of quality, "The best thing about QS-9000 is the continuity and continuous improvement aspect. It keeps our focus year-round and forces us to think about what is next." The plant manager concurs: "Without the QS-9000 effort, it would have been very difficult to keep our lead-dog theme intact. And it would be even harder to generate the kind of ongoing intensity required to sustain a quality organization."

BS&A's next task is to obtain the highest-quality customer-specific ratings possible in order to continue our pursuit of TQL.

In reality, the pursuit of QS-9000 may be a sobering experience for companies that have not made a long-term commitment to their businesses and a strong commitment to their people. But for companies that have in fact properly evolved their quality cultures and invested in their people, systems, and processes, QS-9000 is clearly attainable and, in the end, a highly rewarding journey.

This case study is contributed by Michael Stoeckel, Director of Business Development, MascoTech Body Systems & Assembly, Brighton, Michigan. Special acknowledgment to George Helms, Mike Rhoton, Terry Bell, Oddie Leopando, Rob Janis, and Mark Tomasik.

CHAPTER 11

Driving Excellence

Polywheels Manufacturing Limited

GENERAL

- *Headquarters*   : **Oakville, Ontario, Canada**
- *Year Founded*   : **1986**
- *Number of Employees*   : **146**

QS-9000 SPECIFIC

- *Registered Location(s)*   : **Oakville, Ontario, Canada**
- *Number of Employees*   : **146**
- *Registration Date*   : **October 5, 1994**
- *Product(s)*   : **Compression Molded Products, Front End Panels, Fuel Tank Heat Shields, Fuel Filler Housings**
- *Tier I, II, III Supplier*   : **Tier I and II**
- *Major Customer(s)*   : **Ford**
- *Annual Sales*   : **U.S. $19 Million**

INTRODUCTION

The secret to long-term growth in the business world today is to supply quality products and services at a competitive price. The key to survival in the automotive industry as a supplier today is to produce products and services with superb quality at a low price.

Polywheels Manufacturing Limited has always taken quality very seriously. In the first four years of its existence, high-quality goods were produced without the benefit of a formal quality system. This meant that the company had no methods of calculating cost or ensuring that mistakes were not repeated. In 1991, Polywheels began to assess the quality systems of Ford, General Motors, and Chrysler. It was decided that the Ford Q-101 quality system was best suited for the company's purposes. At that time, Polywheels had no business with any of the automotive companies; the adoption of the Ford system was solely for internal improvement. With the Q-101 system in place, Polywheels began a sales effort with Ford, which resulted in the company becoming a Tier I supplier at a time when Ford was actively reducing its supplier base.

In 1993, Polywheels decided to pursue ISO 9001 in order to improve the effectiveness of the quality assurance function throughout the company. When Polywheels was ready for the ISO 9001 audit in August 1994, the company had a chance to participate in the QS-9000 pilot project. Polywheels took the QS-9000 assessment in September 1994 and officially passed the audit on October 5, 1994. As a result, Polywheels was one of the first known companies worldwide to obtain QS-9000 registration.

This case study describes the process a young and small company used to achieve QS-9000 registration.

BACKGROUND

Frank Milligan, president and chief executive officer, established Polywheels in 1986 in Oakville, Ontario, Canada. In March 1987, Polywheels occupied a 20,000-square-foot facility and employed seven people. In 1993, the company employed 50 people and occupied a 55,000-square-foot building. In October 1995, the company occupied a 340,000-square-foot facility and employed 146 people. Polywheels' strong accent on quality has helped it become one of Canada's largest composites fabricators.

Polywheels manufactures compression-molded automotive parts such as fuel tank heat shields, header panels, and fuel filler supports. Polywheels has been involved in several consumer market products, such as microwave oven cookware, bathroom sinks, outboard motor covers, and snowboards. The company is a Tier I and II supplier. In addition, the distribution network of Polywheels in North America consists of over 100 distributors.

The *Financial Post* and Arthur Andersen named Polywheels one of the top 50 best managed private companies in Canada in 1994. Furthermore, the Oakville Chamber of Commerce named the president of Polywheels as 1993 Entrepreneur of the Year.

Polywheels is a Q1 rated supplier to Ford Motor Company, a major customer of Polywheels. In keeping with the commitment to quality, Polywheels achieved the ISO 9001 registration in 1994.

LEADERSHIP COMMITMENT

The auto industry's systems assessment of its supplier base has become more stringent now than ever before. Suppliers considering their performance excellent today may find their performance inadequate tomorrow. Polywheels is well aware of this.

In late 1993, the president of Polywheels made this statement to his management staff: "Polywheels will obtain the ISO 9001 registration by the end of 1994." The major reason for seeking ISO 9001 registration was Polywheels' continuing drive for improvement. Most of the management staff have grown with the company since its establishment. They have seen the rate at which the company has expanded.

Senior managers have received training in quality improvement tools and techniques. Examples are our problem-solving methodology, design of experiments, and advanced product quality planning (APQP). They demonstrate a commitment to quality improvement through direct involvement in improvement initiatives such as scrap reduction. The president meets with small groups of employees to hear their comments. Managers become involved in improvement initiatives by attending cross-functional teams. Goals reflecting this requirement are established as part of the senior management's tasks, and successes against this are monitored through comments and surveys.

According to the five-year business plan, Polywheels would move to a facility six times its existing size and would triple its labor force in two years. Thus, Polywheels had to adopt a worldwide recognized quality system quickly. Every manager believed that the ISO 9001 standard would be easier to implement when the company was still small.

The management team was responsible for the success of this process; every manager committed to making ISO 9001 registration happen in one year. The quality manager nominated himself as the ISO 9001 champion.

EMPLOYEE AWARENESS AND INVOLVEMENT

"Vision 2000" was presented on a day in August 1994 when Polywheels closed its office and manufacturing facility to let all employees in the organization attend a meeting. In the meeting, the president presented the company's plan between then and the year 2000. He made all employees aware that one of the major upcoming events was the ISO 9001 project. He told the employees the methods Polywheels would use to achieve ISO 9001. All employees participated in the discussions and recognition of the potential problems to be faced.

TRAINING

By reimbursing the tuition fees, Polywheels encourages its people to attend development courses, including quality-related training, at universities and colleges. Annual training needs analysis conducted by the joint workplace training committee is pursued to enhance job-related skills. The approach is used to define the collective and strategic development needs of the organization as well as the individual needs of each employee. The committee is composed of hourly and salaried employees from different departments. Action plans and timing charts are used to implement the training process. Polywheels uses the training survey to study the effectiveness of training.

REGISTRAR SELECTION

Polywheels' quality manual followed the Ford Q-101 system guidelines and requirements. The quality manager believed that the existing quality manual basically met the ISO 9000 requirements with some minor revisions.

An ISO 9000 registration firm had a good reputation and was located reasonably close to Polywheels. The quality manager chose the registration firm to save some traveling cost. After the quality manager signed an agreement with this registration firm, he submitted the quality manual for approval.

The registration firm sent the documentation review report to the quality manager two weeks later. The report indicated that the quality manual submitted did not comply with the ISO 9000 standard. The comments on the report were vague without specifically indicating the noncompliance. An example of a noncompliance was that the quality manual did not meet the requirements of section

2.1 in the ISO 9000 standard. This kind of comment repeated itself in all 20 sections of the ISO standard. Therefore, according to the report, the quality manual submitted failed completely to conform to the ISO 9000 standard.

The quality manager decided he needed some help. What came to his mind was that consultation service was offered through a different division by the same registration firm. Since the quality manager had dealt with the registration firm earlier, he had received much literature from the other division of the registration firm on providing training and consultation service. The price was not cheap.

Auditors from the automakers and other third-party auditors had reviewed the quality manual in the past with excellent comments. The quality manager did not understand why the quality manual deserved to receive the negative ratings given to it by the registration firm.

The quality manager assumed that Polywheels might save some traveling cost by choosing a registration firm locally. Nonetheless, it is extremely important to choose a registration firm that is able to assign auditors experienced in the automotive industry to deal with Polywheels. Otherwise, the traveling cost saved will not compensate for needless expenditure of time and superfluous procedures.

Instead of discussing the report with the registration firm, the quality manager investigated other ISO 9000 registration firms. He had been associated with one laboratory testing company in Michigan for several years and realized that the testing company also provided ISO 9000 registration service. This company has been dealing with the automotive industries for numerous years. It is strictly a registration company; it does not provide any other ISO 9000 consultation services directly or indirectly. The registration cost combined with the traveling cost offered by this company was approximately the same as the cost quoted by the previous registration firm. Consequently, he signed an agreement with the new company and submitted the same quality manual to the new company for approval without any amendments.

DOCUMENTATION REVIEW

The new registration company sent the documentation review report to the quality manager after three weeks. The report stated a few corrective actions required, and the comments were definite. Thus, the quality manager was able to follow the report and make corrections to the quality manual easily. When the documentation approval was obtained from the new registration company, he immediately canceled the contract with the old registration firm.

REGISTRATION PREPARATION

A preliminary assessment for ISO 9001 was scheduled with our new registrar for November 1993. Polywheels demanded that the auditors who performed the preliminary audit be the same ones who would perform the formal audit. This was done so that the high level of discipline in the preliminary audit would be consistent in the formal audit.

Although the preliminary assessment was not a formal registration audit, all managers took it very seriously. Polywheels spent six months in preparation for the assessment. Within those six months, Polywheels successfully built the fundamentals of the ISO 9000 quality system as shown in Figure 11–1.

F I G U R E   11–1

Polywheels' Fundamentals of the ISO 9000 Quality System

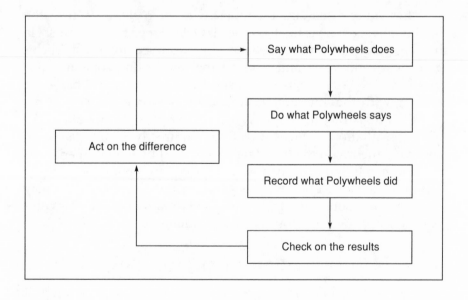

PRELIMINARY ASSESSMENT

It was suggested that Polywheels could have accelerated the process by moving the preliminary assessment date ahead of time. It was said that the company could use the assessment as a trial run and a consultation tool. The quality manager disagreed with that. He considered the preliminary audit formal and Polywheels had to be fully prepared. When the quality manager considered the company was ready for the preliminary assessment, he and the vice president performed an internal quality audit to verify the findings.

The preliminary assessment lasts for only one day. If the auditor writes up a noncompliance report every 10 minutes, one would consider Polywheels incompetent. Also, the auditor would possibly fail to observe some areas in a limited time period. Thus, the probability of passing the formal audit would be low.

Considering the number of employees Polywheels employed at that time, the acceptance criterion was no more than six minor nonconformances and zero major noncompliances. Polywheels failed the preliminary assessment. Document and data control were the areas that needed most attention. However, the quality manager realized that some processes were overdocumented.

After the exercise, all managers and employees involved believed the preliminary assessment was compulsory to the whole ISO 9001 registration process. The noncompliances were not difficult to correct. Therefore, the quality manager scheduled the formal registration in six months.

DOCUMENT CONTROL

The preliminary assessment showed some documents had not been authorized. In addition, some documents used were not at current revision levels. After the assessment, the quality manager bought computer software to address the issues. The quality manager has used the computer program to control all the active quality-related documents and prepare a master list. The list indicated all the current documents and drawings, their revision levels, and their approvals. Any changes to the documents required update in the computer program. This document control method is now more effective.

THE QS-9000 PILOT PROJECT

Polywheels moved to a larger facility in April 1994. Hence, the ISO 9001 registration audit was postponed to September 1994. In August 1994, Chrysler, Ford, and General Motors introduced *Quality System Requirements QS-9000*. The foundation of QS-9000 is ISO 9001 plus sector-specific requirements and customer-specific requirements.

Polywheels was one of the few selected companies to participate in the QS-9000 pilot project. This was a challenge for Polywheels because the company had not achieved ISO 9001 registration. Verification of conformance to ISO 9001 was a necessary condition for registration to QS-9000.

As a pilot project, the registration firm would use the draft QS-9000 requirements to assess Polywheels. Then, Polywheels and the registration firm would offer audibility of the quality system requirements to the QS-9000 task force for comments. The task force would use input received from those who participated in the pilot project to clarify the requirements.

MISCONCEPTIONS ABOUT QS-9000

The misconceptions about QS-9000 in Polywheels were that it would increase paperwork, generate more procedures, reduce flexibility, increase costs, and create no value added.

Obviously, setting up and managing quality system standards requires substantial time. It will take more time if auditors visit regularly and review quality practice in excessive detail. The risk is that Polywheels would lose benefits and regard the whole activity as a deviation from the main course of the business.

The automotive industry has made impressive use of the "team" method of quality improvement. It is a process of problem identification followed by assignment of cross-functional teams to identify root causes and follow through with corrective actions. The team method may sometimes lead to quality improvements. However, a more efficient approach is to first establish a formalized quality system as a foundation and then achieve quality improvement through the team method.

In Polywheels, the senior management team works with the design team in supporting the implementation. The design team studies the present system and recommends how it can be redesigned, then assigns study teams to specific areas to make improvements. The design team represents a cross-section of hourly and salaried employees from all areas within the company. They are chosen from people who volunteer and have an interest in being on the team. Members are selected based on their skills, knowledge of the company, background, and length of service with Polywheels. A study team is made up of people from different job functions who are familiar with some aspects of the area in question. Study teams are assigned a specific task, policy, or procedure to be examined by the design team.

It is necessary to clear up the misconceptions the employees have about QS-9000. To be beneficial, the company must make sure all employees work toward the changes and improvements they represent.

THE CHALLENGE

As indicated in section 4.6.2 of *QS-9000*, Polywheels shall evaluate its own suppliers. According to the requirement, Polywheels must perform subcontractor development using QS-9000 as fundamental quality system requirements. In other words, Polywheels must conduct QS-9000 assessments on its suppliers unless the suppliers are QS-9000 registered.

The biggest challenge facing Polywheels is how to demand the QS-9000 requirements from its own suppliers. Particularly, some small suppliers have never been involved in the ISO 9000 standard and lack the resources to implement QS-9000.

Initially, the purchaser in Polywheels sent the QS-9000 guidelines to all the suppliers. He requested action plans and assigned a due date for response. Some small companies with little annual sales with Polywheels will likely ignore the request. Polywheels does not have an answer to deal with this issue at the present time.

THE THIRD-PARTY AUDIT

From past experience, customers did not perform second-party audits on a regular basis because of limited resources. They applied the resources to companies that were having more difficulties than others. Polywheels did not have a second-party audit done for two years. Polywheels will expect a surveillance audit under the third-party system, once every six months.

The major difference between a second-party audit and a third-party audit is that third-party auditors have a broader focus. Normally, second-party auditors pay less attention to products belonging to other customers. Third-party auditors spend more time surveying all the product lines and study every process, even though the products are nonautomotive products. As a QS-9000 registered firm, Polywheels must apply the QS-9000 quality system requirements to all its products and processes.

Polywheels pays the QS-9000 registration fees. Hence, Polywheels' attitude is to try to learn the most from the third-party audits rather than pure compliance with the requirements.

THE REGISTRATION AUDIT

Three QS-9000 certified auditors spent a few days in Polywheels to assess the company's quality system. Figure 11–2 shows the matrix of the different departments audited against the QS-9000 requirements.

F I G U R E   11–2

Matrix of Different Departments Audited against the QS-9000 Requirements

QS Section	Management	Purchasing	Engineering	Quality Assurance	Sales	Production	Human Resources	Shipping
4.1	X	X	X	X	X	X	X	X
4.2	X							
4.3		X	X	X	X			
4.4	X		X	X	X			
4.5	X	X	X	X		X	X	X
4.6		X						
4.7				X				
4.8		X	X	X		X		X
4.9			X	X		X		
4.10				X		X		
4.11		X		X		X		
4.12				X		X		
4.13				X		X		X
4.14		X	X	X	X	X		
4.15						X		X
4.16	X	X	X	X		X		X
4.17	X			X				
4.18	X		X	X		X	X	
4.19								
4.20	X			X		X		
II.1			X	X		X		
II.2	X	X	X	X	X	X	X	X
II.3	X		X			X		

During the auditing process, Polywheels realized some keys to pass the audit. Every company must show the third-party auditors the following evidence:

1. Good housekeeping.
2. Effective process control techniques.
3. A 100 percent delivery performance or trend of improvement.
4. Zero customer complaints or a trend of improvement.

The means to a successful registration audit is to prove to the third-party auditors that the organization is a quality producer.

USE OF CROSS-FUNCTIONAL TEAMS

Involvement from all departments within the organization is essential to the success of QS-9000 registration. Accounting, engineering, human resources, marketing, production, quality, and sales departments must work together to achieve QS-9000 registration.

For example, a customer complaint may require a change in the manufacturing specification. The sales department initiates the complaint. Engineering suggests the change and alters the manufacturing specification. Quality verifies the corrective actions. Production implements the change, which involves accounting and human resources. Therefore, no department can stand alone.

SUMMARY

Due to the demand of compulsory QS-9000 registration from the automakers, thousands of organizations worldwide are attempting to obtain QS-9000 registration. There is no one answer and no cast-in-stone means by which to obtain QS-9000.

Being registered to QS-9000 does not guarantee quality products. Also, it does not promise 100 percent delivery performance. QS-9000 finds its success only when the suppliers and their employees are using the quality system requirements on a daily basis. Successful registration to QS-9000 is not the end of the journey. The suppliers must eagerly change and see fulfilling customers' needs as the main element of good decision making. Adopting QS-9000 into the corporate culture is a long-term commitment.

Every organization must be a learning organization. It should consist of people capable of questioning every component of what they do and capable of continuously improving. The fundamentals of running a successful company are found in the ability to successfully answer the following questions:

1. Who are the customers and how can their requirements be met?
2. What responsibility should employees have in their organization?
3. Is the mission statement of the company compatible with satisfying customers?
4. How does the leader engage people in accomplishing the mission statement requirements?

The companies with no interest in the QS-9000 process may or may not know the answers to the above questions. However, the companies that have already established the QS-9000 process can definitely answer the above questions.

Customers are satisfied with the quality and delivery Polywheels provides. QS-9000 registration has helped to show a good level in customer confidence and loyalty. As a result, Polywheels has obtained more business from its customers.

This case study is contributed by John Yeung, Quality Manager, Polywheels Manufacturing Limited, Oakville, Ontario, Canada.

CHAPTER 12

Big Achievement for a Tiny Company

Promotional Trim Conversions, Inc.

GENERAL

- *Headquarters* : **Lorain, Ohio, U.S.A.**
- *Year Founded* : **1986**
- *Number of Employees* : **43**

QS-9000 SPECIFIC

- *Registered Location(s)* : **Lorain, Ohio, U.S.A.**
- *Number of Employees* : **18**
- *Registration Date* : **June 19, 1995**
- *Product(s)* : **Decorative Graphics, Service Parts Distribution**
- *Tier I, II, III Supplier* : **Tier I and II**
- *Major Customer(s)* : **Ford**
- *Annual Sales* : **U.S. $5 Million**

INTRODUCTION

Management commitment, documentation, records, training, ISO 9000 based requirements, sector-specific requirements, customer-specific require-ments—if you've already read some of the other case studies in this book, you've no doubt seen these and other terms many times over. These are common elements of the QS-9000 experience, and every QS-9000 registered company has had to wrestle with their meaning as it applies to their unique circumstances. Promotional Trim

Conversions (PTC), Inc., is no exception. What makes our experience a little different from that of others, however, is that PTC is a tiny company whose customer base consists largely of automobile dealerships rather than original equipment manufacturers (OEMs) or their Tier I suppliers. At the time we decided to pursue QS-9000 registration, we were under absolutely no pressure from our customers. Rather, registration was conceived as a strategic initiative that would lead to new business opportunities with the OEMs and their Tier I suppliers that otherwise would remain beyond our grasp. Our goal was to migrate from being a tiny consumer-driven automotive supplier to being a small OEM supplier and to use quality for competitive leverage.

Our case study is not intended to recapitulate the specific paragraphs of *QS-9000*. Rather, it is intended to communicate some of the high points of our own QS-9000 experience and to address some of the issues unique to the very small supplier. The following paragraphs will depict PTC as a diversified automotive services company with a well-conceived vision, highly qualified and motivated people, a sound market strategy, and rigorous systems aimed at providing unparalleled levels of customer satisfaction. As America's first QS-9000 minority business enterprise, strength through diversity has been a hallmark of our corporate philosophy. Our decision to pursue QS-9000 registration was a strategic one. Simply stated, we felt that our marketing effort would benefit mightily from early registration. As we embarked on the QS-9000 journey, however, we learned that there were many other significant benefits that would derive from our efforts. We also encountered some difficulties along the way. We hope that our experience in both of these areas (benefits and difficulties) will help other organizations as they follow their own QS-9000 path.

BACKGROUND

Nineteen hundred ninety-five was a portentous year for PTC, Inc. A tiny company (with annual sales in 1994 of approximately $5 million, and an employment level of 18 people at the Lorain, Ohio headquarters, and an additional 25 people total at branch plants in Louisville, Kentucky, and Detroit, Michigan), Promotional Trim Conversions had been founded in 1986 as an aftermarket franchise of the Trimline corporation. The company's first big break had come in 1989 when founder Paul Hutchins negotiated a "ship-through" program with the Ford Motor Company. Under the terms of this agreement, Ford dealers could order PTC modifications through the Ford order system as original equipment options. PTC drivers would pick up the units to be modified at the local Ford body and assembly plant, drive them to a permanent PTC facility where modification was performed, and return them to the Ford transportation system to be delivered to dealers across the country. The ship-through program proved to be a fabulous success and rapidly grew to a three-plant operation. As PTC established a reputation of reliability within its customer base, new programs of greater technical complexity were added to the decorative trim business. Installation of cellular telephones, auxiliary air conditioners, pop-up sun roofs, and transmission oil coolers joined the company's list of services. Additionally, services were sold directly to OEMs as well as to individual dealerships. In 1990 PTC's Wixom, Michigan, plant was awarded Ford Q1 status, and on June 19, 1995, the company achieved QS-9000 registration at its Lorain facility. What had begun as a local franchise operation had, in nine years, evolved into a respected OEM supplier.

PTC decided early on that the long-term success of any business depends on four key elements: relentless pursuit of a worthy vision; good people; good systems; and the right mix of products and services directed to the right mix of market segments. PTC's vision was simple and focused: to provide long-term job opportunities to people in an economically depressed area, many of whom had experienced the subtle but real hardships of minority status.

PTC targeted two new services that promised to provide stability to the volatile ship-through business: packaging of automotive service parts and delivery of sequenced final assembly parts. The first of these services is directed toward the OEMs—Ford, General Motors, and Chrysler, along with the generic aftermarket. The second is directed toward Tier I suppliers to the OEMs. Although the programs differ substantially at the detail level, they share two essential characteristics that define the strategic niche that PTC has adopted. First, both programs are labor intensive. Second, both involve activities that are not central to the core businesses of those who currently engage in them. Simply stated, car builders build cars and parts makers make parts. Packaging, final assembly, and just-in-time delivery are typically viewed by the OEMs and their Tier I suppliers as necessary evils—distasteful nuisances that detract scarce resources from what they do best.

While discussing this strategy with PTC's owner, Mr. Vernon Wallace, at a staff meeting in December of 1994, the director of quality remarked that the pursuit of the automotive dollar is a little like survival in the jungle. The lions—Ford, General Motors, Chrysler—make the kill and take the lion's share. The hyenas—the major Tier I suppliers—feast on the choice morsels that the lions leave behind. Then we come in to pick the bones clean. Thus, like it or not, we're the buzzards of automotive ecology. Mr. Wallace didn't especially care for the analogy. While he agreed with its accuracy, he thought it unflattering and not consistent with the corporate image we wanted to project. For some eight months we didn't talk much about buzzards around PTC. Then in November at a meeting of the National Minority Supplier Development Council in Detroit, Mr. Wallace introduced PTC to a representative of a potential Tier I customer as "the buzzards of the automotive food chain." "But we're very elegant buzzards," he was quick to add.

GOOD SYSTEMS AND THEIR IMPACT ON DEMORALIZED PEOPLE

The final ingredient in the recipe for success, good systems are the subject of the rest of this study. To be sure, PTC was not without structured management systems prior to our embarkation on the QS-9000 journey. We found, however, that many of our systems were poorly documented or not documented at all. We found that they had evolved out of a sense of need as the proprietary means by which one employee or another solved his or her own recurring problems. In such cases, management as a whole was often unaware of our systems' complexity, their interface with other systems, or in some cases even their existence. We also found that we were already doing a pretty good job of record keeping, especially in matters of financial import and customer dissatisfaction. We weren't, however, squeezing all of the available information out of our records, or using their content to drive the decision-making process.

As a management group, we had tended to stay above the detail level. What we didn't realize is that whether staying above the details is the right or wrong thing to do depends entirely on management's motive. If we were doing it because we had reliable systems in place and we had empowered our employees to make decisions on their own in conformance with these systems, then it was the right thing. If, however, we were doing it because we tended to minimize the importance of these tasks and deemed them so trivial that they could be trusted to our underlings (as was the case), then it was the wrong thing.

Our hearts were in the right place. We told our people how much we appreciated their efforts, and we believed that they really were trying. We also believed that they were handsomely paid for their work, and that their employee benefits were second to none. Although our management had a tendency to use the phrase "All you have to do is . . ." at the drop of a hat, we honestly didn't realize the severe demoralizing effect this had on our employees. It demeaned the importance of people's primary activities and implied that they lacked the mental acuity to recognize what had to be done on their own. It suggested that they lacked initiative and that management was insensitive to their hard work and subsequent frustration. We certainly didn't view our people as experts who could teach us a thing or two about how to improve the business. Instead, we tried to buy our way to better morale with wage increases, bonuses, and further improvements in benefits; these strategies, however, were perceived as overdue fulfillment of past obligation rather than spontaneous gestures of goodwill.

We attributed what we saw as an alarming level of employee dissatisfaction to a lack of appreciation of "all we had done for them." Occasionally our frustration would leak out, and this would only add to the black cloud that seemed to be hanging over everyone's heads. We were guilty not of malice but of ignorance. We were soon to be pleasantly surprised by the effect that involving our people in the arduous task of systems development and implementation would have on their morale. The rain clouds were still there, but they began to move, and a rainbow became faintly visible on the horizon.

As a Ford Q1 supplier, we certainly recognized and accepted the quality imperative as a condition of doing business with the automotive industry. Our senior management felt that continued pursuit of quality was the surest way to increase our business participation among our automotive customer base. In September of 1994 the decision was made to pursue ISO 9001 registration for our Lorain facility. A corporate director of quality was hired to lead the effort and was given nine months to complete the task. We targeted registration against the emerging QS-9000, given that it was more appropriate to our position as an automotive supplier.

AWARENESS

Initially, no one in the management group fully understood the pervasiveness of QS-9000. The prevailing attitude was, "We've hired a new corporate director of quality. He's a top-notch quality man, and he'll take care of this QS-9000 business for us." We soon learned that this attitude wouldn't work. Our problem was that we conceived of QS-9000 as a *quality-management* system rather than a quality *management system.* The requirements are complex, highly detailed, legalistic in form, and consummately thorough. It prescriptively addresses everything from strategic planning to marketing to shipping to customer service. As such, it operationally defines good management practice for the planning, marketing, design, engineering, purchasing, manufacturing, quality control, shipping, and sales functions. It even affects the accounting function. Some managers were a bit put out at the thought of the quality control manager presuming to tell them how to do their jobs. This irritation was normal and appropriate, and actually catalyzed our effort. In order to keep the quality control manager out of the inner workings of their departments, most managers seized the initiative, developing and documenting functional procedures that governed their departments' activities. Their spontaneous participation led quickly to spontaneous cooperation and mutual support. People began to see the common sense of QS-9000. We knew that the standard had evolved over a period of more than 50 years, and that the experience and wisdom of the many who had contributed to its evolution couldn't be disputed. It was a trustworthy road map with clear signposts along the way that could serve as the foundation upon which we could build reliable and durable management systems.

> *We conceived of QS-9000 as a* quality-management *system rather than a* quality management system.

FROM SWISS ARMY KNIFE TO TOOL KIT: MAKING IT OUR SYSTEM

QS-9000 is a little like a Swiss army knife. It covers every need reasonably well, but the fit is always a little less than perfect. Specific objectives within the context of a specific management structure and corporate culture require customized tools. To some extent every company exhibits what some have called the not-invented-here syndrome. Rightly or wrongly, we often believe that methods developed outside our own organization don't quite apply to our unique situations, and we tend to resist them. On the other hand, systems that we develop in-house enjoy a sense of ownership that contributes to their spontaneous and consistent execution. Our first task in implementing QS-9000 was to develop our company's documentation. We needed to customize the generic QS dicta to our own specific context. How we developed our documentation is at least as important as what we did in this regard.

We began by writing a corporate quality policy manual. To a large extent this was a rewrite of QS-9000 itself. Of course we replaced the phrase "The supplier shall . . ." with the phrase "We will . . ." To protect ourselves against errors of omission we also made generous use of the phrase "where necessary and appropriate." Developing a policy manual is very much like writing a contract. We found ourselves struggling with interpretations, seeking to plug potential loopholes, and extrapolating the consequences of our choice of words to the most unlikely and bizarre of possible eventualities. The task took the better part of a week.

While broad-based participation in the actual writing of the policy manual is unnecessary, the communication of its content to senior management is another story. Before we could proceed further with documentation development, we had to make sure that our senior managers fully understood and accepted the commitment they were making and the effects this commitment would have on the day-to-day operation of the business. We planned a one-day off-site retreat to hash through the policy manual. Interestingly, there were few concerns with the details of the individual paragraphs of the document. Likewise, everyone seemed willing to accept the impact that the policy would have on his or her functional sphere of influence. The majority of our time was spent reviewing our corporate vision, mission, supporting values, and strategic plan. Had we gone no further than this in our pursuit of QS-9000 we would already have been the better for our efforts. We ended our session by identifying the next steps in the documentation process and confirming our commitment to the aggressive time line that we had set for implementation.

Next came developing a corporate quality procedures manual as the second of what would be three levels of system documentation. At this level we began to distribute the workload to others in the organization. In a small organization like ours, everyone wears several hats. For example, our chief financial officer coordinates our quotation process, while our sales and marketing director manages the company's purchasing function. In addition to overseeing the quality assurance department, the director of quality is heavily involved in new business start-up. To some extent the fact that we all maintain several functional responsibilities makes cross-disciplinary articulation less of a problem than in a large corporation. Nonetheless, in most cases we took a team approach to procedures development. By way of example, the two aforementioned managers and the director of quality jointly developed our procedures for contract review and purchasing. Other procedures were similarly developed. Both to achieve a consistent style and to articulate the various procedures into a single integrated document, the director of quality handled the writing of all final drafts.

> *To some extent the fact that we all maintain several functional responsibilities makes cross-disciplinary articulation less of a problem than in a large corporation.*

One of our goals during the development of procedures was to make each one a self-contained document. We didn't want people to have to refer back to QS-9000 itself in order to clarify terms or intents. To this end, we spent a lot of time writing definitions of key terms that were referenced in the procedures, and we included these definitions in the procedures themselves. We also enumerated all records that were to be kept to verify compliance with each procedure as the final paragraph of the procedure. This proved to be helpful later on when we developed a companywide document register that catalogued all of our quality records.

In contrast to the writing of the policy manual, the development of systems procedures was a pleasant and rewarding experience. We felt we were accomplishing something that would be highly useful, and we were often gratified to discover that we already had good procedures in place that were fully compliant with QS-9000. However, many of these systems had not been adequately documented in the past. We agreed early on that our first efforts should be to document our systems as they were rather than as we thought they should be. Our logic was that this would provide a good reality check and aid us in subsequent gap analysis. In retrospect this approach served us well. Often we encountered sections of the requirements that seemed not to apply to our business. This was especially true in the sector-specific and customer-specific sections, in which the Swiss-army-knife character is most apparent. When we encountered a requirement that didn't fit, we first verified its inapplicability beyond all reasonable doubt, and then we simply said that it didn't apply. We were somewhat nervous that our registrar would contest our claims of inapplicability, but we certainly didn't want to build unnecessary systems merely for the sake of building systems. Our thinking was that the promulgation of procedures that addressed activities we didn't perform would dilute the procedures that governed activities we did perform. Above all, we didn't want our procedures to represent the way we would do things in an idealized world, but the way we did do things in a real world. Again, our decision in this regard proved to be the right one.

We often wrestled with the question of just how detailed the procedures should be. Since the procedures ultimately directed human decision making, we didn't feel obligated to lock in the ultimate decision. We knew that people would still be the critical link in the decision-making process. We merely wanted them to have the best and most complete information available to help them make the right decision, and to have a structure that would bring their experience and wisdom to bear in the most efficient way. Neither did we want the procedures to be patronizing. Whereas in the past we tended to undervalue the details and complexity of people's day-to-day activities, we now found it necessary to guard against constraining their every move. The confusion of levels—how much detail to include in systems procedures—became even more of a problem as we moved on to the task of writing work instructions, the third level of our QS-9000 documentation.

DEVELOPING WORK INSTRUCTIONS: EMPOWERMENT AT ITS BEST

We began the task of writing work instructions when we were about halfway through the development of our procedures manual.

In retrospect, we're glad we didn't wait until the procedures were finished before we undertook this final task. Our early experience in work instruction development shed some light on the issue of detail that we wouldn't have noticed had we arranged these tasks sequentially. In fact, the rule of thumb that emerged to clarify the question of detail was embarrassingly simple: *Procedures define the responsibility of a department or function, while work instructions define the responsibility of an individual.*

The writing of work instructions was entrusted to the experts—the people in the offices and the plant who actually do the jobs. This is not to say that each employee was permitted to define his job responsibilities arbitrarily or as he saw fit, nor that management abdicated its responsibility to participate in the effort. Rather, we worked in teams to hash out the best way of doing something based on the collective experience of the work group. We always tried to have one person on each team who had absolutely no prior experience with the job in question. The importance of such a person is obvious. He can safely ask all the "dumb" questions that everyone else wants, but is too proud, to ask. He can also challenge the prevailing wisdom, which is often unfounded, and keep the team from jumping to unwarranted conclusions. Perhaps most important, he can learn a great deal from some very fine teachers. We managers gained a new respect for the knowledge, skill, and commitment of our employees as a side benefit of our involvement in these work instruction teams. We agreed on a new management policy that absolutely forbade any of us from using the phrase "All you have to do is . . ." The penalty for using these words was that the offending manager would actually perform the job for one day.

In developing work instructions, we adopted the format of a "process map." For each activity that required work instruction (not all did!), we developed a Level 1 flowchart. This was intended to be a broad overview of the key subprocesses that make up the overall activity. We tried to keep these flowcharts as simple as possible, allowing no more than 12 blocks and limiting the types of blocks to actions (rectangles) and decisions (diamonds). Each block in the Level 1 chart was assigned a two-digit number, xx. We expanded selected blocks in the Level 1 chart into more detailed Level 2 flowcharts where necessary. Similarly, the blocks of the Level 2 charts were assigned two-digit numbers, yy, which we juxtaposed with the number of the Level 1 block from which they derived. Thus, for example, the subactivity number *30.20* refers to Block 20 of the Level 2 flowchart that expands Block 30 of the master chart. Finally, where even more detail was necessary, we wrote simple text paragraphs—Level 3 of the map—corresponding to selected blocks of certain Level 2 charts. As with the first two levels, these paragraphs were assigned a two-digit number, zz. We found that this hierarchy provided a quick and efficient way to track down the exact instruction that was needed to resolve a question. We also found that these process maps were an excellent subject-matter source for training of new employees. The fact that the people who actually do the jobs were the primary authors of the work instructions assured us of strong ownership and spontaneous compliance with their provisions. In fact, the approach was so successful that we actually wrote a procedure to guide us in the process of process mapping.

In summary, we developed our system documentation at three levels: (1) the corporate quality policy manual, (2) the corporate quality procedures manual, and (3) both corporate- and site-specific work instructions. As we moved through the document levels, more and more people, including hourly employees, were involved in the effort. As a side benefit, training per se was largely unnecessary since it occurred spontaneously in the course of document development. In a larger organization formal training would be necessary in order to communicate procedures and work instructions to those who did not participate in their development. The upshot of the documentation phase of our QS-9000 project was that we had exchanged a Swiss army knife for a kit of specialized tools and had enhanced the ability of a group of skilled craftsmen to wield those tools effectively.

CHOOSING YOUR POISON: THE SELECTION OF A REGISTRAR

Contrary to the implications of this section's heading, we found that third-party registrars are not deadly. Nor are their goals at cross-purposes with our own. To be sure, they will not consult or advise. Their job is to evaluate and, in so doing, to confirm success as well as to uncover deficiencies. Appendix B of *QS-9000* clearly defines the role and code of ethical practice for registrars, and provides an initial set of criteria for registrar selection. Our search for a registrar was driven by the need for adequate accreditation (at the time we began our search no registrars had yet been accredited to audit against QS-9000), impeccable reputation in the marketplace, strong references from past clients, proximity to our location, and cost.

While we found that costs do vary somewhat from one registrar to the next, these variations were not so great as to bear significant influence on our selection. We also found that it is important to sense a positive chemistry with representatives from the registrar. After all, we reasoned, they will be visiting our site every six months into perpetuity, delving into every proprietary nook and cranny of our operation. They need to be people we can trust and work with. They also need to be rigorous, thorough, objective, and fair. They are required to assess not only our compliance with the requirements of QS-9000 but also the effectiveness of our implementation. In other words, they have the power to deny or rescind registration based on their perception of how well our system works. The assessment of effectiveness can be very difficult to carry out with full objectivity. In fact, human interpretation both can and should enter the picture. Findings can be challenged, and rebuttals should be welcome. We wanted to make sure that our registrar could accept these provisions.

The ultimate test of a registrar has less to do with whether you pass or fail the initial assessment than with whether you feel you deserved to pass when all is said and done. There really shouldn't be any surprises, and you shouldn't feel that luck had anything to do with the outcome of the assessment. Our own experience was that we had been put through the wringer during our two days of audits. Had we not had this feeling, we probably would not have been getting the quality of service from our registrar that we ultimately wanted. We knew that eventually we would achieve registration, though perhaps not on the first go-around. We were prepared to deal with nonconformances, initiate corrective actions, and invite the auditors back for a confirmatory visit; we also knew that when we finally passed, it would not be because of any special dispensation or good luck. We wanted a rigorous and thorough assessment, and we vowed to do nothing to compromise the independence and integrity of our assessors. The whole enterprise, after all, was directed totally to our own benefit.

STACKING THE ODDS FOR SUCCESS: DOCUMENT REVIEW AND PREASSESSMENT

Subsequent to the development of required documentation, the registration process proceeds in three phases. The first phase is review and approval of documentation by the selected registrar. In our case this involved a meticulous screening of our first two levels of documentation—the quality policy manual and the quality procedures manual—to ascertain that all requirements of QS-9000 had been fully addressed by our internal operating systems. At PTC we went through three iterations before our documentation was finally approved. Because the task of securing document approval fell on the shoulders of the director of quality, he was surprised and frustrated by what he perceived to be pedantic nit-picking on the part of the registrar. He thought that the task of systems development was complete and he was anxious to get on to the next phase. We had a few heart-to-heart phone conversations with our registrar pertaining to this matter. The documentation was finally approved nearly a month behind schedule, and we seriously doubted whether we would be able to hold to our nine-month time line. It was only after our initial assessment that we realized, with much gratitude, that our registrar had done us a great favor by insisting that we polish and refine our documentation. Quality system audits that comprise the initial assessment and all subsequent surveillance audits are conducted against a company's internal policies and procedures, not directly against QS-9000. In short, the company is checked to make sure that it is following its own rules. Had we and the registrar not been totally comfortable that our internal documentation fulfilled all provisions and intents of the requirements prior to the audits, then the audits themselves would have focused unnecessarily on the completeness and acceptability of our system itself rather than on our compliance with the system and the effectiveness of its implementation. Our concern about staying on schedule was somewhat mitigated by the knowledge that we had only three months from the document approval date to undergo the initial assessment. QS-9000 specifies that document approval becomes null and void, and that the review process must be repeated, if assessment does not take place within 90 days.

On-site preassessment, while not required for QS-9000 registration, is absolutely invaluable. Not only does it provide an opportunity for a risk-free dry run, but it also gives managers a chance to get to know the registrar (in our case, the lead assessor), to read and possibly realign priorities, and to rededicate themselves for the final leg of the journey. Our preassessment activity was a desktop audit against the quality systems assessment (QSA) checklist issued by Chrysler, Ford, and General Motors. Auditors are required to use the QSA as part of the initial assessment but are not limited to this instrument. Most of them will delve considerably more deeply into the workings of a company's quality system using a checklist that they have developed from the company's internal documentation and from their own past experience. We found the desktop audit preferable to a full-blown system assessment, which is a second option that most registrars make available to their clients. Even prior to the preassessment we knew pretty much what to expect. By now we were at least ranking amateurs in the QS-9000 arena, if not fledgling professionals. After the preassessment we were confident not only that there wouldn't be any surprises relating to the subject matter of the upcoming audits, but also that we had a good feel for how they would be conducted and how the auditors would interact on a personal level with our staff and employees. We were six weeks away from the real thing, and we still had a lot of work to do shoring up records, finishing training, completing our internal system audits, and evaluating system effectiveness. The preassessment audit had enabled us to sharpen our to-do lists, however, and we really could see the light at the end of the tunnel.

THE INITIAL ASSESSMENT

Everyone in our small organization had contributed mightily to getting ready for the initial assessment day, and all of us were anxious to get on with it. As it happened, the assessment proceeded as expected. It seemed that the auditors were everywhere at once. At the end of the second day, the management team was summoned to the conference room that had become the audit team's home, to receive the final report. We were told that the team had found no nonconformances and that we would be recommended for registration. We reviewed the audit findings in detail with the team and heaved a mighty sigh of relief.

The director of quality didn't anticipate any surprises during the initial assessment. He was wrong. There was one very pleasant surprise of significant proportion, and that was the extent to which the hourly employees, both in the plant and in the office, identified with the outcome of the audits. As management representative, his time was almost fully occupied by the audit process. During those rare moments when he was able to sneak away to the plant to regain his composure, he was immediately accosted by one employee or another asking him, "Did we pass? How's it going? Are we (the plant people) doing OK?" Our audits were conducted in early June. During the summer months our plant crew works from 5:00 AM to 2:00 PM to avoid processing problems caused by the midday heat.

At 5:00 PM on each of the two audit days, every production employee was still in the plant. They were variously edifying one of the auditors relative to the details of their job, relating how great a place PTC was to work, or just milling around, not wanting to leave something as important as QS-9000 registration in the hands of management. Their spontaneous commitment to the success of our company was nothing short of inspiring. When the director of quality congratulated them on their successful completion of the QS-9000 assessment after the management meeting with the audit team, he saw on their faces a sense of pride that he had never before experienced. When the framed certificates arrived, the first one was hung in the plant in recognition their contributions. The second was hung in the staff area as a source of well-deserved pride for our office personnel. Some weeks later we modestly celebrated our accomplishments with a barbecue in our back parking lot. We kept it pretty informal, limiting speeches to those by the director of quality and the company's owner. The director of quality remarked, "we had successfully laid the foundation for an adequate quality system; that our real work was only just beginning and hopefully would never end; that our corporate vision, our ways of doing things, and our overall business strategy were sound; and, most important, that our people were the best in the world. Globally, no one does what you do better than you." It was true.

SOME HIGH POINTS AND ROUGH SPOTS

Since achieving registration five months prior to the writing of this case study, our company has undergone a number of significant changes. We secured an OEM contract in our service parts packaging area that will contribute significantly to our goal of a stable hedge against the volatility of the ship-through conversion business. We are in the process of finalizing a second major contract with a Tier I supplier for final assembly and sequenced delivery of modular components that will firmly establish our presence as a light assembler. It is difficult to say whether we would have gotten either of these contracts without QS-9000 registration. Our belief is that registration was a vital if not deciding factor in both cases.

As a senior manager of a small company, he has had the opportunity to participate in deliberations that extend well beyond the typical role of corporate director of quality in most corporations. Ironically, the view that he has of the overall trends among the major automotive companies and their key suppliers is considerably broader than what he had experienced previously working at the same level in several Fortune 500 companies. Over the past year he has learned that purchasing decisions in the auto industry are more cost-driven than ever before. The logic is that if the quality isn't there, you're not even invited to quote on a business program. The final decision, however, is based less on relative differences in quality than on incremental differences in price. Quality is viewed as a discrete attribute rather than a continuous scale. It's either there or it's not. The dangerous temptation is to view quality as a commodity whose pedigree carries the designator QS-9000.

We have recognized that QS-9000 registration means nothing if it is viewed as anything other than an important milestone on our road to continuous improvement. We did indeed rest on our laurels for a few months following registration, but we're not beating ourselves up unnecessarily for succumbing to this very human tendency. What we are doing, however, is recognizing that it is not QS-9000 registration that represents the ultimate benefit of our efforts, but the systems that we put in place in pursuit of registration. We are in the process of institutionalizing our quality systems—making them the routine way we do business. We're speeding up this effort by carrying out ongoing self-evaluation that is at least as thorough and rigorous as our mandated third-party evaluation.

An example illustrates how this is working. As we entered the service parts packaging business, we didn't do a very good job up front at identifying our production part approval process (PPAP) responsibilities and how they interface with the PPAP responsibilities of our suppliers, the manufacturers of the parts we package. We supply these items to the parts and service division of one of the three major American automotive manufacturers, and we are told by our customer which manufacturers we must purchase them from. These are parts that have been provided to our customer for many years prior to our involvement in their packaging. We assumed that our quality responsibility was limited to our own internal value-added activities (viz., packaging) and that responsibility for the quality of the parts themselves rested solely with the manufacturer. As we got into the business, however, we learned that this is only partly the case. In fact, the chain of responsibility (and potential product liability if there is a failure) involves us to a far greater extent than we had initially thought. Even though we do nothing more than package the parts, if they are defective the onus of rectifying the situation initially falls on us. The concern is not that our quality systems had left us unprepared to deal with this responsibility. Rather, our systems were in place, but we just weren't following them. Rest assured that this chilling realization was a meaningful learning experience for us, that any harm resulting from it was potential rather than real, and that it isn't going to happen again.

We have recognized that there's still a lot of work to do in flawlessly executing our quality systems, especially as we move into product and service niches that are new to PTC. We recognize that, to some extent, our failure to execute sound procedures that are clearly spelled out in our quality planning, contract review, and purchasing documentation is due to members of our core management team having multiple disciplinary responsibilities. We're not using this as an excuse, but we do recognize it as a reality that is typical of very small companies.

SUGGESTIONS FOR OTHER VERY SMALL COMPANIES

Our QS-9000 experiences have taught us many things that would probably have gone unlearned if we had not opted for registration. Many of these experiences are unique to very small organizations, but some apply to all companies regardless of size and organizational complexity. The director of quality has formulated a number of recommendations directed primarily toward companies like PTC—other buzzards in the automotive food chain. These recommendations are based on both his personal experience and the experience of others in his company. He makes no claim as to their originality, wisdom, or applicability to any other organization. They are offered in the spirit of a student who sees the need to continue learning rather than the teacher who has all the answers. Take what's helpful and leave the rest behind.

• Set an aggressive timetable and stick to it. Do a gap analysis, set priorities for filling the major gaps, and schedule the three phases of the assessment process. Incidentally, there's still time to use QS-9000 registration as a strategic advantage, especially in a small company. In two years, what is now an inviting opportunity will become a condition of doing business.

• For a small company, cross-functional linkage is less of a problem than multifunctional responsibility. At PTC our chief accountant is responsible for preparing new business quotations, and therefore for driving the early phases of the advance quality planning process. Our accounts receivable clerk is also our human resources manager. In both cases, the person has one primary function and one or more secondary functions. Where QS-9000 impacts a person's secondary function, it is likely that procedures will not be implemented. Here are a few remedies: First make sure that quality system procedures and work instructions that pertain to the person's secondary role are developed by that person. Second, give high priority to evaluation of conformance to these procedures by the internal audit process and subsequent management reviews. Third, consider changing the person's official job title to reflect the secondary area of responsibility. It doesn't make sense to hire a full-time director of purchasing if the work can be done effectively on a part-time basis by someone who is already on board, but it does make sense to call that person the director of sales, marketing, and purchasing.

• What one does is often less important than why one does it. An organization must be certain of its motives as it undertakes the QS-9000 journey. If the organization is committed to continuous improvement and wants a sensible and complete checklist of conditions necessary for excellence, then QS-9000 will serve it well.

• Develop a detailed procedure for identifying, specifying, and communicating requirements as part of the purchasing functions. An engineering drawing alone isn't sufficient, nor is a detailed but confusing one-size-fits-all specification book. Formal or informal training of supplier personnel is often necessary. Make sure to specify exact PPAP requirements in the purchase order for each new material, component, or service that is purchased, and make sure that they articulate with the PPAP responsibilities to customers. The procedure should mandate review of all purchase orders for new items by the quality assurance function.

• Don't limit trained internal auditors to the quality assurance department. Send salespeople, production managers, engineers, and even accountants to QS-9000 training, and involve them in the ongoing self-assessment process. Remember, QS-9000 is a quality *management system*, not a *quality-management* system.

• Don't just keep records. Use company data to fuel the decision-making process. Company records often contain a wealth of information that can disclose important patterns, trends, and relationships if properly analyzed. Company data are the raw material of continuous improvement.

- Avoid acronyms and abbreviations. They can be misleading and thereby distort effective communication.
- View registration as the beginning of a never-ending process. It's just the first approximation to excellence. It's an important milestone but, once passed, also a responsibility that needs to be maintained.

SUMMARY

Promotional Trim Conversions, a very small minority-owned diversified automotive services company that supplies both the major automotive manufacturers and their Tier I suppliers, made the decision to pursue QS-9000 registration as an element of the company's overall marketing strategy. PTC's tradition of quality leadership had first been established many years before as the company achieved Ford Q1 designation for its Wixom, Michigan plant. While competitive advantage was the primary motive for achieving QS-9000 status, this motive rapidly broadened as our management began to realize that QS-9000 is really a comprehensive road map for designing and executing sound management practices in each of the company's functional areas. Early registration has led to opportunities for the company to expand its offerings into new product and service areas, and the experience we have gained in implementing the specific elements of our program has fortified our commitment to never-ending improvement. In the course of developing procedures for continuous improvement, our management personnel developed a procedure—the process improvement model (PIM)—for staff and administrative processes that has been adopted by several larger companies as their road map for ongoing improvement. As we implemented systematic methods of gauge control and measurement systems analysis, we developed a unique software system that provides for an on-line calibration manual, a dynamic calibration scheduling, and statistical analysis of all types of gauge error data. In 1996 we intend to release this system to both automotive and nonautomotive markets under the auspices of a new company division. Among the primary and secondary benefits we have derived from QS-9000 implementation, the most significant is the true empowerment of our people, salaried and hourly alike. As managers we have gained a new-found respect for the past contributions and future promise of our employees, and as employees we have contributed to making our company a more satisfying and rewarding place to work.

This case study is contributed by Richard A. Shoop, Corporate Director of Quality, Promotional Trim Conversions, Inc., Lorain, Ohio.

CHAPTER 13

Securing the Future

Rouge Steel Company

GENERAL

- *Headquarters*   : **Dearborn, Michigan, U.S.A.**
- *Year Founded*   : **1989**
- *Number of Employees*   : **3,200**

QS-9000 SPECIFIC

- *Registered Location(s)*   : **Dearborn, Michigan, U.S.A.**
- *Number of Employees*   : **3,200**
- *Registration Date*   : **May 18, 1995**
- *Product(s)*   : **Hot Roll, Cold Roll, Electrogalvanized Steel**
- *Tier I, II, III Supplier*   : **Tier I**
- *Major Customer(s)*   : **Ford, Worthington Steel**
- *Annual Sales*   : **U.S. $1.2 Billion**

INTRODUCTION

The purpose of this case study is to demonstrate how Rouge Steel Company was able to become the first fully integrated steel producer to secure QS-9000 registration. The short time we took to achieve this lofty registration is a testament to our existing quality system. This case study will provide an understanding of the process and the tools we used in the design and implementation of the quality system. While some difficult issues had to be resolved in the implementation process, careful planning—as well as the full support of the union leadership and company management—resulted in the implementation of an effective and robust quality system. While we understand that every organization is unique, the quality system in place at Rouge Steel can be adapted to fit the quality requirements of virtually any service or manufacturing process.

In 1990 Rouge Steel's quality system experienced a major shift in focus. Prior to this shift, our focus had been on ensuring that the product met the customer's specifications. This was typically accomplished through inspection. However, discovering that the finished product did not meet customer specifications created problems of reapplication and all the difficulties associated with it. Changing the quality system to focus on the process not only resulted in defect prevention but also allowed employees to better understand how the process and their input affected the final product.

The steel industry is currently facing challenges on several fronts. Competition that comes from within the steel industry is based on product quality and price. Customer demand for higher-quality products has posed a challenge to the entire steel industry. Customers expect, and are entitled to receive, a quality product that is completely usable, with no tolerance for any rejected material. In addition, customers have come to rely on their steel suppliers to provide technical expertise regarding the best application of steel early in the product design stages and in stamping manufacturing processes. Finally, while steel remains the material of choice for the auto industry—due to its cost, strength, formability, recyclability, and environmental advantages—the federally imposed Corporate Average Fuel Economy Standard has significantly contributed to the reduction in the total weight of most vehicles. Vehicle downsizing and substituting of material have decreased the amount of steel consumed in the production of automobiles and light trucks, and the steel industry continues to face the threat of increased use of substitute materials from both the aluminum and the composite industries.

Rouge Steel draws its customer base from four primary markets: automotive original equipment manufacturers (OEMs), converters, service centers, and other end users. Our largest market, automotive OEMs, consumes nearly 55 percent of the company's total production. The domestic auto industry as a whole purchases about 13 percent of its sheet steel needs from Rouge Steel. With the customer base so heavily rooted in automotive OEMs, it was absolutely essential that Rouge Steel attain QS-9000 registration.

We viewed QS-9000 as an opportunity for Rouge Steel to improve and expand its quality system, become a better supplier to the automotive industry, and be proactive in meeting customers' expectations. The goal of the quality system remains the same: to continuously improve product quality through the control of critical process variables.

BACKGROUND

Rouge Steel is a fully integrated flat-rolled steel manufacturer located in Dearborn, Michigan. Annual shipments of approximately 2.6 million tons of flat-rolled steel rank Rouge Steel the eighth largest domestic integrated flat-rolled steel mill. Rouge Steel produces hot-rolled, cold-rolled, and electrogalvanized sheet products. Company sales exceeded $1.2 billion in 1994. Rouge Steel currently employs some 3,200 people, of which 2,500 are represented by the United Auto Workers (UAW).

The company was founded in the 1920s as a division of Ford Motor Company. Steel-making facilities were a piece of Henry Ford's dream of complete vertical integration: the ability to manufacture automobiles completely on a single site. In 1982, the company was made a wholly owned subsidiary of Ford Motor Company and was subsequently purchased by a group of investors in 1989. Rouge Steel became a publicly traded company in 1994 with an initial public offering on the New York Stock Exchange. The proceeds from the public offering were partially used to make Rouge Steel a debt-free company while retaining sufficient cash reserves to meet necessary capital improvements.

QUALITY SYSTEM EVOLUTION

After several years of struggling with various alternative methods of improving product quality, Rouge Steel began its quality system efforts in earnest in 1990. It became clear that there was a need for a well-organized system that focused on the process and drove improvement through a feedback mechanism that monitored for continuous improvement. With those requirements in mind, the new management team of Rouge Steel made a serious commitment to help the company become a producer of top-quality products through the implementation of a quality management system.

Because Rouge Steel had no desire to develop a large quality assurance staff, the implementation efforts were led by the company's president and chief operating officer, who was supported by the quality system implementation manager and the UAW quality representative. Together these three individuals designed a system that, when implemented, placed the responsibility for continuous improvement in the operations—not on the shoulders of some omnipotent quality department. In 1992, a second UAW quality representative was added to this core group with the intention of expanding the quality system to the maintenance functions.

The quality system philosophy is straightforward: If there is going to be meaningful process improvement, the people closest to the operation must have the authority and responsibility to make the necessary changes. For any system, doing without a proper focus of authority or responsibility, or having the authority or responsibility for its success vested in someone outside the affected operation, creates a sense of helplessness. Giving operators the opportunity to react to changes in their processes made them an integral part of the quality system, its implementation, and its success.

Management's commitment to the quality system was demonstrated early on by the high level of involvement and the hands-on approach taken by the company president. He was closely involved in the day-to-day implementation process and took great pains to become knowledgeable in every aspect of the quality system. He often acted as a "reasonability checker" on the suggestions of the implementation manager and UAW quality representative. This served to ensure a balanced approach to implementation and led to a system that is meaningful to operations personnel.

The organization's commitment to quality has not wavered with the success of the system. The determination of senior management to maintain a high level of knowledge on all quality-related issues is most visible in the frequency of the president's quality meetings. The department managers, from each of the company's five operating areas, meet with the president once a month solely for the purpose of addressing quality issues and continuous improvement plans; twice monthly the technical service representatives meet with the president and operating department managers to discuss issues in customer plants; and meetings are held twice weekly with the president, quality assurance manager, and all department managers to discuss and identify corrective actions and to address any new quality issues.

Management's commitment to quality goes far beyond the corporate quality policy posted throughout the plant. The president has publicly stated time and time again that safety is the only thing more important than quality. He has been heard on numerous occasions telling people that they have not only the complete authority but also the responsibility to stop an operation whose product is not of the required quality. Whether through the use of product inspection or process control, any signal of less-than-optimal conditions must be investigated and corrected.

Management has also shown its commitment by designating key quality resource personnel to assist in quality system utilization and implementation at the departmental level. These quality system representatives (QSRs) have been instrumental in the success of the quality system. The QSRs, hourly employees for the most part, received extensive training and have supported the quality system with their dedicated efforts. Their functions include collecting data, conducting design of experiments, maintaining records, assisting in the explanation of the quality system, and maintaining a high level of visibility and quality awareness throughout the plant.

QUALITY TOOLS

The quality system implementation process could never have been completed without a significant number of supporting tools. In a perfect world, a quality system would begin with a careful product failure mode and effects analysis (FMEA). This is an analytical tool that rank-orders the potential, severity, and detectability of a product failure due to a failure in the process. FMEAs are performed first on each product and then on each process. The cause of the failure in the product FMEA becomes the failure mode in the process FMEA. The purpose of this tool is to prevent product failures through understanding the product's use and controlling each part of the process that leads to the desired functionality.

Statistical process control (SPC) was one of the earliest tools used at Rouge Steel to assist in controlling process. The identification of key process variables that were to be monitored with SPC helped increase awareness of the large number of critical points in the process. The implementation of SPC forced the operators to identify key process characteristics within their operation. The process knowledge gained from implementing SPC can be credited with a significant amount of both product and process improvements at Rouge Steel.

A control plan is another tool that was instrumental in the organization's quality system implementation process. Control plans include a summary of major checkpoints in the process for assuring product quality through process management. Control plans also provide a basic guide for how to react when a process change signal is received. One of the requirements of a control plan is that there be documentation of the process statistic and reaction if the process has gone beyond its control limits or specification limits.

A control plan defines the customer characteristic, identifies the key product or process variables, describes what type and how often a measurement is required, outlines the reporting process for the data, and directs the proper response to out-of-control or out-of-specification signals. Rouge Steel has a central database that allows control plans to be printed in either product- or process-specific formats.

In an effort to compile the data collected from the quality system into useful information, a process management capability summary (PMCS) was developed, as shown in Figure 13–1. This summation of data allows for an accurate assessment of the entire operation with just a few pages of information. It allows anyone who has a working understanding of the quality system requirements to identify areas that should be targeted for improvement. This tool is used to track incoming materials, process compliance, measurement system analysis, process stability, and audit results.

COMMUNICATION AND TRAINING

In the early stages, the progress of the quality system at Rouge Steel was painfully slow. It is often difficult to create enthusiasm in a new quality program when people have seen many quality improvement initiatives come and go. One of the first major communication efforts undertaken was to conduct a quality system readiness audit. This procedure consisted of meeting individually with 170 employees for 30 minutes each. The meetings, or interviews, took place over a three-week period, on all three shifts, with a mixture of hourly employees, first-line supervisors, general supervisors, superintendents, and managers. The interviews were conducted by the quality systems implementation manager and the UAW quality representative, and focused on commitment to the quality system, understanding of the tools, and use of the tools.

FIGURE 13-1

Process Management Capability Summary

PROCESS MANAGEMENT CAPABILITY SUMMARY FOR PERIOD ENDING: 31 Aug. 1995
PART B–OPERATION AND PROCESS

OPERATING AREA: BOF **CONTROL PLAN DATE: 1/27/95** **AUTHOR/DATE: Paul Parynik 9/10/95**

Item No.	Operation Description	Customer Character	Key Prod./Proc. Var'ble	Gage or Test Method	Attr/Var Gage Color	% Gage R & R	Date of MSA	MSA Ref No.	Cp	Cpk or % Comp.	Date Calc'd	Type of Control	Freq. of Inspe'n	Related Standard and or Procedure
CP B2 30 14	Pre Teeming Ladle	M3A Clean Steel	Ladle Preheat Performance (degree F)	Preheater Tmp. Gage	Attr. Yellow	N/A	Pending	N/A	N/A	86.30%	9/10/95	Ck Sheet Ht. Log	Each Heat	RO B2-30-02 PO B2-30-35 PO B2-40-27
CP B2 40 01	Ladle Free Open at Teeming Pour Site	IB1 Ladle Open	Free Open Performance	Visual	Attr. Yellow	PO B2-40 6 11 18	Feb-95 Apr-94 Apr-94	LBC-001 B29407B3 B29407B3	N/A	97.2%	9/10/95	Ck Sheet Pit Summary 1st Run	Every Heat x 1	PO B2-40-06, 11 18
CP B2 40 02	Teeming Stream Alum. Kill Ingot Hts.	VIF Surface Steel	Shrouding Alum. Kill Heats Ar Immersed	Visual	Attr. Yellow	PO B2-40 24	Apr-94	B29407B3	N/A	100.0%	9/10/95	Ck Sheet Per Procedure	Every Alum. Killed Ingot	PO B2-40-24
CP B2 40 04	Hot Top Practice Bags Added	IB9 Pipe T1B Coil Wt.	No. of Bags Added Per AK Ingots	Visual	Attr. Yellow	PO B2-40 28	Sep-94	B29409B3	N/A	100.0%	9/10/95	Ck Sheet AA Form	Each Applied Ingot Heat	PO B2-40-28
CP B2 40 05	Post Teeming Ladle	IB9 Pipe T1B Coil Wt.	Alum. Kill Heat Pull Time	Visual	Attr Yellow	PO B2-45 1	Oct-94	B19401B4	N/A	100%	x	Ck Sheet AA Form	Every Alum. Killed Heat	PO B1-45-01, 02 RO B2-40-02
CP B2 40 06	Pre Teeming Ladle	M3A Clean Steel	BOF Ingot Ht. Ladle Temp. (degree F)	Immersion Thermocouple Celox Lab Gage	VAR Orange	20.96%	Mar-95	B2-001	2.23	1.67	9/10/95	Ck Sheet X & MR Chart	Every Ingot Heat	PO B2-30-25, 61
CP B2 40 07	Pre Teeming Ladle	M3A Clean Steel	Ladle Dryout Performance	Ladle Preheat Tmp. Gage	Attr Yellow	N/A	Pending	N/A	N/A	61.0%	9/10/95	Ck Sheet Ht. Log	Each Heat	PO B2-40-03

Additional Notes: Specs. for Ladle Tmp. Ingot Hts. reduced to +/- 25 dg. 1/94

Process Mgr/Supt Approval _____

PT-C-1-09-04
Form B Rev. #2
1/31/95

These interviews revealed a need for immediate action in at least two areas. The first area of concern was the amount of information operators were receiving and how it was distributed. Contrary to what one might expect, the operators were not getting too little information but rather too much. The operators were clear in their request for information of two types: information relevant to their operation and information about how the company was doing as a whole.

To satisfy the operators' request for a manageable amount of information, a plan was implemented to develop department-specific packages that included information on the company's quality performance and financial information. Quality information was provided to the employees on their specific department, the departments that supplied their material, and the departments to which they supplied their product. This information was designed for distribution at crew meetings to answer any questions that might arise.

The second area of concern was the level of quality system awareness at the first-line supervisor level and with the operators. While the general supervisors were less knowledgeable than either the superintendents or managers, they possessed a level of quality system knowledge that would lend itself to improvement through training.

The need to train the general supervisors was addressed through a series of process management guidance sessions (PMGSs). The goal of the training was to increase the general supervisors' knowledge of the quality system tools to the point where they would be comfortable teaching the system to their first-line supervisors and operators. There were seven PMGS modules developed and delivered to the general supervisors. After the completion of the PMGS series, there was a significant increase in both the use and understanding of the quality system at the operating levels throughout the organization.

As an outgrowth of the need to increase communication and to ensure that the proper information was reaching the right people, a communication model was developed as shown in Figure 13–2, to help people visualize how the data they collected would be used and how they would receive feedback. Providing feedback of information is an effective way to develop commitment to the quality system.

Communication Model

Rouge Steel Statistical Control Data Flow and Usage

MEETING THE Q101 REQUIREMENTS

The primary goal of the quality system at Rouge Steel has always been to ensure continuous improvement in our processes and products. However, one of the objectives of the quality system was to meet the quality system (Q101) requirements established by Rouge Steel's largest customer, the Ford Motor Company.

The quality system was patterned to fit the Q101 requirements, and accommodations were made in the system to ensure that the needs of all Rouge Steel's customers were met. Along the way to attaining Q1 status, Rouge Steel received several quality awards from other important customers.

Over the course of three years, the efforts to meet Q101 requirements resulted in continuous improvement in process control, as well as the reduction of internal rejects and customer claims. Rouge Steel received the Q1 Preferred Supplier Award on June 23, 1993.

EMPLOYEE INVOLVEMENT

There is no formal or grandiloquent employee involvement effort associated with the quality system at Rouge Steel. The involvement of operators is solicited on a departmental level rather than by a companywide involvement program. Groups of employees have been brought together to develop FMEAs and control plans, and to solve various types of problems. These groups meet on an as-needed basis and are usually disbanded when the issue is resolved. This type of flexible team membership affords more people the opportunity to be involved in problem solving and reduces the expectation that the group meeting is intended to solve all the quality problems. This approach is patterned after the Japanese "kaizen" process, where incremental improvements lead to continuous improvement.

Rouge Steel's quality system works because it involves the people who produce its steel.

Rouge Steel's quality system works because it involves the people who produce its steel and provides them with clearly defined objectives. It is a dynamic system that allows input at all levels of the organization. Ideas for improvement flow freely between operators, supervisors, managers, vice presidents, and the company's president by way of quality meetings, audits, and line-level quality system usage. The success of this system can be seen as it continues to grow and produce the desired results.

The continuous improvement flow diagram, shown in Figure 13–3, shows the complete loop of the quality system. The macro quality indicators produce facts that are used as feedback to drive improvement in the entire process.

DECISION TO PURSUE QS-9000

Rouge Steel's decision to pursue QS-9000 registration was driven by customer expectations and the company's desire to further advance the quality system. There was some disagreement in the early stages as to whether the company should pursue QS-9000 or ISO 9000. Because QS-9000 encompasses ISO 9000 and measures continuous improvement, the company decided to apply its efforts to attain QS-9000. Rouge Steel could have taken a wait-and-see attitude toward the registration process

> *To be an industry leader, it is important to set the pace rather than follow the pack.*

and sat back until it was clearly established by Chrysler, Ford, and General Motors that all their Tier I suppliers would be required to be QS-9000 registered. However, to be an industry leader it is important to set the pace rather than follow the pack.

QS-9000 ATTAINMENT PLAN

Rouge Steel believed that using the same quality system philosophy that had guided the company through its attainment of Ford's Q1 award and dozens of other customer audits would provide the necessary framework to attain QS-9000 registration. We viewed the attainment of QS-9000 as a necessary and potentially difficult task, but one that could be met relatively quickly given the current implementation methodology of the company's quality system.

The first step in the pursuit of QS-9000 registration was to gain a clear understanding of all its requirements. This was made more difficult by the fact that QS-9000 had not been finalized and was the subject of many public quality debates. While this could have been used as a reason to postpone the effort, we decided that waiting until QS-9000 was finalized would be more harmful than making any necessary adjustments later in the implementation process.

It was clear to everyone associated with Rouge Steel's quality system that the company was positioned to meet the challenges and the intent of any requirements put forth by even the most

FIGURE 13–3

Continuous Improvement Flow Diagram

Rouge Steel Quality System

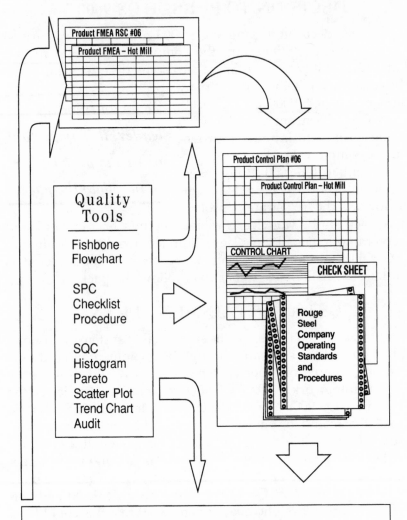

discriminating customer. Continuous improvement in the macro quality indicators had shown that the system is capable and robust. The QS-9000 requirements that were known fit neatly into the existing system, which confirmed our belief that the system was well designed and well implemented.

To begin the selection of an independent registrar, Rouge Steel contacted several organizations qualified to conduct the registration process. Three organizations were interviewed on-site according to seven criteria: auditing experience, automotive requirement knowledge, practical application of QS-9000, stability of the organization, qualifications for QS-9000, service, and professionalism. After the interviews were complete, we decided on a rating for each criterion and company, and then selected the registrar with the highest rating.

Next we needed to determine if it would be necessary to bring in a consultant to evaluate the company's level of readiness for a registration audit or to have the registrar conduct a preliminary assessment.

The same team that led the Q1 efforts was largely intact and eager to face this new challenge. The team determined that the organization would be better served by conducting a thorough self-evaluation than by outsourcing the assessment to a consulting firm and thus losing this educational opportunity. After this critical self-assessment, Rouge Steel determined that the most prudent course of action would be for our registrar to conduct a preliminary assessment.

The first action we took to prepare for QS-9000 registration was to align the existing quality system manual with the 20 elements of Section I and with Section II of QS-9000. The quality system manual in use at Rouge Steel contained 12 sections that encompassed virtually all of the necessary requirements. The procedures in this manual dictated the company's quality system philosophy. Reformatting the manual to better fit the QS-9000 elements brought it up-to-date and ensured that any new requirements were being met. The updated version of the quality manual was provided to our registrar for review and was subsequently approved as meeting all the QS-9000 requirements.

PREASSESSMENT AUDIT PROCESS

The next phase of the registration process began with the registrar conducting an on-site preliminary assessment over a three-day period. It was important to understand exactly what the auditors would be looking for, how they interpreted the elements, and how they would conduct the audit procedure. A significant difference in the QS-9000 preassessment compared to other audits was the large portion of time the auditors spent with the various staff areas. Typically these departments got little more than a cursory glance by auditors; during this assessment, however, nearly 30 percent of the total audit time was spent on the staff departments. It was also clear that the auditors were looking for systemic problems and were interpreting the requirements quite literally.

The audit results indicated that there were at least several minor issues in each department that had to be addressed before the company would be ready for the formal assessment. The two largest areas of concern were document control and proper use of the gauge documentation system.

In typical fashion, the people of Rouge Steel responded to the challenge of correcting the shortcomings uncovered in the audit. In a matter of a few weeks, corrective action plans were developed and implementation of these plans had either begun or was about to begin. Most of the issues were simply a matter of more precisely documenting actions or clarifying procedures. With the exception of traceability of intra- and interdepartmental communications, and the two items mentioned above, there were very few issues that would require a great deal of effort to correct.

The problems associated with company communications included the following: the lack of consistent use of dates on documents, the omission of signatures giving proper authorization for directives, and the lack of clearly identified senders and intended recipients. While these issues may seem minor, their importance cannot be overlooked. The ease of clarifying questions regarding a document is greatly improved when the document is received by the intended person and the sender is readily identified. Documents that supersede previous documents can be positively identified when both documents are dated. To satisfy the requirements of this element, it was a matter of instilling in people the importance of dating, signing, and identifying both who is sending and who should be receiving the communication.

To eliminate redundancy and to ensure the uniformity of implementation, action plans were developed with the input of each involved department. The action plans were administered by the quality system implementation supervisor and the UAW quality representatives. The company's president and his staff fully supported the administration of the action plans and provided any assistance needed by the departments for the development of specific plans.

REGISTRATION ASSESSMENT PROCESS

The registration process began with some apprehension and anxiety on the part of many Rouge Steel employees. The most stressful part of any event is usually the anticipation of it. As the auditors moved from one department to the next, the feeling of relief and the building of confidence became apparent. While there was very little discussion about what the auditors had found, each department felt that its part of the audit went as well as could have been expected. More important, however, were the initiations of corrective actions immediately upon completion of the audit. The efforts to correct deficiencies were under way even before the final audit report was delivered to the company.

The preliminary assessment had been very beneficial to both the company and the auditors. The company had a better understanding of what to expect in the final assessment, and the auditors had become more knowledgeable about the steel-making process. The dress rehearsal had paid a dividend for everyone involved.

The registration process was conducted in a manner very similar to that of the preassessment. The auditors again spent about 30 percent of their time auditing the staff functions. During this time, quality assurance was required to explain its procedures for handling customer claims and responding to requests for data. Advanced engineering members were asked to explain how they are involved in the up-front quality planning. Management responsibility, an area that covers all aspects of the company, required that top management explain how the business plan reflected the company's commitment to continuous improvement.

The auditors spent the balance of the time on the plant floor assessing procedures and evaluating the overall effectiveness of the quality system. They were free to speak to any employee they encountered and took advantage of this at every opportunity. Two of the auditors' common objectives were to ask employees about the company's quality policy and how each person's job impacted quality. Because of the process we had used in the development of the quality system, it was virtually impossible to find anyone who did not know about the company's commitment to quality, and everyone could explain how his or her job impacted quality.

At the end of the three-day audit process, eight minor nonconformances were identified. In order to satisfy the requirements for QS-9000 registration, we had to address these eight findings and submit corrective action plans to the registrar within 30 days of the audit. Each action plan needed to satisfy the auditors as being both practical and effective for correcting the nonconformance. The eight nonconforming issues would be revisited in the six-month follow-up surveillance audits. Rouge Steel was registered to QS-9000 on May 18, 1995.

POST QS-9000 REGISTRATION

The employees of Rouge Steel consider registration to QS-9000 to be an honor worthy of the effort it took to attain it. However, receiving this registration, like other quality awards the company has received, does not permit the company to relax. Rather, it is looked upon as a milestone that can be used to mark the progress toward complete customer satisfaction. Everyone understands that even the highest accolades for past performance will be quickly forgotten unless we are capable of continuously meeting the quality expectations of our customers.

Being one of the first organizations to attain QS-9000, and the first fully integrated steel producer to do so, has generated a great deal of pride in the organization. Everyone loves being associated with a winner, and the quality system designed and implemented by the people of Rouge Steel has created that successful feeling.

The semiannual surveillance audits required by QS-9000 will provide a driver to ensure that the quality system remains effective. The purpose of the surveillance audit is to revisit any issue from the previous audit. This should prevent the possibility of a concern developing into a major quality problem or significant system breakdown.

The ability to supply a worldwide market cannot be overlooked as one of the benefits of achieving QS-9000. Being able to tell a customer anywhere in the world that Rouge Steel is QS-9000 registered has the potential of streamlining what could be a long and arduous sales process. Establishing global standards against which to measure quality system effectiveness is extremely important as the opportunities to compete in the worldwide market continue to increase.

Experiencing the QS-9000 process assisted us in clearly defining some areas of responsibility that we had overlooked in the implementation of the existing quality system. Rewriting the quality manual brought forth several concerns of this type and allowed them to be resolved before they could result in a customer-related concern.

The QS-9000 process highlighted the importance of communication throughout the organization and brought together some parts of the company that previously had very little formal contact. Keeping open the channels of communication, both formal and informal, is often understood to be important but seldom practiced. The efforts necessary to attain QS-9000 registration have offered us an opportunity to establish both formal and informal communication lines between many operations and staff functions.

One of the most significant improvements that QS-9000 has brought to Rouge Steel is the expanded involvement of staff functions in the quality system. Prior to the QS-9000 efforts, many staff functions lacked procedures and staff members viewed themselves as exempt from product quality. With the exception of customer service and sales, many staff members did not see themselves as providing a service to a customer. QS-9000 has clearly established a customer and supplier relationship for every function within the company.

How will Rouge Steel address the future? One possible way to bring the goal of no customer claims into better focus may be to stop measuring defective material in tons or percentages and start measuring in pounds, number of defective parts produced, or defective parts per million. Refining the graduation of the scale used to measure defective products may create a psychological shift in the minds of the workforce in terms of what is considered acceptable by the customer. Rouge Steel fully intends to implement this change in the very near future.

Another issue that needs to be addressed is the development of a supplier management system. Few, if any, processes are totally self-contained. The steel-making process requires virtually thousands of suppliers that provide a broad range of materials and services from iron ore, machine parts, and computer hardware to technical advice and packaging material. The variations in these products are combined in the steel-making process and may impact variations in the final product shipped to the customer. In order to ensure that Rouge Steel receives a high-quality product on a timely and consistent basis, it will be necessary to develop a supplier quality management process that will be an industrywide benchmark.

SUMMARY

Attaining QS-9000 has led to some very useful insights within both Rouge Steel Company and the external environment in which the company competes. Clearly, this award is a coveted honor for the men and women of Rouge Steel. However, the employees of this company know that continuous improvement in both the products they manufacture and the services they provide is the only real key to customer satisfaction.

Many of the QS-9000 requirements and procedures ensure that continuous improvement remains the primary driver for the quality system. The short-term goal of the company is to have zero rejects in customer plants. There is currently a concerted effort to completely separate the customer from any problems that may occur in the steel manufacturing process. Rouge Steel's customers deserve a defect-free product, and our efforts are being directed to ensure that this becomes a reality.

Long-term efforts to ensure that Rouge Steel is capable of meeting its customers' expectations include the addition of new technology and capital improvements. The company is increasing its metallurgical staff and the advanced engineering services we provide to our customers. Our high degree of focus on customer service is continuing with the installation of a highly sophisticated customer order management (COM 2000) system designed to meet customer needs well into the next century.

The quality system and the tools used to implement it will remain at the center of the company's efforts to ensure that the processes we use and the products we produce benefit from continuous improvement. This system is dynamic and robust.

Rouge Steel is already in the process of establishing an environmental management system under the guidelines of ISO 14000. This system will ensure that the company approaches its environmental responsibilities in a practical and systematic manner with the goal of continuous improvement.

Rouge Steel is dedicated to its customers. Our challenge in the years ahead will be to understand the changing demands of our customers and to provide services that exceed their highest expectations.

This case study is contributed jointly by Michael McDonald, QS-9000 Management Representative; and Tom Lareau, United Auto Workers' Quality Representative with Rouge Steel Company, Dearborn, Michigan.

CHAPTER 14

Fast Track to QS-9000

Saturn Electronics & Engineering, Inc.

GENERAL

- *Headquarters* : **Auburn Hills, Michigan, U.S.A.**
  International Locations: Mexico, China, Italy
- *Year Founded* : **1985**
- *Number of Employees* : **1,100**

QS-9000 SPECIFIC

- *Registered Location(s)* : **Coopersville, Michigan, U.S.A.**
- *Number of Employees* : **170**
- *Registration Date* : **February 14, 1995**
- *Product(s)* : **Solenoids and Relays**
- *Tier I, II, III Supplier* : **Tier I**
- *Major Customer(s)* : **Chrysler**
- *Annual Sales* : **U.S. $23 Million**

INTRODUCTION

The purpose of this case study is to describe how Saturn Electronics & Engineering, Inc.'s Coopersville facility achieved QS-9000 registration in an accelerated time frame. The study also illustrates common types of noncompliances found during audits and solutions to obtain corrective action.

QS-9000 registration is extremely important to the organization. It will be one of the requirements for companies that wish to remain in the rapidly shrinking automotive supply base. Our major customer, Chrysler Corporation, has set a deadline of July 31, 1997, to obtain QS-9000 registration for existing suppliers. Coopersville plant personnel work cooperatively to maintain their QS-9000 registration status. The registration of five additional Saturn locations is being aggressively pursued, with the coordination coming from the director of QS-9000 implementation at Coopersville.

BACKGROUND

Saturn Electronics & Engineering, Inc., was founded in 1985 to provide design expertise and assemble electronic products for the automotive, commercial, and military markets. The two original plants are both located in Rochester Hills, Michigan. One is a 12,000-square-foot plant devoted to electronic products for military applications; this plant's 35 employees build multilayer high-density circuit cards and systems for fire control, power control, and multiplexing. The other plant, comprising 33,000 square feet and employing 110 people, builds products for automotive and commercial applications, including disk drive controller boards, "credit card" door locks, electronic modules, sensors, and transmission controllers. Since its founding the company has been profitable every year and has shown exponential sales growth, as indicated in Figure 14–1. The company was ranked number 404 on the 1995 *Inc.* magazine list of America's fastest-growing private companies.

In 1991 the company expanded into the electromechanical field by acquiring plants in the southern United States and Mexico. The Marks, Mississippi, plant manufactures resistor block assemblies; switches; cable releases; underhood and trunk lamp assemblies; subassemblies for the Guadalupe, Mexico, facility; and various other electromechanical products. This 45,000-square-foot plant employs 70 people; its main customers are Chrysler and General Motors. The plant has been recommended to receive Chrysler's Gold Pentastar award for the 1995 model year. The Guadalupe, Mexico, facility employs 80 people and produces switches and wiring harnesses in a 20,000-square-foot facility.

In 1993, MCAM Products, located in Flint, Michigan, was established as a subsidiary to provide value-added plastic components.

FIGURE 14-1

Saturn Electronics & Engineering's Sales Growth

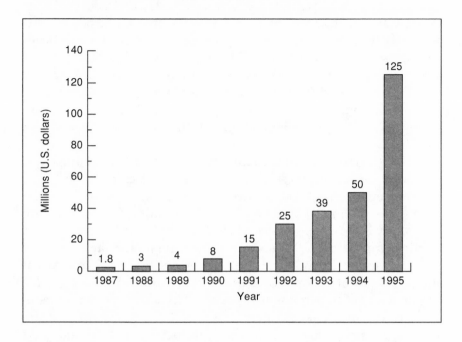

In 1994, a joint venture, Beijing Saturn, was formed to service the Asian market.

The "new" Saturn Electronics & Engineering, Inc., was formed by a merger on March 21, 1995, with Bitron Industries and MascoTech Controls, Inc., a division of MascoTech Corporation. This merger created one of the largest minority-owned automotive suppliers in the United States. Saturn Electronics & Engineering holds a majority stake of 51 percent in the new company. MascoTech Corporation retains a 28 percent equity position, while Bitron holds 21 percent. The new corporation with headquarters in Auburn Hills, Michigan, comprises 10 production facilities in the United States, Mexico, China, and Italy, and employs approximately 1,100 people. To date, the Coopersville plant is the only Saturn Electronics & Engineering, Inc., facility with an ISO 9000 or QS-9000 registration. The three companies complement each other, enabling a total control system to be supplied to the customer rather than individual components. The control system has the capability to take a sensor signal, process the data, and provide actuation function.

The former Bitron plants are located in Rocky Mount, North Carolina, and Torino, Italy. The Torino, Italy, facility is a joint venture that produces electronic components. The Rocky Mount, North Carolina, location employs 184 associates in a 58,000-square-foot facility. Major customers include Chrysler, Ford, Harley Davidson, American Yazaki, John Deere, and OMC. The company was formed as a joint venture between Hi-Ram and OMP of Italy in 1986, and the Rocky Mount facility was opened under the name of Elbi/Hi-Ram in 1988 for the purpose of automatically manufacturing ISO relays. In 1994 the name of the company was changed to Bitron.

The former MascoTech plants are located in Oxford and Coopersville, Michigan. The Oxford, Michigan, facility covers 62,000 square feet and employs 200 people in the production of fuel regulators, fuel dampeners, and motorized actuators. The focus of this case study is the Coopersville, Michigan, plant, a 48,000-square-foot facility employing 170 associates. Main customers are Chrysler, General Motors, Draw-Tite, Borg Warner, and Takata Gateway. The main growth area for the Coopersville plant is the design and manufacture of transmission solenoids. The size of the manufacturing area doubled over the past year due to increased share in this market. Another growth area is the production of electronic brake control modules. Relays and switches are also produced in quantity. The Coopersville, Michigan, facility opened in 1978 under the name of Hi-Ram Corporation. In 1985, Masco Industries acquired the company, allowing Hi-Ram to pursue a more aggressive growth pattern. In 1993, Hi-Ram Corporation and Schmelzer Corporation—another Masco Industries company, located in Oxford, Michigan—merged under the name of MascoTech Controls.

THE STEPPING-STONE

On July 26, 1994, the Coopersville plant became registered to ISO 9001:1987 under the scope of Design & Manufacture of Electrical Components for the Automotive and Commercial Industries. At the time *QS-9000* had not yet been published.

On his first day of work in August 1993 at MascoTech Controls, the new quality manager reported to the Masco corporate offices for a three-day training session in ISO 9001 documentation. Upper management at Masco Corporation was investigating the benefits of obtaining ISO 9001 registration and had contracted a consulting company to provide training in the standard's requirements. The corporation had not yet decided to actively pursue registration for any of its plants.

The Coopersville plant decided to begin modifying its quality system documentation to conform to ISO 9001 requirements. The process to upgrade the quality system was in its infancy when the quality manager was contacted in October of 1993 by a registration firm that was a local ISO 9001 registrar accredited by the Dutch Council for Registration (RvC) and the Registrar Accreditation Board (RAB). Wishing to expand its accreditation scope to include manufacturers of electrical components, the registration firm offered to perform the document review, initial visit, and the assessment audit at no charge if MascoTech Controls would allow representatives from the RvC and the RAB to be present at a witness audit. Normal charges would occur for corrective action verification and surveillances. MascoTech Controls needed to accelerate its ISO 9001 program substantially to take advantage of this offer.

LEADERSHIP COMMITMENT

The Coopersville plant acted independently of the MascoTech Corporation in signing a registration agreement with the registrar in January of 1994. (The MascoTech Corporation had not yet chosen a registrar.) The plant's management team decided that the use of consultants to review the quality system was not necessary. Training would be provided to a limited number of personnel who would educate the rest of the team during management review meetings held to discuss potential noncompliances. In hindsight, more training should have been provided for departmental managers and production supervisors. Most of the noncompliances documented during registrar and internal audits were the result of training deficiencies. However, even without extensive outside training, the plant achieved full registration to QS-9000 in an accelerated time frame.

Aggressive management backing to ensure implementation timetables are met (and not constantly postponed due to other pressing issues, such as new-product launches) is essential in achieving registration to QS-9000. The Coopersville plant's manufacturing area doubled its size during the period in which QS-9000 was implemented. Five new automotive products were launched. Without the full backing of the plant management the process would surely have been delayed. After ISO 9001 registration, many department managers expressed concern about pressing aggressively on to QS-9000 registration, due to the many product launches coming up. The general manager decided that QS-9000 implementation must proceed immediately. Due to rapid growth, postponing the process was only going to make it more difficult.

DOCUMENT PREPARATION AND REVIEW

Many of the requirements of ISO 9001 and QS-9000 were already being met to achieve individual automotive quality system requirements. However, modifications and substantial improvements were required. The new quality system documentation was prepared by the quality manager with significant contributions from the engineering manager. Both men attended statistical process control (SPC) and ISO Network of West Michigan meetings at the Grand Rapids Community College Technical Center. This society presented training in a different element of the ISO 9000 standard each month. The quality manager also attended two three-day seminars on ISO 9001 documentation and internal audits presented by training consultants at Masco headquarters. Each segment of the quality system documentation was reviewed and approved by responsible parties through the companies' engineering change notice (ECN) process.

Any document used to verify the quality of a product or procedure must be controlled. To change a controlled document, approval must be granted by the affected departments. Any person in the organization may submit an ECN to facilitate continuous improvement. The engineering secretary distributes all controlled documents after identifying them as such with a red stamp. The person receiving the new controlled document is responsible for destroying the old copy. One copy of the old document is stamped "obsolete" and stored in an engineering history file by the secretary. All controlled documents are required to have approval signatures with the date noted.

In our registrar's review of MascoTech Controls' quality manual, standard operating procedures, and departmental instructions, 21 noncompliances were documented. These included the absence of a number of procedures, customer quality standards not referenced, special processes not documented, job descriptions with qualifications lacking, and the lack of control of visual aids. Additional procedures were issued and existing procedures updated.

They were then submitted to our registrar for corrective action verification prior to the registration audit.

INITIAL VISIT

The initial visit was carried out in February of 1994 by the registrar's lead assessor for the purposes of discussing the review of the quality documentation, planning the assessment audit, and confirming any obvious nonconformances in the implementation of the system that required attention prior to the registration audit. Another objective of the visit was to familiarize the lead assessor and the company with the processes and facilities to be assessed and the procedure by which the assessment would be carried out. A preassessment is now offered as an option that can be combined with the required man-days of the registration audit if the two are carried out within three months of each other. This method is being chosen for the remaining Saturn Electronics plants that are preparing for registration.

A fairly lengthy list of obvious noncompliances was compiled during the walk-through of the plant. A sampling follows:

- Test equipment not in service required tags indicating "Calibrate before use."
- Test request forms needed to be used to instigate and document prototype testing.
- Acceptance criteria were missing on a number of test stations.
- Thermocouple wire used in testing needed to be tied to a registration.
- Test-related software had to be controlled with revision levels.
- Total measurement range of final testers had to be calibrated.
- Known reject and good parts for verification of testers at start-up had to be on calibration schedule with actual measurements taken; proper storage and identification were required.
- Environmental conditions needed to be controlled during calibration.
- Measurement uncertainty had to be recorded to determine the confidence interval.

- Use of static prevention equipment needed to be described in operator instructions.
- Operators must be registered for special processes.
- Design records, such as meeting minutes, must be retrievable.
- Management review meetings must be documented with minutes.
- Operator instructions were missing at a number of stations.

THE REGISTRATION AUDIT

The ISO 9001 registration audit was performed on April 11 and 12, 1994. A number of working documents were requested by the auditors prior to the assessment. These documents included a plant layout, a production schedule, a product offerings list, a phone list with titles, an approved supplier list, and a print revision level list. An opening meeting was conducted by the registrars with the implementation team present prior to commencing. The format of the audit was explained, including acceptance criteria, and a plan distributed that listed departments to be audited with scheduled times. MascoTech Controls' acceptance limit was 12 minor noncompliances. The number of acceptance criteria depends on the size of the plant and the number of employees. If the number of minor noncompliances is below the set limit and there are not more than three minor noncompliances in any element, corrective action may be submitted in writing and does not need to be verified until the next surveillance. However, if the number of noncompliances exceeds the limit or there are more than three in any category, a corrective action verification assessment is performed on-site by the registrar prior to issuing or renewing registration. An element receives a major noncompliance if there are more than three non-compliances detected.

A guide had to be furnished for each auditor. The guide was present during the entire assessment and helped keep the auditor on the planned time schedule. Observers from the RvC and the RAB were present at the meeting and during the audit.

The auditors documented 33 minor noncompliances. Five non-compliances were found in document control, 12 in measuring and test equipment, and 7 in nonconforming material, resulting in a major noncompliance for each of these elements. Minor noncompliances were also observed in design control, purchasing, material identification and traceability, process control, corrective action, and handling and storage. Thus, MascoTech Controls did not comply with ISO 9001:1987 requirements and was given 60 days in which to provide corrective action. To obtain a registration showing compliance with ISO 9001, an on-site verification of the corrective actions by the registrar was required. After we submitted verification material to our registrar, an on-site corrective action assessment was performed. MascoTech Controls achieved formal registration to ISO 9001 in July of 1994.

THE UPGRADE AND SURVEILLANCE ASSESSMENTS

The surveillance audits do not cover every aspect of QS-9000. However, certain areas will be covered during every audit. All upgrades to quality system documentation will be reviewed during the audit, as will a complete cycle of the company's internal audit documentation. The surveillance audit will be made to the latest revision of QS-9000. An opportunity for improvement is described in the registrar's report following each surveillance assessment. Although some companies view QS-9000 as "say what you do and do as you say," the real focus is continuous improvement and customer satisfaction.

In December of 1994, MascoTech Controls updated its quality system documentation to attempt to comply with QS-9000 requirements. Most of the requirements had previously been incorporated, as the quality manager had obtained a draft copy of *QS-9000* when the original ISO 9001 documentation was being written. A small number of noncompliances were found during our registrar's document review. Two noncompliances were found in the contract review element. We then made modifications to the procedure to more clearly describe how amendments to contracts were made and transferred to concerned functions within the organization. We also had to describe the maintenance and minimum retention time of feasibility commitment review forms used to document contract review. In the process control element we had to add more procedural detail for the verification of job setups. In the handling, storage, packaging, preservation, and delivery element we had to add verification of labels, packing slips, and load sheets from the advanced shipping notices to the procedure. Modified quality system documentation was forwarded to our registrar to verify corrective action for the document review prior to the upgrade assessment.

In January of 1995, an assessment was performed at the Coopersville plant for the purpose of upgrading the plant's registration to ISO 9001:1994 and QS-9000. Three minor noncompliances were found, one in document control and two in process control. Training was listed as an opportunity for improvement in the assessment. Comments were made that the business plan should address the allocation of resources and training programs. It was also felt that the human resources training checklists for new employees could be refined.

An upgrade to the February 1995 revision to *QS-9000* was achieved by the Coopersville plant during the July 1995 surveillance visit. Five minor noncompliances were identified during the surveillance. Since the number was below the acceptance criteria limit, it was acceptable to submit corrective action plans with attached evidence to the registrar. The July surveillance audit listed the identification of work in process as an opportunity for improvement.

CORRECTIVE ACTION USING CROSS-FUNCTIONAL TEAMS

Cross-functional management review teams met weekly to address the items documented during the registrar's initial visit and to address items identified during internal quality audits. The same team was used to address noncompliances documented during registration and surveillance audits. Attendees were the general manager, the plant manager, the quality manager, both engineering managers, the purchasing manager, the human resources manager, the manufacturing manager, and the plant superintendent. Minutes of the meetings were distributed on company bulletin boards throughout the plant to inform all employees on the progress of the effort. Special plantwide meetings were also called to inform every employee of the results of internal quality audits and corrective actions taken and to provide an overview of the QS-9000 requirements.

Prior to the on-site verification, corrective action plans with attached evidence had to be submitted to the registrar for every noncompliance found. All corrective actions submitted had to be in a standard problem-solving format, such as Chrysler's 7-D report. Examples of the attached evidence include updates to standard operating procedures, updates to operator instructions, calibration data sheets, and documented training session sign-in sheets. The following sections describe the noncompliances that were documented and the corrective actions taken.

Design Control

In design control, one noncompliance was detected during the ISO 9001 audit. Critical characteristics identified on one customer drawing were missing from MascoTech Controls' documents. The subject product was in the design stage and had not yet been released to production. Revisions to the design and process review procedure were made to require internal finished goods prints to match the customer's drawing identically.

During recent internal audits, additional weaknesses were found in the company's design control system. Experimental and sketch prints were not controlled with approval signatures and did not list all known special characteristics. Prototype samples made from the prints were not adequately identified to the revision level. This led to propagated errors when the sketches were later upgraded to production prints. Since the experimental prints were not approved by a cross-disciplinary team, many functions in the company were kept in the dark on a design until it reached the point of being approved by the customer. Concurrent multidisciplinary engineering was not being adequately performed. Further revisions were made to the standard operating procedures to form a documented cross-disciplinary engineering review team for each project. All advanced product quality planning (APQP) documentation such as timelines, failure mode effect analysis (FMEA), and design review minutes were distributed to the team to facilitate concurrent engineering and detect inadequacies prior to reaching the product approval stage.

Document and Data Control

Noncompliances observed in the element of document control included operator instructions not agreeing with actual practice or customer revision level, missing operator instructions, missing approval signatures, and operators using handwritten instructions they prepared themselves for reference. The use of obsolete or uncontrolled drawings and standards was also detected.

Production supervisors and operators were given a documented training session on the document control requirements. The operators reviewed their instructions and identified many omissions and mistakes. Copies of the instructions were marked up by the operators and given to their supervisor to complete engineering change notice (ECN) requests.

All documents in controlled file areas were verified for the correct revision level and proper approval signatures by secretarial staff. All obsolete documents were purged. All staff using controlled prints and standards were also trained in document control practices and how to verify that the correct revision level was being used. The document control procedure and ECN request form were revised to better address the distribution of internal and external design changes. All related documents—such as control plans, FMEAs, audit lists, operator instructions, and flowcharts—have boxes included on the form requiring a Y or N entry to indicate if they are affected by the change. Each of these items is tracked until its completion by the engineering secretary. A list is published at the end of each month of any open engineering change items exceeding 30 days. If the items are not closed within 10 additional days, the general manager is notified for follow-up.

Purchasing

One purchasing noncompliance documented during the registration audit was the omission of suppliers of material used in the finished product, such as solder and flux, from the approved supplier list. The procedure was updated to correct this oversight. All existing suppliers were grandfathered into the approved supplier list. In Saturn Electronics' system, a potential new supplier must be surveyed. If the supplier does not meet acceptance criteria, a corrective action plan must be submitted and approved before the supplier may be added to the list.

The biggest opportunity for improvement at Saturn Electronics is in the reduction of the parts per million (PPM) defective shipments from suppliers. Active development of Saturn Electronics' supplier base is being pursued using QS-9000 as fundamental quality system requirements. Saturn Electronics' supplier quality engineer has set a schedule to assess each supplier to QS-9000. Suppliers of critical components and suppliers with low ratings are being targeted first. After the assessment, each supplier is given 30 days to submit a corrective action plan with timelines. Documentation of each corrective action is required to be submitted following completion. A supplier rating system with quality system requirements was first developed by the Coopersville plant in October of 1993. The supplier general quality system requirements manual was later upgraded to meet QS-9000 requirements. The rating system was not enforced until January 1995 because we wished to give suppliers one year to become familiar with the requirements and address their shortcomings. If ratings drop below 80 percent, an assessment visit is scheduled with the supplier to identify areas that need to be improved to address its ratings problem. Suppliers are not permitted to quote on new jobs if their rating is below 70 percent. New sources are approached as possible replacements after a first-quarter score below 70 percent. Suppliers are also often called in or visited if problems are experienced on the line with their product. After two consecutive quarters of nonsatisfactory ratings (below 70 percent), the supplier is dropped from the approved supplier list.

Product Identification and Traceability

During the first ISO 9001 audit, a noncompliance was written for inadequate traceability through the subsupplier for a safety product. A receiver number is issued for each lot of purchased material. Lot traceability logs were issued to each line for recording the receiver number of each batch of material brought to the production line. All product produced at Saturn Electronics has a Julian date code lot number stamped on the product or on the box in which the product is packed. Through the lot traceability log it is possible to determine which receiver number of purchased material is in an applicable date code. Recently, a computerized inventory control system has been introduced at Saturn Electronics. Individual lot numbers are now tracked through the computer system on any product with safety designations.

During the QS-9000 surveillance audit, a noncompliance was issued due to material in bins at the end of a semiautomated line having no identification showing test status or part number. Saturn's procedure to store passed parts in gray trays and rejected parts in yellow trays was not an adequate indication of test status. This area was also listed as an opportunity for improvement in the assessment report. The standard operating procedure was revised to require the use of routing tickets or tags with part numbers. The tickets and tags have spaces for operator signatures and dates to indicate test status.

Process Control and Manufacturing Capabilities

During the first audit, it was discovered that setup instructions performed by operators were not adequately covered. For example, instructions on the welder did not describe the method to adjust for a one-quarter-inch pinch point. Now instructions and control plans contain all the information needed by an operator to set up the machine. Setups performed by maintenance men and supervisors are not described in detail, as the ability to set up noncomplex machinery is one of their job description requirements. Control plans and instructions also detail any preventive maintenance that affects product quality. The instructions do not detail maintenance requirements to prevent machine breakdown.

In process control, no method was found to obtain the latest updated safety regulations. A subscription service for safety and environmental regulations was obtained and the standard operating procedure updated. On a soldering operation it was found that the solder being used had a slightly different composition from that called for on the instruction. It turned out that the composition of the solder being used agreed with the ranges allowed on the part print but that the instruction was written by a technician who obtained the solder information from actual material. The manufacturing and quality system procedure was revised to stipulate that instruction data had to be verified from the control plan and from controlled part prints. The subject instruction was revised to agree with the part print.

One process control noncompliance was detected during the QS-9000 upgrade audit. It involved components sensitive to electrostatic discharge (ESD); the ESD-sensitive components were being stored in an approved storage tray but on unapproved foam. Approved ESD foam was purchased, along with an ESD training video. All personnel working in ESD-sensitive areas now watch the video. All training sessions are documented.

A noncompliance was written up for manufacturing capabilities during the last surveillance audit. No documented method was in place to evaluate the effectiveness of existing operations and processes in reference to plant layout and efficiency of process flow. A new procedure with an evaluation form was added to close out the noncompliance.

Control of Inspection, Measuring, and Test Equipment

Noncompliances observed in inspection, measuring, and test equipment included the following:

- Fixtures not routinely verified via preventive maintenance or gauge control schedule.
- Measurement of uncertainty not included in gauge control system.
- Temperature and humidity chart recorder not included in gauge control system.
- Rented oscilloscope had no certificate of calibration on-site (calibration sticker on the piece of equipment was current); the company from which the equipment was rented was not on the approved supplier list.
- Test software revision on final tester did not agree with revision on master list.
- Test fluid temperature limits not specified on final tester.
- Previous test results were not analyzed after it was found that a piece of equipment was out of acceptance during scheduled gauge calibration.
- Weld controllers were not calibrated; SPC charts maintained for weld pull force were not viewed as sufficient to control the process.

A separate heating and air conditioning system was purchased for the quality assurance lab to provide a temperature- and humidity-controlled environment. A documented training session was held for all employees to detail the standards for calibrating product and process gauges. Employees in all areas helped identify other gauges that were missing calibrations. A gauge-tracking computer program is used by Saturn Electronics to positively recall any gauges before their calibration expires. Procedures controlling inspection equipment were modified to add calibration sources to the approved supplier list and to address the noncompliances referenced above.

Nonconforming Product and Corrective Action

Violations found for the control of nonconforming product were mainly limited to missing reject tags and missing rework instructions. During the QS-9000 upgrade assessment, it was discovered that scrap was not adequately segregated in the warehouse. One skid of scrap material was sitting next to a skid of production inventory. A separate scrap area was added in the warehouse, and a documented training session held for material control personnel to close out the violations to control of nonconforming product.

During the QS-9000 audit, a noncompliance was written for the corrective action element due to nontimely response to corrective actions from suppliers. Another corrective action noncompliance was charged to the handling, storage, packaging, and delivery element due to no action being taken toward customer receiving discrepancy reports. The corrective and preventive action procedure was updated to add a tracking and follow-up procedure for all internal and external corrective action requests. In addition, the on-time response to corrective action requests was added as an element in the supplier rating system. The procedure was also updated to require a formal corrective action plan for any deficiency in customer rating reports, such as delivery or receiving discrepancies.

A "quality alert" procedure exists at Saturn Electronics to enable any employee to request corrective action for noncompliances or questionable procedures or product specifications. Approximately 15 quality alerts are responded to each month. Frequently, the corrective action includes an update to standard operating procedures or department instructions. The updates to these quality system documents make them more efficient and clear.

INTERNAL QUALITY AUDITS

At Saturn Electronics, rigorous internal quality audits have been instrumental in both obtaining and maintaining QS-9000 registration. A list of internal auditors is maintained with qualifications and exclusions detailed. It is imperative to maintain auditor independence.

Auditor meetings are held prior to the actual audit. Notes are compared, and areas in which auditors are aware of possible noncompliances are discussed to ensure they are investigated. To make the internal audit more strenuous than the surveillance audits by the registrar, any situation in which there is a suspected non-compliance is written up for the application of corrective action. If an improvement to a procedure or process is evident, it is documented whether the process is in compliance or not. This robustness keeps the company ahead of the game.

Weekly management review meetings are held to discuss and implement corrective action for each of the internal audit noncompliances. Meetings are continued until each noncompliance is closed. It is mandatory for each department manager to attend the meetings. A copy of the meeting minutes is displayed on each bulletin board within the plant to inform all employees of the progress made.

TRAINING AND EDUCATION

An area in which opportunity for improvement exists is identified after each surveillance audit. After the January 1995 surveillance audit, the area of training was identified as an opportunity. The training and education area remains the major threat to maintenance of QS-9000 registration. In all of the audits performed by our registrar, and in all of Saturn Electronics' internal audits, the root cause of the majority of noncompliances is training deficiencies. A documented training session is then required as a part of the corrective action plan. The rapid growth of the Coopersville plant has necessitated the addition of a number of salaried personnel whose training has been neglected. In addition, there is rapid turnover of hourly personnel. Policies may need to be reevaluated to retain hourly personnel and involve them more in continuous improvement projects. During rapid turnover situations, it is very difficult to train employees and evaluate the effectiveness of the training. A computer program was purchased to track training requirements; however, it has not been implemented to date.

SUMMARY

An organization cannot become complacent after achieving QS-9000 registration. Surveillance audits are performed every six months to confirm continuous conformance and improvement to the system. The biggest challenge to maintaining QS-9000 registration status at Saturn Electronics & Engineering, Inc., will be the implementation and maintenance of an effective training system. The root cause of the majority of noncompliances found during internal quality audits was training deficiencies. Recurring types of noncompliances are found due to inadequate orientation training of new employees. Rapid growth and high turnover rates of hourly employees make training effectiveness a challenge.

The registration of the Guadalupe, Marks, Oxford, Rochester Hills, and Rocky Mount plants to QS-9000 is being actively pursued. Coopersville's quality manager was promoted to director of QS-9000 implementation and is coordinating the effort from that facility, where he also retains the position of quality manager. Marks's target is August of 1996 to become the next plant to achieve registration, with Guadalupe following close behind in September.

Delays in implementing QS-9000 are being experienced at three of the plants where key personnel turnover and new product launches have been a factor. The company hopes to attain QS-9000 registration of these three plants by December of 1996. It is imperative that upper plant management provide visible backing of the project to ensure that implementation schedules are met. Postponements only send the message to people that management is not really serious about the importance of QS-9000. Plants that are not serious about QS-9000 will be left out of the automotive supplier chain in the near future.

This case study is contributed by Brent Godfrey, Director of QS-9000 Implementation, Saturn Electronics & Engineering, Inc., Coopersville, Michigan.

CHAPTER 15

Team Approach to QS-9000

Stemco Inc.

GENERAL

- *Headquarters* : **Longview, Texas, U.S.A.**
- *Year Founded* : **1951**
- *Number of Employees* : **450**

QS-9000 SPECIFIC

- *Registered Location(s)* : **Longview, Texas, U.S.A.**
- *Number of Employees* : **450**
- *Registration Date* : **May 9, 1995**
- *Product(s)* : **Wheel-End Products, Exhaust Systems**
- *Tier I, II, III Supplier* : **Tier I and II**
- *Major Customer(s)* : **Ford, Navistarr, Paccar, Rockwell**
- *Annual Sales* : **U.S. $80 Million**

INTRODUCTION

Stemco's approach to QS-9000 used an 18-step method that coordinated four support areas as important foundations for achieving registration: quality management system design and implementation; education and training; registrar interaction and coordination; and internal and external support services. These support areas developed communication across organizational lines via the presence of senior management leadership commitment and employee awareness and involvement. QS-9000 became important for Stemco in strengthening our market presence with the original equipment manufacturers (OEMs) and improving our internal quality system.

BACKGROUND

Stemco Inc. is a division of Coltec Industries, a Fortune 1000 company, and represents a major segment of Coltec's automotive group (truck products). Stemco, founded in 1951, initially manufactured two products: mufflers and oil reservoirs. Four decades later, Stemco now designs and manufactures wheel-end products (including oil seals, hubcaps, and hubodometers), heavy-duty exhaust system products, and brake system accessories (including moisture ejectors and low-pressure indicators) for the medium- to heavy-duty truck market. Our customers are considered to be after-market distributors, international manufacturers, and original equipment manufacturers.

In 1993, Stemco began its journey to achieve ISO 9001 registration at its manufacturing facility in Longview, Texas. Later, in 1994, Stemco chose to pursue QS-9000 registration concurrently. What was the catalyst for Stemco's success? In large part, it can be attributed to the foundation laid in place for a total quality management system called total customer value (TCV). The company empowered its employees and involved them in quality teamwork. The 18-step implementation plan enacted to achieve registration is described in Figure 15–1.

MANAGEMENT OVERVIEW AND COMMITMENT

The first step of the process involved leadership commitment. Stemco began training the senior management team on the QS-9000 process and its benefits. The outcome initiated ownership of the process and quickly focused people on the job at hand. The management overview focused on two segments: (1) customer expectations and strategic business objectives, as Stemco wanted to become a significant player in the OEM market, and (2) the bottom-line benefits to be derived by achieving QS-9000 registration.

In the next phase, the senior management team fostered the registration process by selecting a cross-functional team and a management representative to establish and implement a QS-9000 plan. The cross-functional QS-9000 team members represented all

Stemco's ISO/QS-9000 Model Implementation Plan

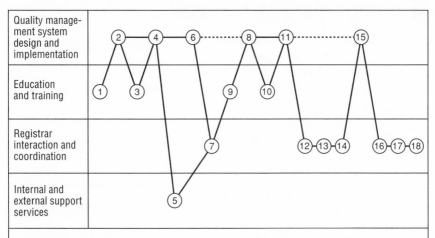

Quality manage- ment system design and implementation		
Education and training		
Registrar interaction and coordination		
Internal and external support services		

1. Management overview

2. Form steering committee, assign project personnel

3. Implementation and employee awareness training

4. Set implementation schedule

5. Gap analysis audit and corrective action plan

6. Submit registrar questionnaire and quotation

7. Registrar selection

8. Document quality system, implement corrections and conduct implementation

9. Documentation and job skills training

10. Auditor training

11. Conduct internal audits–corrective actions

12. Adequacy audit–corrective actions

13. Pre-registration audit (Registrar)– corrective actions

14. Assessment (Registrar)

15. Implement corrective actions and submit report to registrar

16. Review corrective actions

17. Issue certificate

18. Surveillance

levels and areas of the company. The team approach (TCV culture) provided a strong foundation for members to work as a cohesive group to resolve problems. Each of these members possessed skills in leadership, project management, communication, and documentation. It should be noted that the latter skill, documentation, was taught to each team member. The roles and responsibilities of the team included reviewing and approving procedures, setting priorities, selecting the registrar, providing training, and performing internal audits. A preselection of registration agencies was conducted to obtain literature and material.

EMPLOYEE AWARENESS, TRAINING, AND EDUCATION

Perhaps the single most important activity involves training and education. Throughout the entire implementation plan and even after registration, training was conducted and considered to be a never-ending journey. In the first phase of training, a QS-9000 overview was conducted for all employees in the company to achieve employee awareness. The second phase consisted of element-specific training conducted for each department (e.g., design and development for the product engineering de-

Perhaps the single most important activity involves training and education.

partment). The final phase was to train the QS-9000 team in the following areas: QS-9000, project management skills, documentation skills, team-building skills, and auditing skills.

By far, the most effective way of training is to "train the trainer." Stemco's management representative was the ISO facilitator who provided the bulk of training for the disciplines mentioned above. The ISO facilitator had the combined qualifications and skills of a quality auditor, total quality management facilitator, and a quality engineer. The team had to be knowledgeable about the elements of QS-9000 to accurately interpret and communicate information to the employees.

IMPLEMENTATION SCHEDULE AND GAP ANALYSIS

Step 4 of our implementation plan involved the team establishing the implementation schedule by mapping out the remaining activities needed to obtain registration. The schedule used ballpark dates and had flexibility. Again, training is the biggest hurdle. Once it is accomplished, the organization is ready to move forward with implementing the plan.

A system adequacy audit or gap analysis is performed to assess the organization's ability to meet the requirements of QS-9000. Usually, the audit is performed by an outside agency (consultant) or an unbiased third party. However, in Stemco's case, the gap analysis audit was performed by the QS-9000 management representative. The analysis worked out well, since the management representative was a new employee and had no perceived ideas or biases concerning Stemco's quality system. The audit revealed numerous areas for improvement, including document and data control, engineering design and development, manufacturing capabilities, and process control. In all, over 63 nonconformances or findings were documented for corrective action. The company took over six months to complete corrective action on 70 percent of the findings.

REGISTRAR SELECTION

The next process in the implementation plan involved following up preselection of registrars. Stemco chose four registrars and invited them to come to our facility and make a presentation. The QS-9000 team evaluated each registrar based on established criteria such as industry knowledge and reputation, location, accreditation body, costs, and ability to partner with our company. Each registrar was rated and given a score, and the highest scorer was awarded the business. After registrar selection, an established date for the final assessment and a tentative date for the preassessment was agreed upon. Stemco felt that a preassessment was required to familiarize the registrar with our process and to prepare our employees for the actual audit.

DOCUMENTATION AND TRAINING

Steps 8 and 9 of the implementation plan happen synergistically to start addressing concerns of the recent gap analysis audit. Therefore, the organization began documenting the quality system and implementing corrections. Stemco adopted the quality system documentation progression table from the *Quality System Requirements QS-9000* (August 1994 edition) as the foundation for the documentation system. The QS-9000 team completed training documentation (procedural writing). For example, the gap analysis uncovered that no procedures existed for design and development of new products. Therefore, we began drafting procedures for design and development. The product engineering group was responsible for drafting these procedures. We gained a complete buy-in from the engineers and instituted training. Afterward, the QS-9000 team representative for that area followed the procedures when launching a newly designed product.

Job skills training was conducted simultaneously to ensure that all employees had been properly trained or made aware of changes in procedures. Over 150 procedures were either written (newly created) or revised. After training, the employees were more inclined to formulate ideas to help the process. Everyone got on board the QS-9000 bandwagon for improvement. During this activity, a sense of ownership was felt by each employee of the organization since everyone had provided input. In addition, an auditor training course was conducted in-house for the QS-9000 team members to certify their knowledge of the requirements and the auditing process. The QS-9000 team was eager to go out and perform an audit.

INTERNAL AUDIT

The first internal system audit conducted by the QS-9000 team uncovered 48 major findings. The newly trained auditors documented findings against elements of QS-9000 and established procedures. Areas such as product engineering showed no evidence of the design development activity following newly established procedures for other (new) product launches. A major product development project lacked evidence of advanced product quality planning (APQP) activities such as design and process failure mode and effect analysis and design review.

Other areas, such as manufacturing and engineering, lacked control over drawings and specifications and changes associated with these documents. In the quality assurance area, evidence clearly showed that assigned corrective actions were not completed in a timely fashion according to procedure; some were shown to be outstanding for several months when the procedure required 30 days for completion. This internal system audit opened the eyes of our team members who function as auditors. The experience provided them with a deeper appreciation of how our quality system stacked up against QS-9000. Simply put, we had a tremendous opportunity ahead of us. The company took another six months to complete the corrective action plan on 75 percent of the findings. Most of this activity was conducted by small cross-functional teams (eight teams of four individuals) dedicated to resolve the findings. During that time, the QS-9000 team monitored the corrective action plans.

ADEQUACY AND PREREGISTRATION AUDIT

Stemco submitted the quality manual to the registrar for review. The registrar responded with minor corrections, then conducted a preassessment audit and found some major concerns. For example, a major finding in the design and development area was discrepancies in Stemco's internal audit that showed engineering procedures were not being followed. Two third-party auditors spent three days and uncovered 24 findings. The company took 45 days to complete corrective actions on 60 percent of the findings. It should be noted that the percentage of findings completed was based on activities completed in a normal span of time. However, other corrective actions requiring an extended time frame used a Gantt chart to illustrate steps taken for completion.

ASSESSMENT: THE REGISTRATION AUDIT

Stemco underwent the assessment in less than 45 days from the preassessment. Normally, an organization would require three months, minimum, after a preassessment to conduct a final assessment. Nevertheless, Stemco felt it was ready for the audit. The outcome cited four major areas for improvement, which delayed our recommendation for registration. In other words, Stemco did not receive registration on the first try.

The four areas cited as showstoppers were document and data control, corrective and preventive action, production part approval process, and internal audits.

CONFORMANCE PLAN

The document and data control issue exposed our system merging over to a new on-line computer system. The changes to documents such as drawings were not updated in the new system. To resolve this problem, the following corrective action plan was initiated: (1) update all engineering print files on the new computer system as well as each control area, (2) procedually change and address how control files will be handled and who will be responsible, and (3) provide training for employees responsible for document control. Document and data control is a never-ending gap to try to close; continued area awareness training on a quarterly basis helped reduce document and data control issues.

The corrective and preventive action system encompasses four areas of the company: customer complaints, warranty and product returns, internal process and product, and external supplier. The problem of closure was not evident for each area. The solution was to verify closure and implementation effectiveness. In the internal process and product, warranty, and product return process, the corrective actions are placed in Pareto format and then acted upon. This process lessens the repetitive offenders and focuses on root causes to solve the biggest problems. In the customer complaints area, corrective action is handled in a timely manner. The sales representative communicates Stemco's corrective action process back to the customer for closure. The supplier corrective action closures are monitored on an individual basis, which involves a number of successful shipments. In other words, by monitoring these shipments, we can tell whether the supplier has corrected the problem based on the response and several successful shipments.

Another area for improvement was internal audits. All too often, we assume corrective action has been taken and closed out, when nothing could be further from the truth. Repeatedly we found closure to audits incomplete. A signal was uncovered during our first internal system audit that identified lack of control for drawings. This same problem was cited in the registration audit. To resolve this issue, an auditor would verify closure within a time frame of 30 to 60 days. Enough time has elapsed to verify closure and system effectiveness. If closure is not accomplished, the auditor will reissue an audit finding to show that corrective action is still open.

The production part approval process was revised to reflect that document changes to production parts will be communicated to the customer and submission level status approval will be obtained from the customer.

The above resolution to the four areas was completed in 45 days. Later, a limited registration audit was conducted by the registrar for compliance of the four areas. The audit was successful, and Stemco was recommended for registration to ISO 9001 and QS-9000. From start to finish, the entire process took 18 months.

SUMMARY

Any organization undergoing a registration audit would do some things differently if it had another chance. Our organization learned several things to improve upon. The first improvement is to continue to monitor audits on a frequent basis to check how well the organization is doing. Quarterly audits are effective because the organization and employees see continued activities for improvement. The second improvement involves closure of audits to verify implementation effectiveness. We must continue to evaluate the system to see if improvements are worthwhile and contributing to the bottom line. And last, senior management must continue to foster improvement by training our employees on tools for improving the process and product innovation.

The future of our company relies on employees possessing the entrepreneurial spirit to take us into the 21st century. The QS-9000 quality system lays that foundation.

This case study is contributed by Michael S. Winters, Quality Manager with Stemco Inc., Longview, Texas.

CHAPTER 16

Journey to Registration

Zener Electronics

GENERAL

- *Headquarters* : **Houston, Texas, U.S.A.**
- *Year Founded* : **1976**
- *Number of Employees* : **300**

QS-9000 SPECIFIC

- *Registered Location(s)* : **Houston, Texas, U.S.A.**
- *Number of Employees* : **200**
- *Registration Date* : **May 5, 1995**
- *Product(s)* : **Engine Control Modules**
- *Tier I, II, III Supplier* : **Tier II**
- *Major Customer(s)* : **Delco Electronics Corporation**
- *Annual Sales* : **Not Provided**

INTRODUCTION

The purpose of this case study is to share our journey to QS-9000 registration. QS-9000 registration can mean different things to different companies. It can mean prestige, consistency, higher quality, less scrap, or higher profits. At Zener Electronics it means that we have proved to ourselves and our customers that we are fully committed to installing and maintaining an outstanding quality system. This results in higher customer satisfaction. It means that we have a quality system that it is very important in opening doors to potential new business.

Initially Zener Electronics decided to pursue General Motors' Targets for Excellence, then ISO 9002 registration, but later changed to QS-9000. It took us 16 months from the time of the management decision to become ISO 9002 registered to the day of QS-9000 third-party assessment. Companies can take different routes on their own journey, different avenues, and different approaches.

BACKGROUND

Zener Electronics was founded in October 1976 in Houston, Texas, as an AC-Delco sales and service representative. As Zener grew and added new employees, management instilled a philosophy of quality first in a can-do company. In 1981 Zener commenced working with electronic control modules for Delco Electronics Corporation. The continued growth of Zener Electronics has been steady, from a single figure start to almost 300 employees, owing it all to the philosophy of quality first.

In January 1992, Fred Jones Enterprises, Inc., headquartered in Oklahoma City, Oklahoma, purchased Zener Electronics. Zener became part of the Fred Jones electronics division. Currently Zener has four operating divisions. The electronic control module division is ISO 9002 and QS-9000 registered.

The leadership and management of Zener Electronics are fully committed and involved in the quality process of the company. From its founding 19 years ago, Zener has striven to be a leader in customer service and satisfaction in the automotive industry. Company senior managers have created an environment in which quality of products and service to the customer are the key objectives.

GETTING STARTED

In early 1991, the management of Zener Electronics began pursuing Targets for Excellence. In 1992 plans were changed to pursue ISO 9002 registration. It was apparent that the road to registration would lead us into many areas of quality that would need to be addressed by an expert in the quality area. After analyzing the ISO 9002 requirements, managers decided they needed more expertise if they were to succeed in this endeavor. Zener hired a quality systems manager to head the quest for registration.

After a few weeks of investigation, the quality systems manager arrived at a decision-making point. In order to meet ISO 9002 requirements, certain areas of the operation needed to be separated from the main manufacturing department and two new departments would need to be formed. The separations from the manufacturing department included the stockroom and quality assurance personnel. The new departments developed were purchasing and document control. The separation and addition of these departments gave Zener Electronics a better structure to build from and added clarity to the operation. Once these basic items were established, the journey to registration was well under way.

In April 1994, Delco Electronics Corporation informed us that we needed to change from ISO 9002 to the new upcoming quality system requirements, and in November 1994 sent us the latest version of *QS-9000*. Our first step was to find out what QS-9000 requirements were. At the time, our quality system setup for ISO 9002 was nearing completion. We now had to interpret the new requirements and make any necessary adjustments and additions.

LEADERSHIP COMMITMENT

One problem that we encountered was continuous involvement. We had to constantly remind each other that this was a new way of life. Everyone had to stay abreast of what was going on, provide ideas, and provide guidance. We all had to access our system every day, make improvements, and share information.

To make this journey successful, there has to be total commitment from top management. This commitment must then filter down through the ranks, to the next levels of management, and so on until everyone is informed, involved, and committed to the journey.

To make this journey successful, there has to be total commitment from top management.

One item that everyone needs to remember is that this is not a quality assurance program. It does not belong to the quality department. It is a process involving everyone, and that means *everyone*. It belongs to the company.

MANAGEMENT RESPONSIBILITIES

One of the first items accomplished by our management was defining and documenting its policy for quality and its commitment to quality. Management wrote the mission statement and the quality policy. This was a team effort of all managers.

The next phase was to ensure that the quality policies were understood and implemented at all levels of our organization. We have a diverse group of employees, and one of the problems we faced was a slight language barrier. To overcome this, we had our quality policies translated into the native languages of the three main groups of people. Once this was done, we had volunteers from those groups hold meetings with the employees to explain the purpose of the policies and what it meant to each worker.

Our original plan was to have each employee memorize the mission statement. We then asked ourselves, "Does this really accomplish the goal?" The answer was no. We then changed our approach to having employees tell us what the mission statement meant to them. How did each employee's work fit into the words of the statement? What did the employee do or need to do to meet the needs of the mission statement? From our experience, we recommend that all employees should interpret the mission statement or quality policy. They can express how they and their work tie in, instead of merely repeating a memorized statement.

When studying element 4.1 (Management Responsibility), we took a close look at subelement 4.1.2 (Organization). We reviewed all of our employees' job descriptions. Some of them were modified to include responsibility, authority, and interrelationship of other personnel. Our quality systems manager was appointed as the company's management representative. The process of ISO 9002, and later QS-9000, was his primary function. This does not mean that the management representative must always do all of the work; the management representative's main function is to guide everyone's efforts in the right direction.

One area to pay particular attention to is management review. When writing the quality systems manual or procedures, make sure it defines the intervals of the review and sticks to those intervals. If a section is included about reporting or reviewing of activities at the management review in the procedures or even job instructions, we recommend that a checklist be maintained to make sure all activities are actually reviewed. We included a reporting activity in several procedures and job instructions, but at first we did not have a checklist. We overlooked some items that we had said were going to be reviewed. We now maintain a checklist that includes the activities, a section for management approval for every item, and a date when the approval took place. This checklist also forms part of the records of the management review.

When reviewing the quality system, we recommend that part of the management review contain trends in quality and operational performance. The trends should be compared with progress toward overall business objectives. If the trends are favorable, continue with what is being done. If they are not favorable, develop priorities for prompt solutions and even longer-term planning.

USE OF CONSULTANTS

At Zener we considered using the services of consultants, but eventually decided against it. We felt that we would take more ownership of this process if we did it on our own. We also felt that we had enough expertise and experience, and that instead of paying for a consultant we could use those moneys elsewhere in this process.

The following are some deciding factors in whether to use a consultant:

1. What is the level of experience at the facility?
2. What amount of time does the company have available to thoroughly investigate and understand the requirements of the QS-9000?
3. Can the company afford the services of a consultant?
4. Will the company follow the recommendations of the consultant?
5. Will the employees be involved and committed if a consultant is used?

QUALITY PLANNING

A large part of the journey to registration is defining and documenting how the requirements for quality will be met or achieved.

If a company prepares control plans (quality plans), make sure that each plan is workable. In other words, don't make the control plan so large or so difficult that it can't be achieved.

Delco Electronics Corporation mainly defines the control plan with help from Zener. There were a few items that we thought were good ideas at the time, but to complete the plan would have taken thousands of dollars and the full-time effort of one to two people. Then there was the possibility that the process or product wouldn't improve. Don't have a control plan just to say there is one. Make sure that it is workable, that it is feasible, and that good benefits will come from it.

Part of the quality planning process includes the identification of suitable verification at appropriate stages in the realization of product. At Zener we use a unit traveler to identify verification of various stages of product flow. After product passes an operation or inspection station, the traveler is initialed by the operator. Our operation is a batch process, but similar techniques can be used for continuous flow operations.

Clarification of standards' acceptability is another important part of quality planning. Delco Electronics Corporation provides workmanship standards, but if there is any question we have the standard clarified.

When developing procedures and job instructions, if a quality record is needed or required, we identify what it is, how it is prepared, who keeps it, how long is it kept, and how or where it is kept.

GAP ANALYSIS

During the early stages of our journey, a gap analysis was performed. The purpose of this was to figure out where we were in relation to the requirements; in other words, we determined the gap between what was and what needed to be. If a very good operating quality system is in place, the gap will be less. There will probably have to be changes or modifications made, but not as many as in a company starting from scratch. During the gap analysis, many opportunities for improvements surfaced. These opportunities were assigned to teams as well as individuals for resolution.

EMPLOYEE AWARENESS AND INVOLVEMENT

Employee awareness and involvement are very important at the beginning of this process. Employees are the ones who will make this system work or not. Without their involvement and ideas, this would be a program with an ending, and not a process that will go on forever. The employees know better than anyone else their own methods for getting things done. They can provide the details of how their jobs are performed. They can try out procedures and job instructions before official finalization. Also, they must adhere to the procedures and job instructions regularly.

At the beginning of our journey, we at Zener made sure that all employees had the opportunity to provide their thoughts and ideas. This provided a basis for standardization for like jobs and shift-to-shift standardization. Some employees wrote their own job instructions.

During the past year, our training department has set up a continual training and employee involvement schedule. During these sessions, the procedures and job instructions are reviewed. Any new ideas are investigated for improvement and, if feasible, incorporated into revised procedures and job instructions. This method keeps all employees aware of what is going on and keeps them involved in the process.

Executive leadership and other management levels are also very important in this process. They must show that they are aware of the process and that they are continuously involved. They provide guidance and help remove obstacles.

DOCUMENT AND DATA CONTROL

At the beginning, there were a few procedures and job instructions already in place, but these documents were not under any type of control system. There were old versions as well as new versions being used. The formation of a document control system occurred in the early stages of our journey.

The first step in setting up our document control system was to define the format as well as what was required in all documents. Our document control process is formally written in five different procedures, described in the following paragraphs.

1. *Document control system*: Our first official "controlled" procedure, this system details the requirements for writing and controlling all levels of internal procedures. It defines the various steps of submission to document control, our numbering system, new procedures, modifying procedures, deleting procedures, formal approvals, and document release. It also describes how master documents are kept.

2. *Document change request*: This procedure describes the requirements for the document change request (DCR) form. This form is used whenever new documents are introduced into the quality management system, modifications have to be made to existing documents, or documents become obsolete and require removal from the system.

3. *Master document setup and serialization*: This procedure outlines the requirements in laying out formal procedural documents. It also includes the requirements for assigning and maintaining master document control numbers. The main format we have used is the military format, which is as follows:

    1.0 Topic/Section

      1.1 Subsection/Main Paragraph

        1.1.1 Subsection/Paragraph

          1.1.1.1 Paragraph

            1, 2, 3 or **A, B, C,** etc.   List

4. *Forms control*: This procedure outlines the requirements and responsibilities for submitting forms to the document control system. We have further defined that only forms that meet either of the following two requirements be controlled:

    a. The usage of the form must result in the form being retained as a company/quality record.

    b. The structure or layout of the form is so important to the user that controls must be placed over its alterations.

5. *Manuals*: This procedure outlines the requirements and responsibilities for controlling internal and external manuals. A few guidelines for our internal manuals are as follows:

    a. The manuals must contain a control page, introduction page, history page, and a table of contents.

    b. An appendix and glossary are optional.

    c. The manuals must be bound.

    d. Manuals submitted to document control with a document change request (DCR) will be controlled manuals.

    e. Manuals must be signed for by the recipient.

Externally controlled documentation is defined in a separate procedure. Our engineering group does this function. The procedure defines their responsibilities for routing and implementing customer-supplied controlled documents. We receive these documents either by fax or by mail. Their responsibilities include the following:

1. Verify that all copies are legible and that there are no typographical errors.
2. Check that any changes will not adversely affect production.
3. Check that any changes will not adversely affect operating costs.

If a discrepancy is noted or a question is raised during the verification and checking of the documents, the customer is notified by phone call, fax, or mail.

When no discrepancies are noted, the documentation is forwarded to document control for updating and distribution.

When setting up our document control system, we decided that there would be a full-time person in document control. We knew that there would be changes to procedures, new procedures added, and obsolete procedures that needed to be purged from the system. At times we have had to add additional help in this area due to the work load. Other organizations may use the same approach. Some factors to consider would be company size, how many procedures exist, and how often changes are expected.

PROCESS CONTROL

Delco Electronics Corporation's policy and procedures manual defines many of our processes. We have elected to use these documents as Level 2 procedures (quality operating procedures). We further describe processes that directly affect quality and have Level 3 procedures (job instruction sheets) written on these areas. The job instructions are written in detail so that a substitute person could read and follow the instructions and do the job without adversely affecting quality.

Delco Electronics Corporation has also provided criteria for workmanship that we must follow. These criteria are in the form of a workmanship standards manual. We have further enhanced this by adding representative samples and illustrations.

A QS-9000 company must have a process to ensure compliance with all applicable government safety and environmental regulations. We thought that we were in full compliance, but there was one thing we overlooked—an out-of-date fire inspection certificate. All local, state, and federal operating permits and inspection certificates must be up-to-date to be in full compliance with QS-9000.

We developed several job instructions as part of our preventive maintenance system. We have job instructions for the different types of equipment and tools we use. These job instruction sheets describe what maintenance activities are to take place, along with the time intervals. When setting up the procedures or job instructions, remember that records must be maintained. We have set up a recording sheet for each piece of equipment and tool. On that sheet is the date that preventive maintenance was performed, any adjustments that had to be made, and any parts that had to be replaced.

In each of our job instructions we have documented what each operation is responsible for. We also use travelers to maintain the flow of products, what has happened to the products, and what needs to happen. The traveler is a piece of paper that has check-off blocks to be initialed by operators as the unit is processed through their area of operation. If corrective action is needed at any stage of operation, we have detailed instructions on how it is to be performed, who performs it, and, if necessary, what means to use to prevent recurrence.

Our control plan contains process performance requirements for various characteristics. Delco Electronics Corporation defines most of the performance requirements. Whenever there are characteristics with performances that are either unstable or not capable, a reaction plan is initiated. These reaction plans are reviewed with the customer. Delco Electronics Corporation is always willing to help us with any problem or concern we may have. They listen to our suggestions as well as vice versa. It is to our mutual benefit to work things out together.

TRAINING

In any type of business, training is a key item whether it is formal training, one-on-one training, or on-the-job training. Before Zener decided to pursue ISO 9002 and QS-9000, we had already established a training department. Some training items were in procedure-type format, but most were not. Those that were in procedure-type format were documented through our document control system; those that were not, were documented and submitted through the document control system. We had to modify a basic training record activity. We now have records of training as part of each employee's personnel record and computerized training records. We had to develop a system for evaluating the training effectiveness. This is proving to be very successful. It enables us to modify any existing training we have as well as to add items to our training program.

CONTROL OF INSPECTION, MEASURING, AND TEST EQUIPMENT

In our journey to registration, one of the many areas that required our careful attention was the calibration of measurement and test equipment. Due to the extensive QS-9000 requirements for this area, a complete assessment of our existing calibration procedures needed to be performed. After performing the assessment, our shortcomings were revealed and areas that needed development and adjustments were identified.

Before our journey had begun, we had an in-house calibration system. We had personnel who checked and adjusted test and measuring equipment. The problem was that these in-house calibrations were not made against certified equipment having a known valid relationship to internationally or nationally recognized standards.

The first step in the control of equipment was to identify what measurements had to be made and what accuracy was required. Then appropriate equipment was selected that was capable of the needed accuracy and precision. All inspection, measuring, and testing equipment that could affect product quality was identified. Each piece of equipment had its own unique identifier. Procedures and job instructions were then written on the method of calibration for all equipment. Part of our calibration system includes the safeguarding of the equipment from adjustments that would invalidate the calibration settings. We use a "void seal" method of ensuring that adjustments cannot be made. These seals are placed in locations where, if they are broken, the equipment will be placed out of service until rechecked.

One of the areas where modifications needed to be made was maintaining all calibration records. From the surface, the record-keeping process seemed tedious and unnecessary, but after record-keeping procedures were implemented, they proved to be very helpful. When used properly, calibration records provide a variety of information. The information can range from determining calibration schedules to identifying trends. This information is vital for the quality of any product. If the test equipment being used is not reliable, there will always be a question of quality.

Another area revealed to us by our initial assessment of our calibration system was the realization that some equipment would slip through the cracks and never be calibrated. Two procedures were developed in order to prevent this from happening. First, an equipment-receiving inspection process was developed for any new equipment arriving at our facility. The purpose of this process was to identify all new equipment and its need for calibration. The process entails assigning the equipment a unique number for identification purposes and building a physical file in order to include the equipment with all other calibratable items. Second, a database was developed in order to track all of our equipment. All relevant equipment information is kept in the database, which in turn provides a variety of report options available to us. Basically, what was accomplished by developing the two processes listed above was an identification and tracking system that ensures the calibration of all measurement and test equipment.

INTERNAL QUALITY AUDITS

Internal audits form an integral part of the quality system. At Zener, we conducted four separate internal audits in 10 months. The first audit was an adequacy audit for ISO 9002. The purpose of an adequacy audit is to check that the documentation system addresses all of the requirements of the standard. The second audit was a compliance audit for ISO 9002. In the compliance audit, we checked that our quality system is operating and meeting the requirements of the standard, or determining its effectiveness. The third audit was a compliance audit for QS-9000, and our fourth audit was a second compliance audit for QS-9000.

In our procedure for internal audits, we state that our auditors will be trained by either an external or an internal training program. We currently send our auditor candidates to an external training program. After successful completion of the training program, the auditors are placed on the audit team.

QS-9000 requires that the internal audits be scheduled on the basis of the status and importance of the activity to be audited. For the first three audits, we decided that all areas were of equal status and importance. The fourth audit was performed by a new group of internal auditors, and because of this we again decided to treat all areas as having equal status and importance. The new audit group needed the experience, and we wanted them to see how everything tied together. Based on our own internal audits and our third-party audit, we can modify our method of determining status and importance.

The results of the internal audits have to be recorded and brought to the attention of the personnel having responsibility in the area being audited. Then the management personnel responsible for the area must take timely corrective action on any deficiencies found. Part of the corrective action should include the methods used in determining the corrective actions. Once corrective actions have taken place, there must be follow-up activities to verify and record those corrective actions taken. We make sure we checked and recorded the effectiveness of the corrective actions taken. Another item of awareness is that the internal auditor must be independent of those having direct responsibility for the activity being audited.

The results of any internal audits must be part of the regularly scheduled management review activities. During this review, we covered any deficiencies that were found, corrective actions taken, actions to prevent recurrence, and the effectiveness of the corrective actions. At Zener, we use what we call an NCR, or nonconformance report. There are areas on the NCR for the deficiencies found, corrective action, and actions to prevent recurrence, but no place for verifying the effectiveness of the corrective actions. Our NCR is being modified. By doing this all on one form, we are creating a checklist for closing out a deficiency.

REGISTRAR SELECTION

At Zener, we spent quite a bit of time on the registrar selection phase. Registrars were contacted for interviews. We also requested names of companies that the registrars had registered. Some contact was made to a few of these companies. We asked the companies if they would recommend the registrar and for any likes and dislikes. We wanted a registrar that was accredited in both the United States and in the European arena to assure that our registration would be recognized worldwide. We were also in favor of the registrar being in close proximity.

Cost of services is a big item to consider. Different registrars charge different rates for basically the same services. When requesting quotes from registrars, we made sure that we thoroughly understood what the charges were for and exactly how they were calculated. We received quotes from three different registrars that showed several thousands of dollars' difference. We learned that sometimes what appears to be the high quote turns out to be the low quote. There may be extensive travel involved that has been left off the quote, the number of audit days needed may be incorrect, special reports may have been included in one quote but not others, and so on.

Another key item is customer service of the registrar. If it takes a considerable amount of time for a registrar to return calls or memos, considering a different registrar may be beneficial.

THE REGISTRATION AUDIT

Once a registrar is selected, an audit schedule is developed. The first step of the audit process is the audit of the quality manual. This normally will take place at least two weeks prior to the on-site audit. We felt that we had a very good quality manual, but many questions were raised. All questions had to be answered prior to the on-site audit.

Our registration audit covered a three-day period by two auditors. It is an experience. We had opening and closing meetings each day, with the final closing meeting on the third day.

We had selected several people to be guides or escorts. These people escorted the auditors throughout the process. They answered many questions themselves, provided records, gathered procedures for review, and stood by while the auditors addressed other employees. To us, it seemed that those three days during the audit were the longest days in history. We knew we had a good system in place, but we were always anxious for the final results. The auditors were very thorough in their audit. It seemed like they had the knack for finding that one error on that one record out of hundreds of records.

At the end of the third day came the moment of truth. All of our managers were in the conference room awaiting the final results. Although the meeting lasted only 30 minutes, it seemed like hours. All of the managers were deep in thought about the last 16 months. Did we truly have a quality system worthy of registration to QS-9000? Did we overlook anything? Was there anything that we could have or should have done differently? Will we make it or not? The auditors told us the results. We had some nonconformances, but we were recommended for a conditional pass. This meant that we had 30 days to address the nonconformances and provide written results of our actions to the registrar. We addressed the nonconformances well within the 30-day time frame. We waited again for results. They came: We had to revise our corrective actions on some of the nonconformances. We did. We waited for results. They came: Again, it was revision time. The time frame from the on-site audit to the day of official registration was 48 days, or 35 working days. We made it!

THE SURVEILLANCE AUDIT

Six months after registration, it was time for the surveillance audit. I am writing this portion four days after our first surveillance audit. This time the audit lasted one day with two auditors. Like that of the original audit, this was a long day. We have spent the last six months refining, redefining, addressing, and keeping everyone involved in this process. We were hoping that all of our efforts over the last six months were fruitful. We gathered in the conference room for the results. The auditors expressed their thanks to the escorts and managers for all of their help. They went over a few nonconformances. In our minds we were thinking, "Did we make it?" The recommendation from the lead auditor was that we keep our registration pending corrective actions on the nonconformances. We made it again! Because most of the nonconformances are minor in nature, we will have no trouble making the few corrections.

Even though the first surveillance audit was only four days ago, we have already identified items that we want to modify and improve, and are making plans for the next six months.

SUMMARY

We have achieved QS-9000 registration. Not many companies can say this yet. It is not an easy task. It takes dedication, involvement, motivation, leadership, and commitment. It is the work of everyone.

We are starting the QS-9000 registration process in another area of our business. We have given ourselves a six-month time frame to get it accomplished. This may sound aggressive, but we have much of the foundation already. A whole different group will be involved, but it can be done.

The following are some lessons we have learned:

1. Stay committed to this process at all times.
2. Keep everyone informed and up-to-date.
3. Always look for better ways of doing things.

4. Always search for improvement ideas.

5. Periodically reread the *Quality System Requirements QS-9000*.

When deciding whether to pursue QS-9000 registration, keep in mind that it is not a program with an end. It is a process that keeps going. It is not a quality assurance process. It is the function and responsibility of everyone in the company. One person can lead the efforts, but one person cannot do it alone.

This case study is contributed jointly by Roger W. Koepp, Quality Systems Manager, and Robert Burdett, Assistant Manager of Technology, with Zener Electronics, Houston, Texas.

APPENDIX A

Case Contributors

Robert Burdett is Assistant Manager of Technology with Zener Electronics, Houston, Texas. He has been involved with the technical area in manufacturing for five years and has been active in the setup and implementation of process changes and additions, statistical process control, and the adherence to customer requirements. Mr. Burdett is currently performing various quality engineering tasks and ensuring the maintenance of the QS-9000 quality system.

Richard H. Busch II is TQM Manager and Excellence Facilitator with J. B. Tool & Machine, Inc., Wapakoneta, Ohio. He is a panel member of Lima Technical College and Apollo Vocational School in Ohio. Mr. Busch is a requested speaker at universities and manufacturing convention seminars and a recipient of numerous awards nationally and internationally for exceptional performance in the manufacturing arena.

David M. Carter is Quality Assurance Senior Administrator with Delphi Saginaw Steering Systems, Saginaw, Michigan. He has a bachelor of science degree in mechanical engineering from Michigan Technological University, Houghton, Michigan. He currently serves on the divisional quality assurance staff and has been engaged in the QS-9000 implementation process from its beginning.

Diane M. Fries is Quality Assurance Manager with Delphi Saginaw Steering Systems, Saginaw, Michigan. Sloan Fellow Ms. Fries holds a master of science degree in management from the Massachusetts Institute of Technology, Cambridge, Massachusetts, and a master of business administration degree and a bachelor of business administration degree in accounting from Ohio University, Athens, Ohio. She is a certified public accountant and belongs to the Michigan Association of CPAs and the American Society for Quality Control. Ms. Fries, Manager, QS-9000 Implementation, is the executive champion of the registration effort.

Brent Godfrey is Director of QS-9000 Implementation for Saturn Electronics & Engineering, Inc., Coopersville, Michigan. He has been quality manager for their Coopersville, Michigan, plant since August 1993. He holds bachelor of science degrees in mechanical engineering and in bioengineering from the University of Michigan at Ann Arbor. Mr. Godfrey is also a quality engineer, certified by the American Society for Quality Control, and is licensed as a professional engineer by the State of Michigan.

Richard H. Hamood is General Supervisor of Quality Assurance with Delphi Saginaw Steering Systems, Saginaw, Michigan. He is currently serving as Divisional QS-9000 Joint Coordinator. Mr. Hamood has been working for General Motors for 23 years in various capacities. He holds an associate degree from Macomb College, Macomb, Michigan. Mr. Hamood is a Certified ISO 9000 lead auditor, a member of the American Society for Quality Control, and a senior member of the Society of Manufacturing Engineers.

Daniel J. Henry, Jr., is President and Chief Executive Officer of Laser Specialists, Inc., Fraser, Michigan. He has a BA and a JD from the University of Detroit, Michigan, and an MA from the University of Wyoming, Laramie, Wyoming. Through Laser Specialists, Inc., Mr. Henry is a member of the American Society for Quality Control, the Automotive Industry Action Group, the Michigan Tooling Association, and the Precision Metalforming Association.

James F. Jackson is UAW QS-9000 Coordinator with Delphi Saginaw Steering Systems, Saginaw, Michigan. He has an AS in management and supervision, and a visual communication degree from Calhoun College, Alabama. Mr. Jackson is a member of the American Society for Quality Control. He has been working for Delphi Saginaw Steering Systems for more than 16 years.

Bruce G. Janowsky is Chief Financial Officer of the Jamestown Container Companies, Falconer, New York. Mr. Janowsky has a master of science degree in business administration from Carnegie-Mellon University and a bachelor of science degree in economics from Allegheny College.

Roger W. Koepp is Quality Systems Manager with Zener Electronics, Houston, Texas. He was the quality assurance assistant manager during the implementation phase at Zener Electronics and was promoted to his current position after QS-9000 registration. Mr. Koepp was selected as an honored member of Who's Who Worldwide for 1993–94.

Tom Lareau is the United Auto Workers' Quality Representative at Rouge Steel Company, Dearborn, Michigan. He has been employed by Rouge Steel since 1972. Mr. Lareau holds a master of arts degree in education from the University of Michigan, a master of science degree in administration from Central Michigan University, and a bachelor of general studies degree from the University of Michigan at Dearborn. He is a member of the Iron and Steel Society, and the American Arbitration Association.

Edward Lawson is Vice President of Quality Assurance for Aetna Industries, Inc., which is based in Center Line, Michigan. He has been working in the field of quality management for more than 20 years, both in the United States and in Europe. Mr. Lawson is a senior member of the American Society for Quality Control and the Society of Manufacturing Engineers. He is certified by the American Society for Quality Control as a quality engineer and quality auditor.

Michael McDonald is QS-9000 Management Representative for Rouge Steel Company, Dearborn, Michigan. He holds a bachelor of science degree in metallurgical engineering from Michigan Technological University, Houghton, Michigan. Mr. McDonald is a member of the American Society for Quality Control, and the Iron and Steel Society, and is active in the American Iron and Steel Institute.

Joseph M. Palmeri is Corporate Quality Director with Jamestown Container Companies, Jamestown, New York. He holds a master's degree in package engineering from the Rochester Institute of Technology, and a bachelor's degree in economics from Niagara University.

John A. Paroff is Technical Director with Drake Products Corporation, Grand Rapids, Michigan. He has a bachelor's degree in chemical engineering from Pennsylvania State University and a master's degree in mathematics from the University of Akron. Mr. Paroff is a senior member of the American Society for Quality Control. He is certified by the American Society for Quality Control as a quality engineer and a certified reliability engineer. He is also a registered professional engineer.

Richard A. Shoop is Corporate Director of Quality at Promotional Trim Conversions, Inc., Lorain, Ohio. He holds a PhD in mathematics from Kent State University, where he served as a tenured member of the faculty for 14 years prior to founding a quality systems consulting group, Shoop/Symons & Company, in 1981. Dr. Shoop is a member of the American Society for Quality Control. He is certified by the American Society for Quality Control as a quality engineer.

Michael Stoeckel is Director of Business Development for MascoTech Body Systems & Assembly, Brighton, Michigan. He holds a bachelor of science degree in business administration from Ohio State University. He is currently an executive member of the American Marketing Association, an associate member of the Society of Automotive Engineers, and a member of the Automotive Market Research Council.

Brian H. Storms is Packaging Engineer with Jamestown Container Companies, Jamestown, New York. He holds a bachelor of science degree in packaging science from Rochester Institute of Technology, and an associate degree in applied science in mechanical engineering technology from the State University of New York.

Michael S. Winters is Quality Manager with Stemco Inc., Longview, Texas. He holds a bachelor's degree from the University of Missouri and a master of business administration degree from Amber University. Mr. Winters is a member of the American Society for Quality Control, and a Registrar Accreditation Board auditor.

John Yeung is Quality Manager with Polywheels Manufacturing Ltd., Oakville, Ontario, Canada. He holds a bachelor's degree in chemical engineering from the University of Toronto, Ontario, Canada. He is a licensed professional engineer of the Province of Ontario, Canada. Mr. Yeung is also a member of the American Society for Quality Control and the Society of Automotive Engineers.

APPENDIX B

QS-9000 Registrars

Appendix B contains a list of registrars offering third-party auditing and registration services to QS-9000. As of this writing, the following registrars are QS-9000 qualified. This list is provided for information purposes only and may change over time. Internet users can access ASQC's home page at http://www.asqc.org/9000/qsregist. html for the latest information on QS-9000 registrars.

ABS Quality Evaluations, Inc.
16855 Northchase Drive
Houston, TX 77060-6008, USA
Tel: (713) 873-9400
Fax: (713) 874-9564
Accrediting body: RvA, RAB

A.G.A. Quality
8501 E. Pleasant Valley Road
Cleveland, OH 44131, USA
Tel: (216) 524-4990
Fax: (216) 642-3463
Accrediting body: RvA, RAB

American Quality Assessors (AQA)
1201 Main Street, Suite 2010
Columbia, SC 29202, USA
Tel: (803) 779-8150
Fax: (803) 779-8109
Accrediting body: RAB

AT&T Quality Registrar (AT&T QR)
650 Liberty Avenue
Union, NJ 07083, USA
Tel: (908) 851-3058
Fax: (908) 851-3158
Accrediting body: RAB

British Standards Institution (BSI QA)
P.O. Box 375
Milton Keynes, MK14 6LL, United Kingdom
Tel: 44-90-822-0908
Fax: 44-90-823-1826
Accrediting body: RvA, UKAS

British Standards Institution (BSI QA)
8000 Towers Crescent Drive, Suite 1350

Vienna, VA 22182, USA
Tel: (703) 760-7828
Fax: (703) 761-2770
Accrediting body: RvA

Bureau Veritas Quality International (BVQI)
West Blaak 7
3012 KC Rotterdam
Post Box 2705
3000 CS Rotterdam
The Netherlands
Tel: 31-10-403-1666
Fax: 31-10-414-5763
Accrediting body: RvA

Bureau Veritas Quality International (North America), Inc. (BVQI)
North American Central Offices
509 North Main Street
Jamestown, NY 14701, USA
Tel: (716) 484-9002
Fax: (716) 484-9003
Accrediting body: RAB

Det Norske Veritas Certification, Inc. (DNV)
16340 Park Ten Place, Suite 100
Houston, TX 77084, USA
Tel: (713) 579-9003
Fax: (713) 579-1360
Accrediting body: RAB

Det Norske Veritas Industry, Inc. (DNVI)
Haasprechtstraat 7
P.O. Box 9599
3007 AN Rotterdam
The Netherlands
Tel: 31-10-479-8600
Fax: 31-10-479-7141
Accrediting body: RvA

Entela, Inc.
Quality System Registration Division
3033 Madison Avenue SE
Grand Rapids, MI 49548, USA
Tel: (616) 247-0515 / (800) 888-3787
Fax: (616) 247-7527
Accrediting body: RvA, RAB

Inchcape Testing Services
Intertek Services Corporation
313 Speen Street, Suite 200
Natick, MA 01760, USA
Tel: (508) 647-5147
Fax: (508) 647-6714
Accrediting body: RvA, RAB

KPMG Quality Registrar
150 John F. Kennedy Parkway
Short Hills, NJ 07078, USA
Tel: (800) 716-5595 or (201) 912-6552
Fax: (201) 912-6050
Accrediting body: RvA, RAB

Lloyd's Register Quality Assurance Limited (LRQA)
33–41 Newark Street, Riverview Historical Plaza II
Hoboken, NJ 07030, USA
Tel: (201) 963-1111
Fax: (201) 963-3299
Accrediting body: RAB

Lloyd's Register Quality Assurance Limited (LRQA)
Norfolk House, Wellesley Road
Croydon, CR9 2DT, United Kingdom
Tel: 44-1-816-886882
Fax: 44-1-816-818146
Accrediting body: RvA

National Quality Assurance, Ltd. (NQA)
Gainsborough House
Houghton Regif
Dunstable, LU5 5ZX
United Kingdom
Tel: 44-1-582-866766
Fax: 44-1-582-866700
Accrediting body: UKAS

NSF International
3475 Plymouth Road
P.O. Box 130140
Ann Arbor, MI 48113-0140, USA
Tel: (313) 769-8010
Fax: (313) 769-0109
Accrediting body: RvA

OMNEX Automotive Quality Systems Registrar, Inc.
P.O. Box 15019
Ann Arbor, MI 48106, USA
Tel: (313) 480-9940
Fax: (313) 480-9941
Accrediting body: RAB

Quality Management Institute (QMI)
Sussex Centre
90 Burnhamthorpe Road West, Suite 300
Mississauga, Ontario L5B 3C3, Canada
Tel: (905) 272-3920
Fax: (905) 272-8503
Accrediting body: RvA, RAB

Quality Systems Registrars, Inc. (QSR)
13873 Park Center Road, Suite 217
Herndon, VA 22071-3279, USA
Tel: (703) 478-0241
Fax: (703) 478-0645
Accrediting body: RvA, RAB

SGS International Certification Services, Inc.
Meadow Office Complex
301 Route 17 North
Rutherford, NJ 07070, USA
Tel: (800) 747-9047 or (201) 935-1500
Fax: (201) 935-4555
Accrediting body: RAB

SGS Yarsley International Certification Services Ltd.
Trowers Way
Redhill Surrey RH1 2JN
United Kingdom
Tel: 44-1-737-768445
Fax: 44-1-737-761229
Accrediting body: UKAS

Smithers Quality Assessments, Inc. (SQA)
425 West Market Street
Akron, OH 44303-2099, USA
Tel: (216) 762-7441 or 4231
Fax: (216) 762-7447
Accrediting body: RvA

Steel Related Industries Quality System Registrars (SRI)
2000 Corporate Drive, Suite 450
Wexford, PA 15090, USA
Tel: (412) 934-9000
Fax: (412) 935-6825
Accrediting body: RvA, RAB

TUV America, Inc.
5 Cherry Hill Drive
Danvers, MA 01923, USA
Tel: (508) 777-7999
Fax: (508) 762-8414
Accrediting body: RAB

TUV Essen
2099 Gateway Place, Suite 200
San Jose, CA 95110, USA
Tel: (408) 441-7888
Fax: (408) 441-7111
Accrediting body: RAB

TUV Rheinland of North America, Inc.
North American Headquarters
12 Commerce Road
Newtown, CT 06470, USA
Tel: (203) 426-0888
Fax: (203) 270-8883
Accrediting body: RvA, RAB

Underwriters Laboratories Inc. (UL)
1285 Walt Whitman Road
Melville, NY 11747-3081, USA
Tel: (516) 271-6200
Fax: (516) 423-5657
Accrediting body: RvA, RAB

APPENDIX C

QS-9000 Accreditation Bodies

Appendix C contains a list of accreditation bodies recognized by Chrysler, Ford, and General Motors to qualify registrars for QS-9000. As of this writing, these accreditation bodies are recognized worldwide. This list is provided for information purposes only and may change over time. Internet users can access ASQC's home page at http://www.asqc.org/9000/accredit.html for the latest information on QS-9000 accreditation bodies.

Australia and New Zealand

Joint Accreditation System of Australia and New Zealand (JAS-ANZ)
P. O. Box 164
Civic Square Act 2608, Australia
Tel: 61-6-276-1999
Fax: 61-6-276-2041

Canada

Standards Council of Canada (SCC)
45 O'Connor Street, Suite 1200
Ottawa, Ontario, Canada K1P 6N7
Tel: (613) 238-3222
Fax: (613) 995-4564

Finland

Finnish Accreditation Service (FINAS)
P.O. Box 239
Lonnrotinkatu 37
Fin-00181 Helsinki, Finland
Tel: 358-0-616-71
Fax: 358-0-616-73-41

Germany

TGA - Tragergemeinschaft für Akkreditierung GmbH
Stresemannallee 13
60596 Frankfurt/M, Germany
Tel: 49-69-6300-9111
Fax: 49-69-6300-9144

Italy

Sistema Nazionale per l'Accreditamento degli Organismi di Certificazione (SINCERT)
Via Battistotti Sassi 11
20133 Milano, Italy
Tel: 39-2-71-92-02 or 39-2-71-96-64
Fax: 39-2-71-90-55

Japan

Japan Accreditation Board (JAB)
Akasaka Royal Building Annex
6-18 Akasaka 7 Chrome, Minato-ku
Tokyo 107, Japan
Tel: 81-3-556-103-75
Fax: 81-3-556-103-76

Netherlands

Raad voor Accreditatie (RvA)
Postbus 2768
3500 GT Utecht
The Netherlands
Tel: 31-30-239-45-00
Fax: 31-30-239-45-39

Norway

Justervesenet-Norweigian Metrology and Accreditation Service (NMAS)
P.O. Box 6832 St. Olavs Plass
N-1030 Oslo, Norway
Tel: 47-22-20-02-26
Fax: 47-22-20-77-72

Spain

Entidad Nacional de Acreditacion (ENAC)
CL. Serrano, 240-7th Floor
Madrid 28016, Spain
Tel: 34-1-457-32-89
Fax: 34-1-458-62-80

Sweden

Swedish Board for Accreditation and Conformity Assessment (SWEDAC)
P. O. Box 878
SE-501 15
Boras, Sweden
Tel: 46-33-17-77-45
Fax: 46-33-10-13-92

Switzerland

Swiss Accreditation Service (SAS)
Swiss Federal Office of Metrology
Lindenweg 50
3084 Wabern, Switzerland
Tel: 41-31-963-31-11
Fax: 41-31-963-32-10

United Kingdom

United Kingdom Accreditation Service (UKAS)
Audley House
13 Palace Street
London SW1E 5HS, United Kingdom
Tel: 44-1-712-337111
Fax: 44-1-712-335115

United States of America

Registrar Accreditation Board (RAB)
611 East Wisconsin Avenue
P. O. Box 3005
Milwaukee, WI 53201-3005, USA
Tel: (414) 272-8575 or (800) 248-1946
Fax: (414) 765- 8661

Resources

American Association for Laboratory Accreditation (A2LA)
656 Quince Orchard Road, #620
Gaithersburg, MD 20878-1409, USA
Tel: (301) 670-1377
Fax: (301) 869-1495

American National Standards Institute (ANSI)
11 West 42nd Street, 13th floor
New York, NY 10036, USA
Tel: (212) 642-4900
Fax: (212) 398-0023
Web site: http://www.ansi.org

American Society for Quality Control (ASQC)
611 East Wisconsin Avenue
P.O. Box 3005
Milwaukee, WI 53202, USA
Tel: (414) 272-8575 or (800) 248-1946
Fax: (414) 765-8661
Web site:
http://www.asqc.org/~9000

Automotive Industry Action Group (AIAG)
26200 Lasher Road, Suite 200
Southfield, MI 48034, USA
Tel: (810) 358-3570
Fax: (810) 358-3253
Web site: http://www.aiag.org

Canadian Standards Association (CSA)
178 Rexdale Boulevard
Rexdale, Ontario, M9W 1R3, Canada
Tel: (416) 747-4000
Fax: (416) 747-4149

European Organization for Testing and Certification (EOTC)
Rue Stassart 33, 2nd floor
B-1050 Brussels, Belgium
Tel: 32-2-519-6969
Fax: 32-2-519-6917

International Automotive Sector Group (IASG)
To obtain a latest IASG-sanctioned QS-9000

interpretations, call ASQC at (800) 248-1946.

To submit questions or issues to the IASG for consideration, fax inquiries, in English, to Fax Voice Mail Box (614) 847-8556.

Web site: http://www.asqc.org/9000/saninttc.html

International Organization for Standardization (ISO)
Rue de Varembe 1
Case postale 56
CH-1211 Geneva 20, Switzerland
Tel: 41-22-7490111
Fax: 41-22-7333430
Web site: http://www.iso.ch

National Institute of Standards and Technology (NIST)
TRF Building, Room A163
Gaithersburg, MD 20899, USA

Tel: (301) 975-4040
Fax: (301) 926-1559
Web site: http://www.nist.gov

National ISO 9000 Support Group
9864 Cherry Valley SE, Suite C
Caledonia, MI 49302, USA
Tel: (616) 891-9114
Fax: (616) 891-9462
Web site: http://www.cris.com/~isogroup

Quality Systems Update (QSU)
Irwin Professional Publishing
11150 Main Street, Suite 403
Fairfax, VA 22030-5066, USA
Tel: (703) 591-9008 or (800) 773-4607
Fax: (703) 591-0971 or (800) 926-9495
Web site: http://www.irwinpro.com

APPENDIX E

Acronyms

A2LA	American Association of Laboratory Accreditation
AIAG	Automotive Industry Action Group
ANSI	American National Standards Institute
APQP	advanced product quality planning
ASN	advance shipping notification
ASQC	American Society for Quality Control
ASTM	American Society for Testing of Materials
BSI	British Standards Institution
CAD	computer-aided design
CAE	computer-aided engineering
CC	critical characteristic
CFT	cross-functional team
CSA	Canadian Standards Association
CUSUM	cumulative sum
DFA	design for assembly
DFM	design for manufacturing
DFMEA	design failure mode and effects analysis
DOE	design of experiments
EAPA	engineering approved product authorization
ECN	engineering change notice
EOTC	European Organization for Testing and Certification
EU	European Union
EVOP	evolutionary operation of processes
FMEA	failure mode and effects analysis

FTC	first time capability
GD&T	geometric dimensioning and tolerancing
GR&R	gauge repeatability and reproducibility
IAAR	Independent Association of Accredited Registrars
IASG	International Automotive Sector Group
IIOC	Independent International Organization for Certification
ISO	International Organization for Standardization
MBNQA	Malcolm Baldrige National Quality Award
MSA	measurement systems analysis
NACCB	National Accreditation Council for Certification Bodies (UK) *(at present UKAS)*
NAFTA	North American Free Trade Agreement
NIST	National Institute of Standards and Technology
OEM	original equipment manufacturers
PFMEA	process failure mode and effects analysis
PPAP	production part approval process
PQP	product quality planning
QA	quality assurance
QC	quality control
QFD	quality function deployment
QOS	quality operating system
QS	quality system
QSA	quality system assessment
QSR	quality system requirements
RAB	Registrar Accreditation Board
RvA	Raad voor Accreditatie (Dutch Council for Accreditation)
RvC	Raad voor de Certificate (Dutch Council for Certification) *(at present RvA)*
SAS	Swiss Accreditation Service
SCC	Standards Council of Canada
SFMEA	system failure mode and effects analysis
SIC	Standard Industrial Classification
SPC	statistical process control
SQA	supplier quality assurance
TAG	technical advisory group/truck advisory group (AIAG)
TC	technical committee, as in TC 176
TQM	total quality management
UKAS	United Kingdom Accreditation Service
VA	value analysis
VE	value engineering

APPENDIX F

Glossary

The intent of this glossary is to assist the reader in understanding the material covered in this publication, not to provide definitions for all acronyms and technical language related to the automotive industry.

ANSI American National Standards Institute (ANSI) is a privately funded federation of leaders representing both the private and the public sectors. ANSI assures that member organizations that write standards follow rules of consensus and broad participation by interested parties. (ANSI HomePage)

ASQC ASQC is the leading quality improvement organization in the United States, with more than 130,000 individual and 1,000 sustaining members worldwide. A not-for-profit professional association headquartered in Milwaukee, Wisconsin, ASQC carries out a variety of professional, educational, and informational programs. (ASQC HomePage)

assessment An evaluation process including a document review, an on-site audit, an analysis, and a report. Customers may also include a self-assessment, internal audit results, and other associated materials in the assessment.

audit An on-site verification activity used to determine the effective implementation of a supplier's documented quality system. (QS-9000:1995)

audit program The organizational structure, commitment, and documented methods used to plan and perform audits. (ASQC Quality Auditing Technical Committee)

BSI British Standards Institution. This is the United Kingdom's standards-writing body.

compliance An affirmative indication or judgment that the supplier of a product or service has met the requirements of the relevant specifications, contract, or regulation; also the state of meeting the requirements. (ANSI/ASQC A3)

conformance An affirmative indication or judgment that a product or service has met the requirements of the relevant specifications, contract, or regulation; also the state of meeting the requirements. (ANSI/ASQC A3)

consulting The provision of training, documentation development, or assistance with implementation of quality systems to a specific customer. If these activities are open to the public, advertised, and not customer specific, they are considered training rather than consulting. (QS-9000:1995)

corrective action plan A plan for correcting a quality-related issue.

documentation Material defining the process to be followed (e.g., quality manuals, operator instructions, graphics, pictorials). (QS-9000:1995)

environment All of the process conditions influencing the manufacture and quality of a part or product.

EOTC European Organization for Testing and Certification; set up by the European Union and European Free Trade Association to focus on conformity assessment issues in the nonregulated spheres.

EU European Union; a framework within which member states have agreed to integrate their economies and eventually form a political union. Current members are Belgium, Denmark, France, Germany, Greece, Ireland, Italy, Luxembourg, the Netherlands, Portugal, Spain, and the United Kingdom.

follow-up audit An audit whose purpose and scope are limited to verifying that corrective action has been accomplished as scheduled and to determining that the action effectively prevented recurrence. (ASQC Quality Auditing Technical Committee)

ISO International Organization for Standardization; a worldwide federation of national standards bodies from 92 countries (as of this writing), one from each country. The ISO is a nongovernmental organization established in 1947. The mission of the ISO is to promote the development of standardization and related activities in the world with a view to facilitating the international exchange of goods and services, and to developing cooperation in the spheres of intellectual, scientific, technological and economic activity. (ISO HomePage)

nonconformance Product or material that does not conform to the customer requirements or specifications. (QS-9000:1995)

nonconformity A process that does not conform to a quality system requirement. (QS-9000:1995)

organization A company, corporation, firm, enterprise, or association, or part thereof, whether incorporated or not, public or private, that has its own functions and administration. (ISO 8402:1994)

procedures Documented processes that are used when work affects several functions or departments of an organization. Procedures are considered to be Level 2 quality system documentation.

process A set of interrelated resources and activities that transform inputs into outputs. (ISO 8402:1994)

quality The totality of features and characteristics of an entity that bear on its ability to satisfy stated or implied needs. (ISO 8402:1994)

quality assurance All the planned and systematic activities implemented within the quality system and demonstrated as needed to provide adequate confidence that an entity will fulfill requirements for quality. (ISO 8402:1994)

quality control The operational techniques and activities that are used to fulfill requirements for quality. (ISO 8402:1994)

quality manual A document that describes the elements of the quality system used to assure that customer expectations, needs, and requirements are met. The quality manual is considered to be Level 1 quality system documentation.

quality planning The structured process for defining the methods (i.e., measurements, tests) that will be used in the production of a specific product or family of products (i.e., parts, materials). Quality planning focuses on the concepts of defect prevention and continuous improvement rather than defect detection.

quality policy The overall quality intentions and direction of an organization with regard to quality, as formally expressed by top management. (ISO 8402:1994)

quality records Documented evidence that processes were executed according to the quality system documentation and records results.

RAB Registrar Accreditation Board; a private, not-for-profit organization and an affiliate of ASQC. The RAB's primary mission is to provide assurance of the competence and reliability of third-party organizations (registrars) that audit and register quality systems to recognized standards, specifically those in the ISO 9000 series. RAB accredits registrars using criteria based on internationally recognized standards and guides. (ASQC HomePage)

registrar A company that conducts quality system assessments to the quality system requirements. (QS-9000:1995)

registrar *(accredited)* A qualified organization certified by a national body to perform audits to the quality systems requirements and to register the audited facility as meeting these requirements.

registration Procedure by which a body indicates relevant characteristics of a product, process, or service, or particulars of a body or person, and then includes or registers the product, process, or service in an appropriate publicly available list. (ISO/IEC Guide 2)

Registration and certification are often used interchangeably. In the U.S., quality systems registration is used more widely than quality system certification, which is the preferred European terminology.

repair Action taken on nonconforming product so that the product will fulfill the intended usage although the product may not conform to the original requirements. (QS-9000:1995)

rework Action taken on nonconforming product so that it will meet the specified requirements. (QS-9000:1995)

RvA Raad voor Accreditatie; the Dutch Council for Accreditation for recognizing the competence and reliability of organizations that perform third-party certification of products, accreditation of laboratories, and registration of quality systems. Effective September 14, 1995, Raad voor de Certificate (RvC) merged with the Foundation for Accreditation of Laboratories (STERLAB) to become RvA.

subcontractors Providers of production parts, materials, or service parts directly to a supplier; to Chrysler, Ford, General Motors; or to other customers subscribing to QS-9000. Providers of heat treating, painting, plating, or other finishing services are included. (QS-9000:1995)

suppliers Providers of production materials, production, or service parts; heat treating; and plating, painting, or other finishing services directly to Chrysler, Ford, General Motors, or other customers subscribing to QS-9000. (QS-9000:1995)

Suppliers can be Tier I, II, or III depending on the situation.

UKAS United Kingdom Accreditation Service; the British authority for recognizing the competence and reliability of organizations that perform third-party certification of products and registration of quality systems. In August 1995, the National Accreditation Council for Certification Bodies (NACCB) in the United Kingdom was merged with the National Measurement Accreditation Services (NAMAS) to form the UKAS.

Bibliography

Chrysler, Ford, General Motors. 1994. *Quality System Assessment.* Southfield, MI: Automotive Industry Action Group, August.

———. 1995. *Advanced Product Quality Planning and Control Plan.* Southfield, MI: Automotive Industry Action Group, February.

———. 1995. *Measurement Systems Analysis* (2d ed.). Southfield, MI: Automotive Industry Action Group, February.

———. 1995. *Potential Failure Mode and Effects Analysis* (2d ed.). Southfield, MI: Automotive Industry Action Group, February.

———. 1995. *Production Part Approval Process* (2d ed.). Southfield, MI: Automotive Industry Action Group, July.

———. 1995. *Quality System Requirements: QS-9000* (2d ed.). Southfield, MI: Automotive Industry Action Group, February.

———. 1995. *Statistical Process Control.* Southfield, MI: Automotive Industry Action Group, March.

Benson, Roger S., and Richard W. Sherman. 1995. "ISO 9000: A Practical Step-by-Step Approach." *Quality Progress,* October, pp. 75–78.

Bounds, Gregory. 1996. *Cases in Quality.* Burr Ridge, IL: Richard D. Irwin.

Brumm, Eugenia K. 1995. *Managing Records for ISO 9000 Compliance.* Milwaukee, WI: ASQC Quality Press.

Chauvel, A. M. 1994. "Quality in Europe: Toward the Year 2000." *Quality Management Journal,* January, pp. 71–77.

Dargaty, Zane D. 1995. "Most Common Nonconformances." *Quality System Update,* October, p. 17.

Deming, W. Edwards. 1992. *Out of the Crisis.* Cambridge, MA: Massachusetts Institute of Technology, Center for Advanced Engineering Study.

Dickinson, James, and Timothy Hubbard. 1995. "Making Up Your Mind Set: Creating A Culture Conducive to QS-9000." *Proceedings of the Jump-Start QS-9000 Conference.* Subir Chowdhury and Ken Zimmer, eds. September, pp. 36–41.

Durant, A. C., and I. Durant. 1993. "The Role of ISO 9000 Standards in Continuous Improvement." *Quality Systems Update,* October, pp. 19–24.

Dusharn, Dirk. 1995. "ISO 9000 Certification Costs." *Quality Digest,* January, p. 8.

Feigenbaum, Armand V. 1983. *Total Quality Control.* New York: McGraw-Hill.

Harmon, Marion. 1994. "First There Was ISO 9000, Now There's . . . ISO 14000." *Quality Digest,* July, pp. 24–31.

Higgason, Larry. 1995. "AIAG 1995 Quality Survey Results Summary." *Proceedings of the Jump-Start QS-9000 Conference.* Subir Chowdhury and Ken Zimmer, eds., September, pp. 75–90.

Hilary, Rachel. 1996. "Behind the Stars and Stripes: Quality in the USA." *Quality Progress,* January, pp. 31–35.

Holdredge, Mark. 1995. "Poco a Poco: Ideas for Effective Implementation of QS-9000." *Proceedings of the Jump-Start QS-9000 Conference.* Subir Chowdhury and Ken Zimmer, eds., September, pp. 50–60.

International Automotive Sector Group (IASG). 1995. *IASG Sanctioned QS-9000 Interpretations.* International Automotive Sector Group, November.

Jaeger, Martin J. 1995. "The Bottom Line on QS-9000." *Quality System Update,* November, pp. 23–25.

Keenan, Tim. 1995. "Quest for QS-9000: Suppliers Begin Long Journey to Compliance." *Ward's AutoWorld,* November, pp. 41–43.

Martin, Tripp, et al. 1995. "QS-9000 and Automotive Quality." *Proceedings of the ASQC 49th Annual Quality Congress,* May, pp. 782–786.

Martin, Tripp. 1996. "Seeking a Registrar for QS-9000." *Automotive Excellence,* January, pp. 8–9.

Peach, Robert W, ed. 1995. *The ISO 9000 Handbook* (2d ed.). Fairfax, VA: Irwin Professional Publishing.

Pernik, Cornelia A. 1995. "Beating the QS-9000 Deadline." *Actionline,* April, pp. 28–31.

Pray, Hal W. 1995. "Overcoming the Three Biggest Obstacles to QS-9000." *Proceedings of the Jump-Start QS-9000 Conference.* Subir Chowdhury and Ken Zimmer, eds. September, pp. 42–49.

Sayle, Allan J. 1989. *Management Audits: the Assessment of Quality Management Systems.* Milwaukee, WI: ASQC Quality Press.

Stamatis, D. H. 1995. "QS-9000 Revisions: Not Far Enough." *Quality Digest,* December, pp. 46–49.

Stamatis, D. H. 1995. *Integrating QS-9000 with Your Automotive Quality System.* Milwaukee, WI: ASQC Quality Press.

Stephens, Kenneth S. 1994. "ISO 9000 and Total Quality." *Quality Management Journal,* October, pp. 57–71.

Struebing, Laura. 1996. "9000 Standards." *Quality Progress,* January, pp. 23–28.

Weston, F. C., Jr. 1995. "What Do Managers Really Think of the ISO 9000 Registration Process." *Quality Progress,* October, pp. 67–73.

Zottola, Vincent. 1995. "How to Implement ISO 9000 and Not Go Broke." *Quality System Update,* August, p. 12.

Zuckerman, Amy. 1995. "9 Steps to QS-9000." *Actionline,* November, pp. 28–31.

Zuckerman, Amy. 1995. "International Standards." *Quality Digest,* September, pp. 21–22.

INDEX